TRANSLATING
STRATEGY
INTO ACTION

The

BALANCED
SCORECARD

Robert S. Kaplan
David P. Norton

HARVARD BUSINESS SCHOOL PRESS
BOSTON, MASSACHUSETTS

Library of Congress Cataloging-in-Publication Data

Kaplan, Robert S.
   The balanced scorecard : translating strategy into action / Robert S. Kaplan, David P. Norton.
      p.   cm.
   Includes index.
   ISBN 0-87584-651-3 (alk. paper)
   1. Industrial productivity—Measurement.   2. Strategic planning.
   3. Organizational effectiveness—Evaluation.   I. Norton, David P.
   II. Title.
   HD56.K35   1996
   658.4'012—dc20   96-10216
                                                                          CIP

Contents

Preface

THE ORIGINS OF THIS BOOK can be traced back to 1990 when the Nolan Norton Institute, the research arm of KPMG, sponsored a one-year multicompany study, "Measuring Performance in the Organization of the Future." The study was motivated by a belief that existing performance-measurement approaches, primarily relying on financial accounting measures, were becoming obsolete. The study participants believed that reliance on summary financial-performance measures were hindering organizations' abilities to create future economic value. David Norton, CEO of Nolan Norton, served as the study leader and Robert Kaplan as an academic consultant. Representatives from a dozen companies[1]—manufacturing and service, heavy industry and high-tech—met bi-monthly throughout 1990 to develop a new performance-measurement model.

Early in the project, we examined recent case studies of innovative performance-measurement systems. One, the Analog Devices case,[2] described an approach for measuring rates of progress in continuous improvement activities. The case also showed how Analog was using a newly created "Corporate Scorecard" that contained, in addition to several traditional financial measures, performance measures relating to customer delivery times, quality and cycle times of manufacturing processes, and effectiveness of new product developments. Art Schneiderman, then vice president of quality improvement and productivity at Analog Devices, came to one meeting to share his company's experiences with the scorecard. A variety of other ideas were presented during the first half of the study, including shareholder value, productivity and quality measurements, and new compensation plans, but the participants soon focused on the multidimensional scorecard as offering the most promise for their needs.

The group discussions led to an expansion of the scorecard to what we labeled a "Balanced Scorecard," organized around four distinct perspectives—financial, customer, internal, and innovation and learning. The name reflected the balance provided between short- and long-term objectives, between financial and nonfinancial measures, between lagging and leading indicators, and between external and internal performance perspectives. Several participants experimented with building prototype Balanced Scorecards at pilot sites in their companies. They reported back to the study group on the acceptance, the barriers, and the opportunities of the Balanced Scorecard. The conclusion of the study, in December 1990, documented the feasibility and the benefits from such a balanced measurement system.

We summarized the findings of the study group in an article, "The Balanced Scorecard—Measures That Drive Performance," *Harvard Business Review* (January–February 1992). At that time, we were contacted by several senior executives to help them implement the Balanced Scorecard in their organizations. These efforts led to the next round of development. Two executives, Norman Chambers, then chief executive officer of Rockwater, and Larry Brady, then executive vice president (subsequently promoted to president) of the FMC Corporation stand out as particularly effective in extending the application of the scorecard. Chambers and Brady saw the scorecard as more than a measurement system. They both wanted to use the new measurement system to communicate and align their organizations to new strategies: away from the historic, short-term focus on cost reduction and low-price competition, and toward generating growth opportunities by offering customized, value-added products and services to customers. Our work with Chambers and Brady, and with the managers in their organizations, highlighted the importance of tying the measures in the Balanced Scorecard to an organization's strategy. While seemingly an obvious insight, in fact most organizations, even those implementing new performance-measurement systems, were not aligning measurements to strategy. Most companies were trying to improve the performance of existing processes—through lower cost, improved quality, and shortened response times—but were not identifying the processes that were truly strategic: those that must be performed exceptionally well for an organization's strategy to succeed. We described the importance of choosing measures based on strategic success in a second HBR article, "Putting the Balanced Scorecard to Work," published in September–October 1993.

By mid-1993, Norton was CEO of a new organization, Renaissance Solutions, Inc. (RSI), one of whose primary services was strategic consulting, using the Balanced Scorecard as a vehicle to help companies translate and implement strategy. An alliance between Renaissance and Gemini Consulting opened up opportunities for integrating the scorecard into major transformation programs. These experiences further refined the strategic linkages of the scorecard, demonstrating how even 20 to 25 measures across the four perspectives, could communicate and help implement a single strategy. So rather than view the multiple measures as requiring complex trade-offs, the strategic linkages enabled the scorecard measures to be tied together in a series of cause-and-effect relationships. Collectively, these relationships described the strategic trajectory—how investments in employee re-skilling, information technology, and innovative products and services would dramatically improve future financial performance.

The experiences revealed that innovating CEOs used the Balanced Scorecard not only to clarify and communicate strategy, but also to manage strategy. In effect, the Balanced Scorecard had evolved from an improved *measurement system* to a core *management system*. In addition to our initial group of companies, including Brown & Root Energy Services (the parent division of Rockwater) and FMC, we observed the evolving Balanced Scorecard process in several companies mentioned throughout this book: Metro Bank, National Insurance, Kenyon Stores, and Pioneer Petroleum (names have been disguised to preserve confidentiality). The senior executives in these companies were now using the Balanced Scorecard as the central organizing framework for important managerial processes: individual and team goal setting, compensation, resource allocation, budgeting and planning, and strategic feedback and learning. We summarized these developments in a third article, "Using the Balanced Scorecard as a Strategic Management System," *Harvard Business Review* (January–February 1996).

The rapid evolution of the Balanced Scorecard into a strategic management system led us to realize that we had learned far more than we were able to communicate in a series of articles. Also, we were receiving numerous requests for additional information about how to build and implement Balanced Scorecards. The combination of an ample supply of rich, detailed implementation experiences and a perceived demand for additional information led us to write this book.

The book, while as comprehensive and complete as we could make it, is still a progress report. During the past three years, we have seen new developments and applications as the scorecard concept takes hold in more and more organizations. Our hope is that the observations reported in this book will help more executives to launch and implement Balanced Scorecard programs in their organizations. And we are confident that many of them will be innovating companies, like the ones we have been fortunate to learn from during the past five years, that will expand the structure and use of the scorecard even further. So perhaps in a few years readers can look forward to *Balanced Scorecard: The Sequel.*

We are clearly indebted to many people and organizations who have assisted us in our intellectual journey. They include executives and project leaders at FMC (Larry Brady and Ron Mambu), Rockwater (Norm Chambers and Sian Lloyd Rees), and Analog Devices (Ray Stata, Jerry Fishman, and Art Schneiderman). We wish we could acknowledge the executives at Metro Bank, National, Kenyon Stores, Pioneer Petroleum, and several other companies by name, but for reasons of confidentiality, we cannot. Through their leadership and actions, all these executives have showed how the Balanced Scorecard can become the cornerstone of an organization's management systems.

We have also benefited immeasurably from efforts of many professionals at RSI who have worked with their clients to widen the envelope of Balanced Scorecard applications. In particular, Michael Contrada and Rebecca Steinfort synthesized the experiences of a diverse set of clients into a living body of knowledge within RSI. Laura Downing and Marissa Hendrickson showed us how to apply the Balanced Scorecard in a not-for-profit setting, the Massachusetts Special Olympics, to which they devote much of their personal time. RSI co-founders, Harry Lasker and David Lubin, helped us extend implementation into technology-based solutions, including the strategic feedback and learning system described in Chapter 11. This extension enabled us to embed the scorecard concept into the meetings, information systems, and everyday life of organizations. Our relationship with Gemini Consulting, particularly the support of Francis Gouillart, created further opportunities to expand the scorecard concept into complex transformational processes. From all these professional partnerships, we found the true meaning of learning organizations.

Several people played important roles in the preparation of the book. Carol Franco, director of the Harvard Business School Press, gave enthusiastic endorsement and editorial assistance throughout the project. Hollis Heim-bouch, our editor, gave invaluable and insightful comments on initial and subsequent drafts that significantly improved the book's organization and contents. Thoughtful comments from Ted Francavilla, Tom Valerio, and Professors William Bruns, Robert Simons, and Robin Cooper enabled us to make important improvements in the final manuscript.

Natalie Greenberg applied her usual painstaking and thorough copy-editing skills that, among many other benefits, eliminated our tendency toward repetition. Barbara Roth kept us on schedule by managing effectively the production process and gave excellent advice in art production and editing. Rose Fitzpatrick of Renaissance Solutions supported us by translating crude hand-written notes and roughly scrawled figures and tables into a polished final manuscript. Her patience through many iterations and refinements was a source of strength. To all these people we say thank you.

Robert S. Kaplan and David P. Norton
Boston and Lincoln, Mass., February 1996

NOTES

1. The companies included Advanced Micro Devices, American Standard, Apple Computer, Bell South, CIGNA, Conner Peripherals, Cray Research, DuPont, Electronic Data Systems, General Electric, Hewlett-Packard, and Shell Canada.
2. R. S. Kaplan, "Analog Devices: The Half-Life Metric," Harvard Business School Case #9-190-061, 1990.

Measurement and Management in the Information Age

IMAGINE ENTERING THE COCKPIT of a modern jet airplane and seeing only a single instrument there. How would you feel about boarding the plane after the following conversation with the pilot?

> Q: I'm surprised to see you operating the plane with only a single instrument. What does it measure?
>
> A: Airspeed. I'm really working on airspeed this flight.
>
> Q: That's good. Airspeed certainly seems important. But what about altitude. Wouldn't an altimeter be helpful?
>
> A: I worked on altitude for the last few flights and I've gotten pretty good on it. Now I have to concentrate on proper air speed.
>
> Q: But I notice you don't even have a fuel gauge. Wouldn't that be useful?
>
> A: You're right; fuel is significant, but I can't concentrate on doing too many things well at the same time. So on this flight I'm focusing on air speed. Once I get to be excellent at air speed, as well as altitude, I intend to concentrate on fuel consumption on the next set of flights.

We suspect that you would not board the plane after this discussion. Even if the pilot did an exceptional job on air speed, you would be worried about colliding with tall mountains or running low on fuel. Clearly, such a conversation is a fantasy since no pilot would dream of guiding a complex vehicle like a jet airplane through crowded air spaces, with only a single instrument. Skilled pilots are able to process information from a large number of indicators to navigate their aircraft. Yet navigating today's organizations through complex competitive environments is at least as complicated as flying a jet. Why should we believe that executives need anything less than a full battery of instrumentation for guiding their companies? Managers, like pilots, need instrumentation about many aspects of their environment and performance to monitor the journey toward excellent future outcomes.

The Balanced Scorecard (BSC) provides managers with the instrumentation they need to navigate to future competitive success. Today, organizations are competing in complex environments so that an accurate understanding of their goals and the methods for attaining those goals is vital. The Balanced Scorecard translates an organization's mission and strategy into a comprehensive set of performance measures that provides the framework for a strategic measurement and management system. The Balanced Scorecard retains an emphasis on achieving financial objectives, but also includes the performance drivers of these financial objectives. The scorecard measures organizational performance across four balanced perspectives: financial, customers, internal business processes, and learning and growth. The BSC enables companies to track financial results while simultaneously monitoring progress in building the capabilities and acquiring the intangible assets they need for future growth.

COMPETING IN THE INFORMATION AGE

Companies are in the midst of a revolutionary transformation. Industrial age competition is shifting to information age competition. During the industrial age, from 1850 to about 1975, companies succeeded by how well they could capture the benefits from economies of scale and scope.[1] Technology mattered, but, ultimately, success accrued to companies that could embed the new technology into physical assets that offered efficient, mass production of standard products.

During the industrial age, financial control systems were developed in companies, such as General Motors, DuPont, Matsushita, and General

Electric, to facilitate and monitor efficient allocations of financial and physical capital.[2] A summary financial measure such as return-on-capital-employed (ROCE) could both direct a company's internal capital to its most productive use and monitor the efficiency by which operating divisions used financial and physical capital to create value for shareholders.

The emergence of the information era, however, in the last decades of the twentieth century, made obsolete many of the fundamental assumptions of industrial age competition. No longer could companies gain sustainable competitive advantage by merely deploying new technology into physical assets rapidly, and by excellent management of financial assets and liabilities.

The impact of the information era is even more revolutionary for service organizations than for manufacturing companies. Many service organizations, especially those in the transportation, utility, communication, financial, and health care industries, existed for decades in comfortable, noncompetitive environments. They had little freedom in entering new businesses and in pricing their output. In return, government regulators protected these companies from potentially more efficient or more innovative competitors, and set prices at a level that provided adequate returns on their investment and cost base. Clearly, the past two decades have witnessed major deregulatory and privatization initiatives for service companies throughout the world as information technology created the "seeds of destruction" of industrial-era regulated service companies.

The information age environment for both manufacturing and service organizations requires new capabilities for competitive success. The ability of a company to mobilize and exploit its tangible or invisible assets has become far more decisive than investing and managing physical, tangible assets.[3] Intangible assets enable an organization to:

- develop customer relationships that retain the loyalty of existing customers and enable new customer segments and market areas to be served effectively and efficiently;
- introduce innovative products and services desired by targeted customer segments;
- produce customized high-quality products and services at low cost and with short lead times;
- mobilize employee skills and motivation for continuous improvements in process capabilities, quality, and response times; and
- deploy information technology, data bases, and systems.

New Operating Environment

Information age organizations are built on a new set of operating assumptions.

CROSS-FUNCTIONS

Industrial age organizations gained competitive advantage through specialization of functional skills: in manufacturing, purchasing, distribution, marketing, and technology. This specialization yielded substantial benefits, but, over time, maximization of functional specialization led to enormous inefficiencies, hand-offs between departments, and slow response processes. The information age organization operates with integrated business processes that cut across traditional business functions.[4] It combines the specialization benefits from functional expertise with the speed, efficiency, and quality of integrated business processes.

LINKS TO CUSTOMERS AND SUPPLIERS

Industrial age companies worked with customers and suppliers through arm's-length transactions. Information technology enables today's organizations to integrate supply, production, and delivery processes so that operations are triggered by customer orders, not by production plans that push products and services through the value chain. An integrated system, from customer orders upstream to raw material suppliers, enables all organizational units along the value chain to realize enormous improvements in cost, quality, and response times.

CUSTOMER SEGMENTATION

Industrial age companies prospered by offering low-cost but standardized products and services; recall Henry Ford's famous dictum, "They can have whatever color they want as long as it is black." Once consumers have satisfied their basic needs for clothing, shelter, food, and transportation, they want more individualized solutions to their wants. Information age companies must learn to offer customized products and services to its diverse customer segments, without paying the usual cost penalty for high-variety, low-volume operations.[5]

GLOBAL SCALE

Domestic borders are no longer a barrier to competition from more efficient and responsive foreign companies. Information age companies compete against the best companies in the world. The large investments required for new products and services may require customers worldwide to provide adequate returns. Information age companies must combine the efficiencies and competitive honing of global operations with marketing sensitivity to local customers.

INNOVATION

Product life cycles continue to shrink. Competitive advantage in one generation of a product's life is no guarantee of product leadership in the next technological platform.[6] Companies that compete in industries with rapid technological innovation must be masters at anticipating customers' future needs, devising radical new product and service offerings, and rapidly deploying new product technologies into efficient operating and service delivery processes. Even for companies in industries with relatively long product-life cycles, continuous improvement in processes and product capabilities is critical for long-term success.

KNOWLEDGE WORKERS

Industrial age companies created sharp distinctions between two groups of employees. The intellectual elite—managers and engineers—used their analytical skills to design products and processes, select and manage customers, and supervise day-to-day operations. The second group was composed of the people who actually produced the products and delivered the services. This direct labor work force was a principal factor of production for industrial age companies, but used only their physical capabilities, not their minds. They performed tasks and processes under direct supervision of white-collar engineers and managers. At the end of the twentieth century, automation and productivity have reduced the percentage of people in the organization who perform traditional work functions, while competitive demands have increased the number of people performing analytic functions: engineering, marketing, management, and administration. Even individuals still involved in direct production and service delivery are valued for their suggestions on how to improve quality, reduce costs, and decrease cycle times. As the plant manager of a refurbished Ford engine plant declared, "The machines are designed to run automatically. The people's job is to think, to problem solve, to ensure quality, not to watch the parts go by. Here, people are viewed as problem-solvers, not variable costs."[7]

Now all employees must contribute value by what they know and by the information they can provide. Investing in, managing, and exploiting the knowledge of every employee have become critical to the success of information age companies.

As organizations attempt to transform themselves to compete successfully in the future, they are turning to a variety of improvement initiatives:

- Total quality management
- Just-in-time (JIT) production and distribution systems
- Time-based competition
- Lean production/lean enterprise
- Building customer-focused organizations
- Activity-based cost management
- Employee empowerment
- Reengineering

Each of these improvement programs has had demonstrated success stories, champions, gurus, and consultants. Each competes for the time, energy, and resources of senior executives. And each offers the promise of breakthrough performance and enhanced value creation for many, if not all, of a company's constituencies: shareholders, customers, suppliers, and employees. The goal of these programs is not incremental improvement or survival. The goal is discontinuous performance, enabling an organization to succeed in the new information age competition.

But many of these improvement programs have yielded disappointing results. The programs are often fragmented. They may not be linked to the organization's strategy, nor to achieving specific financial and economic outcomes. Breakthroughs in performance require major change, and that includes changes in the measurement and management systems used by an organization. Navigating to a more competitive, technological, and capability-driven future cannot be accomplished merely by monitoring and controlling financial measures of past performance.

TRADITIONAL FINANCIAL ACCOUNTING MODEL

All the new programs, initiatives, and change management processes of information age companies are being implemented in an environment governed by quarterly and annual financial reports. The financial-reporting process remains anchored to an accounting model developed centuries ago for an environment of arm's-length transactions between independent entities. This venerable financial accounting model is still being used by information age companies as they attempt to build internal assets and capabilities, and to forge linkages and strategic alliances with external parties.[8]

Ideally, this financial accounting model should have been expanded to incorporate the valuation of a company's intangible and intellectual assets, such as high-quality products and services, motivated and skilled employees, responsive and predictable internal processes, and satisfied and loyal customers. Such a valuation of intangible assets and company capabilities would be especially helpful since, for information age companies, these assets are more critical to success than traditional physical and tangible assets. If intangible assets and company capabilities could be valued within the financial accounting model, organizations that enhanced these assets and capabilities could communicate this improvement to employees, shareholders, creditors, and communities. Conversely, when companies depleted their stock of intangible assets and capabilities, the negative effects could be reflected immediately in the income statement. Realistically, however, difficulties in placing a reliable financial value on such assets as the new product pipeline; process capabilities; employee skills, motivation, and flexibility; customer loyalty; data bases; and systems will likely preclude them from ever being recognized in organizational balance sheets. Yet these are the very assets and capabilities that are critical for success in today's and tomorrow's competitive environment.

THE BALANCED SCORECARD

The collision between the irresistible force to build long-range competitive capabilities and the immovable object of the historical-cost financial accounting model has created a new synthesis: the Balanced Scorecard. The Balanced Scorecard retains traditional financial measures. But financial measures tell the story of past events, an adequate story for industrial age companies for which investments in long-term capabilities and customer relationships were not critical for success. These financial measures are inadequate, however, for guiding and evaluating the journey that information age companies must make to create future value through investment in customers, suppliers, employees, processes, technology, and innovation.

The Balanced Scorecard complements financial measures of past performance with measures of the drivers of future performance. The objectives and measures of the scorecard are derived from an organization's vision and strategy. The objectives and measures view organizational performance from four perspectives: financial, customer, internal business process, and learning and growth. These four perspectives provide the framework for the Balanced Scorecard (see Figure 1-1).

The Balanced Scorecard expands the set of business unit objectives beyond summary financial measures. Corporate executives can now measure how their business units create value for current and future customers and how they must enhance internal capabilities and the investment in people, systems, and procedures necessary to improve future performance. The Balanced Scorecard captures the critical value-creation activities created by skilled, motivated organizational participants. While retaining, via the financial perspective, an interest in short-term performance, the Balanced Scorecard clearly reveals the value drivers for superior long-term financial and competitive performance.

The Balanced Scorecard as a Management System

Many companies already have performance measurement systems that incorporate financial and nonfinancial measures. What is new about a call for a "balanced" set of measures? While virtually all organizations do indeed have financial and nonfinancial measures, many use their nonfinancial measures for local improvements, at their front-line and customer-facing operations. Aggregate financial measures are used by senior managers as if these measures could summarize adequately the results of operations performed by their lower and mid-level employees. These organizations are using their financial and nonfinancial performance measures only for tactical feedback and control of short-term operations.

The Balanced Scorecard emphasizes that financial and nonfinancial measures must be part of the information system for employees at all levels of the organization. Front-line employees must understand the financial consequences of their decisions and actions; senior executives must understand the drivers of long-term financial success. The objectives and the measures for the Balanced Scorecard are more than just a somewhat ad hoc collection of financial and nonfinancial performance measures; they are derived from a top-down process driven by the mission and strategy

Figure 1-1   The Balanced Scorecard Provides a Framework to Translate a Strategy into Operational Terms

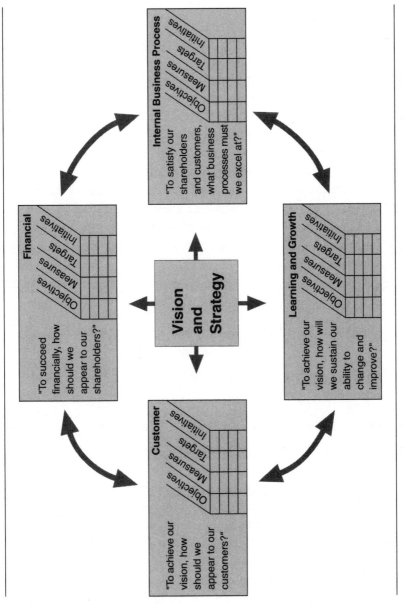

Source: Robert S. Kaplan and David P. Norton, "Using the Balanced Scorecard as a Strategic Management System," *Harvard Business Review* (January–February 1996): 76. Reprinted with permission.

of the business unit. The Balanced Scorecard should translate a business unit's mission and strategy into tangible objectives and measures. The measures represent a *balance* between external measures for shareholders and customers, and internal measures of critical business processes, innovation, and learning and growth. The measures are *balanced* between the outcome measures—the results from past efforts—and the measures that drive future performance. And the scorecard is *balanced* between objective, easily quantified outcome measures and subjective, somewhat judgmental, performance drivers of the outcome measures.

The Balanced Scorecard is more than a tactical or an operational measurement system. Innovative companies are using the scorecard as a *strategic management system,* to manage their strategy over their long run (see Figure 1-2). They are using the measurement focus of the scorecard to accomplish critical management processes:

1. Clarify and translate vision and strategy
2. Communicate and link strategic objectives and measures
3. Plan, set targets, and align strategic initiatives
4. Enhance strategic feedback and learning

CLARIFY AND TRANSLATE VISION AND STRATEGY

The scorecard process starts with the senior executive management team working together to translate its business unit's strategy into specific strategic objectives. To set financial goals, the team must consider whether to emphasize revenue and market growth, profitability, or cash flow generation. But especially for the customer perspective, the management team must be explicit about the customer and market segments in which it has decided to compete. For example, one financial institution thought its top 25 senior executives agreed about its strategy: to provide superior service to targeted customers. In formulating customer objectives for the scorecard, however, it became clear that each executive had a different definition as to what superior service represented and who were the targeted customers. The process of developing operational measures for the scorecard brought consensus among all 25 executives as to the most desirable customer segments, and the products and services the bank should offer to those targeted segments.

With financial and customer objectives established, an organization then identifies the objectives and measures for its internal business process. Such identification represents one of the principal innovations and benefits of the scorecard approach. Traditional performance measurement systems, even those that use many nonfinancial indicators, focus on improving the cost, quality, and cycle times of existing processes. The Balanced Scorecard highlights those processes that are most critical for achieving breakthrough performance for customers and shareholders. Often this identification reveals entirely new internal processes that the organization must excel at for its strategy to be successful.

Figure 1-2   The Balanced Scorecard as a Strategic Framework for Action

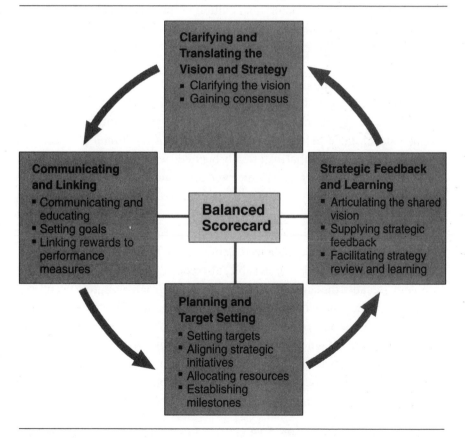

Source: Robert S. Kaplan and David P. Norton, "Using the Balanced Scorecard as a Strategic Management System," *Harvard Business Review* (January–February 1996): 77. Reprinted with permission.

The final linkage, to learning and growth objectives, reveals the rationale for significant investments in reskilling employees, in information technology and systems, and in enhanced organizational procedures. These investments—in people, systems, and procedures—generate major innovation and improvement for internal business processes, for customers, and, eventually, for shareholders.

The process of building a Balanced Scorecard clarifies the strategic objectives and identifies the critical few drivers of the strategic objectives. In our experience with the design of scorecard programs, we have never encountered a management team that had reached full consensus on the relative importance of its strategic objectives. In general, these are harmonious teams in well-managed organizations. The reason for the lack of consensus can usually be related to the functional history and culture of the organization. Executives tend to build careers within a single function. Certain functions tend to dominate the priorities. For example, oil companies tend to be dominated by the technical and cost focus of the refineries, at the expense of marketing, while consumer goods companies tend to be dominated by a marketing and sales focus, at the expense of technology and innovation. High-tech companies have a strong engineering and technology culture, with manufacturing often being a stepchild. When executives from different functional perspectives, especially in companies that historically operated with strong functional silos, attempt to work together as a team, there are blind spots—areas of relative ignorance around which it is difficult to form teams and create consensus because so little shared understanding exists about overall business objectives and the contribution and integration of different functional units.

The development of a Balanced Scorecard, while making such lack of consensus and teamwork more visible, also contributes to the solution of the problem. Because the scorecard is developed by a group of senior executives, as a team project, the scorecard creates a shared model of the entire business to which everyone has contributed. The scorecard objectives become the joint accountability of the senior executive team, enabling it to serve as the organizing framework for a broad array of important team-based management processes. It creates consensus and teamwork among all senior executives, regardless of previous employment experience or functional expertise.

COMMUNICATE AND LINK STRATEGIC OBJECTIVES AND MEASURES

The Balanced Scorecard's strategic objectives and measures are communicated throughout an organization via company newsletters, bulletin boards, videos, and even electronically through groupware and networked personal computers. The communication serves to signal to all employees the critical objectives that must be accomplished if an organization's strategy is to succeed. Some organizations attempt to decompose the high-level strategic measures of the business unit scorecard into specific measures at the operational level. For example, an on-time delivery (OTD) objective on the business unit scorecard can be translated into an objective to reduce setup times at a specific machine, or to a local goal for rapid transfer of orders from one process to the next. In this way, local improvement efforts become aligned with overall organizational success factors. Once all employees understand high-level objectives and measures, they can establish local objectives that support the business unit's global strategy.

The scorecard also provides the basis for communicating and gaining commitment to a business unit's strategy with corporate-level executives and the board of directors. The scorecard encourages a dialogue between business units and corporate executives and board members, not just about short-term financial objectives, but about the formulation and implementation of a strategy for breakthrough performance for the future.

At the conclusion of the communication and linkage process, everyone in the organization should understand the business unit's long-term goals, as well as the strategy for achieving these goals. Individuals have formulated local actions that will contribute to achieving business unit objectives. And all organizational efforts and initiatives will be aligned to the needed change processes.

PLAN, SET TARGETS, AND ALIGN STRATEGIC INITIATIVES

The Balanced Scorecard has its greatest impact when it is deployed to drive organizational change. Senior executives should establish targets for the scorecard measures, three to five years out, that, if achieved, will transform the company. The targets should represent a discontinuity in business unit performance. If the business unit were a public company, target achievement should produce a doubling or more of the stock price. Organizational financial targets have included doubling the return on invested capital, or a 150% increase in sales during the next five years. An electronics company set a financial target to grow at a rate nearly double the expected growth rate of its existing customers.

To achieve such ambitious financial objectives, managers must identify stretch targets for their customer, internal-business-process, and learning and growth objectives. These stretch targets can come from several sources. Ideally, the targets for the customer measures should be derived from meeting or exceeding customer expectations. Both existing and potential customer preferences should be examined to identify the expectations for outstanding performance. Benchmarking can be used to incorporate existing best practice and to verify that internally proposed targets will not keep the business unit trailing in strategic measures.

Once targets for customer, internal-business-process, and learning and growth measures are established, managers can align their strategic quality, response time, and reengineering initiatives for achieving the breakthrough objectives. Thus, the Balanced Scorecard provides the front-end justification, as well as focus and integration for continuous improvement, reengineering, and transformation programs. Rather than just apply fundamental process redesign to any local process where gains might be easily obtained, managerial efforts are directed to improving and reengineering processes that are critical for the organization's strategic success. And unlike conventional reengineering programs, where the objective is massive cost cutting (the slash and burn rationale), the reengineering program's objective need not be measured by cost savings alone. The targets for the strategic initiative are derived from such scorecard measures as dramatic time reductions in order fulfillment cycles, shorter time-to-market in product development processes, and enhanced employee capabilities. These time compressions and expanded capabilities, of course, are not the ultimate objective. Through a series of cause-and-effect relationships embodied in the Balanced Scorecard, these capabilities eventually become translated into superior financial performance.

The Balanced Scorecard also enables an organization to integrate its strategic planning with its annual budgeting process. At the time when a business establishes 3–5 year stretch targets for the strategic measures, managers also forecast milestones for each measure during the next fiscal year—how far along they expect to be during the 12 months of year one of the plan. These short-term milestones provide specific targets for assessing progress in the near term along the business unit's long-term strategic trajectory.

The planning and target-setting management process enables the organization to:

- quantify the long-term outcomes it wishes to achieve,
- identify mechanisms and provide resources for achieving those outcomes, and

- establish short-term milestones for the financial and nonfinancial measures on the scorecard.

ENHANCE STRATEGIC FEEDBACK AND LEARNING

The final management process embeds the Balanced Scorecard in a strategic learning framework. We consider this process to be the most innovative and most important aspect of the entire scorecard management process. This process provides the capability for organizational learning at the executive level. Managers in organizations today do not have a procedure to receive feedback about their strategy and to test the hypotheses on which the strategy is based. The Balanced Scorecard enables them to monitor and adjust the implementation of their strategy, and, if necessary, to make fundamental changes in the strategy itself.

By having near-term milestones established for financial, as well as other BSC measures, monthly and quarterly management reviews can still examine financial results. More important, however, they can also examine closely whether the business unit is achieving its targets for customers, for internal processes and innovation, and for employees, systems, and procedures. Management reviews and updates shift from reviewing the past to learning about the future. Managers discuss not only how past results have been achieved but also whether their expectations for the future remain on track.

The process of strategic learning starts with the first process in Figure 1-2, the clarification of a shared vision that the entire organization wants to achieve. The use of measurement as a language helps translate complex and frequently nebulous concepts into a more precise form that can gain consensus among senior executives. The communication and alignment process, the second process in Figure 1-2, mobilizes all individuals into actions directed at attaining organizational objectives. The emphasis on cause and effect in constructing a scorecard introduces dynamic systems thinking. It enables individuals in various parts of an organization to understand how the pieces fit together, how their role influences others and, eventually, the entire organization. The planning, target setting, and strategic initiative process—the third process in Figure 1-2—defines specific, quantitative performance goals for the organization across a balanced set of outcomes and performance drivers. A comparison of the desired performance goals with current levels establishes the performance gap that strategic initiatives can be designed to close. Thus the Balanced Scorecard not only measures change; it fosters change.

The first three critical management processes shown in Figure 1-2 are vital for implementing strategy. But, by themselves, they are insufficient. For a simpler world, they would be adequate. The theory behind the top-down command-and-control model is that the captain of the ship (the CEO) determines the direction and speed of the ship (the business unit). The sailors (the managers and front-line employees) carry out the orders and implement the plan determined by the captain. Operational and management control systems are established to ensure that the managers and employees act in accordance with the strategic plan established by senior executives. This linear process of establishing a vision and strategy, communicating and linking the vision and strategy to all organizational participants, and aligning organizational actions and initiatives to achieving long-run strategic goals is an example of a single-loop feedback process. With single-loop learning, the objective remains constant. Departures from planned results do not cause people to question whether the planned results are still desirable. Nor do they question whether the methods being used to accomplish the objectives are still appropriate. Departures from the planned trajectory are treated as defects, with remedial actions launched to bring the organization back onto the intended path.

The strategies for information age organizations, however, cannot be this linear or this stable. Today's information age organizations operate in more turbulent environments, and senior managers need to receive feedback about more complicated strategies. The planned strategy, though initiated with the best of intentions and with the best available information and knowledge, may no longer be appropriate or valid for contemporary conditions. The metaphor is closer to that of sailing in a highly competitive race, under changing weather and sea conditions, than that of steering an isolated ship, through a stable environment, to a destination. In a sailboat race, a chain of command still exists. But the captain is constantly monitoring the environment, being highly sensitive and often responding tactically and strategically to shifts in competitors' behavior, team and boat capabilities, wind conditions, and water current. And the captain must receive information from a myriad of sources, such as personal observation, instrumentation and measurements, and, especially, the advice of tacticians on the boat who also survey the conditions so that they can devise plans to take advantage of environmental changes and to counter competitor behavior.

In such constantly shifting environments, new strategies can emerge from capitalizing on opportunities or countering threats that were not anticipated when the initial strategic plan was articulated. Frequently, ideas for seizing new opportunities come from managers farther down in the organization.[9] Yet traditional management systems do not encourage nor facilitate the formulation, implementation, and testing of strategy in continually changing environments.

Organizations need the capacity for double-loop learning.[10] Double-loop learning occurs when managers question their underlying assumptions and reflect on whether the theory under which they were operating remains consistent with current evidence, observations, and experience. Of course, managers need feedback about whether their planned strategy is being executed according to plan—the single-loop learning process. But even more important, they need feedback about whether the planned strategy remains a viable and successful strategy—the double-loop learning process. Managers need information so that they can question whether the fundamental assumptions made when they launched the strategy are valid.

A properly constructed Balanced Scorecard articulates the theory of the business. The scorecard should be based on a series of cause-and-effect relationships derived from the strategy, including estimates of the response times and magnitudes of the linkages among the scorecard measures. For example, how long before improvements in product quality and on-time delivery will lead to an increased share of customers' business and higher margins on existing sales, and how large will the effect be? With such quantification of the linkages among scorecard measures, periodic reviews and performance monitoring can take the form of hypothesis testing.

If an organization's employees and managers have delivered on the performance drivers—such as reskilling of employees, availability of information systems, development of new products and services—then failure to achieve the expected outcomes—for example, higher sales or multiple products sold per customer—signals that the theory embodied in the strategy may not be valid. Such disconfirming evidence should be taken seriously. Managers must then engage in an intense dialogue to review market conditions, the value propositions they are delivering to targeted customers, competitor behavior, and internal capabilities. The result may be to reaffirm belief in the current strategy but to adjust the quantitative relationship among the strategic measures on the Balanced Scorecard. Alternatively, the intensive strategic reviews may reveal that an entirely new strategy is required—a double-loop learning outcome—in light of the new knowledge about market conditions and internal capabilities. In either case, the scorecard will have stimulated learning among key executives about the viability and validity of their strategy. In our experience, this process of data gathering, hypothesis testing, reflection, strategic learning, and adaptation is fundamental to the successful implementation of business strategy.

This strategic feedback and learning process completes the loop embodied in Figure 1-2. The strategic-learning process feeds into the next vision and strategy process where the objectives in the various perspectives are reviewed, updated, and replaced in accordance with the most current view of the strategic outcomes and required performance drivers for the upcoming periods.

SUMMARY

Information age companies will succeed by investing in and managing their intellectual assets. Functional specialization must be integrated into customer-based business processes. Mass production and service delivery of standard products and services must be replaced by flexible, responsive, and high-quality delivery of innovative products and services that can be individualized to targeted customer segments. Innovation and improvement of products, services, and processes will be generated by reskilled employees, superior information technology, and aligned organizational procedures.

As organizations invest in acquiring these new capabilities, their success (or failure) cannot be motivated or measured in the short run by the traditional financial accounting model. This financial model, developed for trading companies and industrial age corporations, measures events of the past, not the investments in the capabilities that provide value for the future.

The Balanced Scorecard is a new framework for integrating measures derived from strategy. While retaining financial measures of past performance, the Balanced Scorecard introduces the drivers of future financial performance. The drivers, encompassing customer, internal-business-process, and learning and growth perspectives, are derived from an explicit and rigorous translation of the organization's strategy into tangible objectives and measures.

The Balanced Scorecard, however, is more than a new measurement system. Innovative companies use the scorecard as the central, organizing framework for their management processes. Companies can develop an initial Balanced Scorecard with fairly narrow objectives: to gain clarification, consensus, and focus on their strategy, and then to communicate that strategy throughout the organization. The real power of the Balanced Scorecard, however, occurs when it is transformed from a measurement system to a management system. As more and more companies work with the Balanced Scorecard, they see how it can be used to

- clarify and gain consensus about strategy,
- communicate strategy throughout the organization,
- align departmental and personal goals to the strategy,
- link strategic objectives to long-term targets and annual budgets,
- identify and align strategic initiatives,
- perform periodic and systematic strategic reviews, and
- obtain feedback to learn about and improve strategy.

The Balanced Scorecard fills the void that exists in most management systems—the lack of a systematic process to implement and obtain feedback about strategy. Management processes built around the scorecard enable the organization to become aligned and focused on implementing the long-term strategy. Used in this way, the Balanced Scorecard becomes the foundation for managing information age organizations.

NOTES

1. A. D. Chandler, Jr., *Scale and Scope: The Dynamics of Industrial Capitalism* (Cambridge, Mass.: Harvard University Press, 1990).
2. See A. D. Chandler, Jr., *The Visible Hand: The Managerial Revolution in American Business* (Cambridge, Mass.: Harvard University Press, 1977) and T. H. Johnson and R. S. Kaplan, *Relevance Lost: The Rise and Fall of Management Accounting* (Boston: Harvard Business School Press, 1987).
3. H. Itami, *Mobilizing Invisible Assets* (Cambridge, Mass.: Harvard University Press, 1987).
4. J. Champy and M. Hammer, *Reengineering the Corporation: A Manifesto for Business Revolution* (New York: HarperBusiness, 1993).
5. Industrial age companies used traditional production and service delivery processes to supply different models and options to diverse consumers. This high-cost approach was not made visible until the development of activity-

based cost systems in the mid-1980s; see R. Cooper and R. S. Kaplan, "Measure Costs Right: Make the Right Decisions," *Harvard Business Review* (September–October 1988): 96–103. Now companies recognize they must either achieve greater focus in the customer segments they choose to serve or deploy technology-based product and service delivery processes that enable high-variety outputs to be supplied at low resource costs.

6. J. L. Bower and C. M. Christensen, "Disruptive Technologies: Catching the Wave," *Harvard Business Review* (January–February 1995): 43–53.

7. R. S. Kaplan and A. Sweeney, "Romeo Engine Plant," 9-194-032 (Boston: Harvard Business School, 1994).

8. R. K. Elliott, "The Third Wave Breaks on the Shores of Accounting," *Accounting Horizons* (June 1992): 61–85.

9. R. Simons, *Levers of Control: How Managers Use Innovative Control Systems to Drive Strategic Renewal* (Boston: Harvard Business School Press, 1995), 20.

10. For an extensive discussion of single- and double-loop learning in management processes, see Chris Argyris and Donald A. Schön, *Organizational Learning II: Theory, Method, and Practice* (Reading Mass.: Addison-Wesley, 1996); and "Teaching Smart People How to Learn," *Harvard Business Review* (May–June 1991): 99–109.

Why Does Business Need a Balanced Scorecard?

MEASUREMENT MATTERS: "If you can't measure it, you can't manage it." An organization's measurement system strongly affects the behavior of people both inside and outside the organization. If companies are to survive and prosper in information age competition, they must use measurement and management systems derived from their strategies and capabilities. Unfortunately, many organizations espouse strategies about customer relationships, core competencies, and organizational capabilities while motivating and measuring performance only with financial measures. The Balanced Scorecard retains financial measurement as a critical summary of managerial and business performance, but it highlights a more general and integrated set of measurements that link current customer, internal process, employee, and system performance to long-term financial success.

FINANCIAL MEASUREMENT

Historically, the measurement system for business has been financial. Indeed, accounting has been called the "language of business." Bookkeeping records of financial transactions can be traced back thousands of years, when they were used by Egyptians, Phoenicians, and Sumerians to facilitate commercial transactions. A few centuries later, during the age of exploration, the activities of global trading companies were measured and monitored by accountants' double-entry books of accounts. The Industrial Revolution, during the nineteenth century, spawned giant textile, railroad, steel, machine-tool, and retailing companies. Innovations in measuring the financial performance of these organizations played a vital role in their successful growth.[1] And financial innovations, such as the return-on-investment (ROI) metric, and operating and cash budgets, were critical to the great success of early-twentieth century enterprises like DuPont and General Motors.[2] The post–World War II trend to diversified enterprises created an intracorporation demand for reporting and evaluation of business unit performance, a practice used extensively by diversified companies like General Electric and made famous, if not notorious, by the rigorous financial reporting and controls of Harold Geneen at IT&T.

Thus, as we stand at the end of the twentieth century, the financial aspect of business unit performance has been highly developed. Many commentators, however, have criticized the extensive, even exclusive use of financial measurements in business.[3] At its heart, an overemphasis on achieving and maintaining short-term financial results can cause companies to overinvest in short-term fixes and to underinvest in long-term value creation, particularly in the intangible and intellectual assets that generate future growth.

As a specific example, the FMC Corporation through the 1970s and 1980s produced one of the best financial performances of any large U.S. corporation. Yet in 1992, a new management team performed a strategic review to determine the best future course to maximize shareholder value. The review concluded that while excellent short-run operating performance was still important, the company had to launch a growth strategy. Larry Brady, president of FMC, recalled:

As a highly diversified company, . . . the return-on-capital-employed (ROCE) measure was especially important to us. At year-end, we rewarded division managers who delivered predictable financial performance. We had run the company tightly for the past 20 years and had been successful. But it was becoming less clear where future growth would come from and where the company should look for breakthroughs into new areas. We had become a high return-on-investment company but had less potential for further growth. It was also not at all clear from our financial reports what progress we were making in implementing long-term initiatives.[4]

Inevitably, as managers are pressured to deliver consistent and excellent short-term financial performance, trade-offs are made that limit the search for investments in growth opportunities. Even worse, the pressure for short-term financial performance can cause companies to reduce spending on new product development, process improvements, human resource development, information technology, data bases, and systems as well as customer and market development. In the short run, the financial accounting model reports these spending cutbacks as increases in reported income, even when the reductions have cannibalized a company's stock of assets and its capabilities for creating future economic value. Alternatively, a company could maximize short-term financial results by exploiting customers through high prices or lower service. In the short run, these actions enhance reported profitability, but the lack of customer loyalty and satisfaction will leave the company highly vulnerable to competitive inroads.

As another example, Xerox, up through the mid-1970s, enjoyed a virtual monopoly on plain paper copiers. Xerox did not sell its machines; it leased them and earned revenues on every copy made on these machines. Sales and profits from leasing machines, and those of supporting items like paper and toner, were large and growing. But customers, apart from concern about high copying costs, for which no ready alternative was available, were disgruntled about the high breakdown rates and malfunctions of these expensive machines.[5] Rather than redesign the machines so that they would break down less frequently, Xerox executives saw an opportunity to enhance their financial results even further. They permitted direct purchase of their machines, and then established an extensive field service force as a separate profit center, to repair broken machines at customer locations. Given the demand for its services, this division soon was a substantial contributor to Xerox's profit growth. Furthermore, since no output could be produced while waiting for the service person, companies bought additional machines as backups, so sales and profits grew even higher. Thus, all the financial indicators—sales and profit growth, return on investment—were signaling a highly successful strategy.

But customers were still unhappy and surly. They did not want their supplier to excel at having a superb field service force. They wanted cost-efficient machines that did not break down. When Japanese and American entrants were eventually able to offer machines that produced comparable or even better quality copies, that did not break down, and that were lower priced, they were embraced by Xerox's dissatisfied and disloyal customers.

Xerox, one of the most successful U.S. companies from 1955 to 1975, almost failed. Only under a new CEO, with a passion for quality and customer service that he communicated throughout the organization, did the company make a remarkable turnaround in the 1980s.

Financial measures are inadequate for guiding and evaluating organizations' trajectories through competitive environments. They are lagging indicators that fail to capture much of the value that has been created or destroyed by managers' actions in the most recent accounting period. The financial measures tell some, but not all, of the story about past actions and they fail to provide adequate guidance for the actions to be taken today and the day after to create future financial value.

THE BALANCED SCORECARD

The Balanced Scorecard provides executives with a comprehensive framework that translates a company's vision and strategy into a coherent set of performance measures. Many companies have adopted mission statements to communicate fundamental values and beliefs to all employees. The mission statement addresses core beliefs and identifies target markets and core products. For example,

To be the most successful company in the airline business.

To be the best broad-based financial institution in our chosen markets.

Mission statements should be inspirational. They should supply energy and motivation to the organization.[6] But inspirational mission statements and slogans are not sufficient. As Peter Senge observed: "Many leaders have personal visions that never get translated into shared visions that galvanize an organization. What has been lacking is a discipline for translating individual vision into shared vision."[7]

As a specific example, Norman Chambers, the chief executive officer of Rockwater, an undersea construction company, led a two-month effort among senior executives and project managers to develop a detailed mission statement. Shortly after distributing this mission statement, Chambers received a phone call from a project manager on a drilling platform in the middle of the North Sea. "Norm, I want you to know that I believe in the mission statement. I want to act in accordance with the mission statement. I'm here with my customer. What am I supposed to do? How should I be behaving each day, over the life of this project, to deliver on our mission statement?" Chambers realized that there was a large void between the mission statement and employees' day-to-day actions.

The Balanced Scorecard translates mission and strategy into objectives and measures, organized into four different perspectives: financial, customer, internal business process, and learning and growth. The scorecard provides a framework, a language, to communicate mission and strategy; it uses measurement to inform employees about the drivers of current and future success. By articulating the outcomes the organization desires and the drivers of those outcomes, senior executives hope to channel the energies, the abilities, and the specific knowledge of people throughout the organization toward achieving the long-term goals.

Many people think of measurement as a tool to control behavior and to evaluate past performance. As we discussed in Chapter 1, the measures on a Balanced Scorecard should be used in a different way—to articulate the strategy of the business, to communicate the strategy of the business, and to help align individual, organizational, and cross-departmental initiatives to achieve a common goal. Used in this way, the scorecard does not strive to keep individuals and organizational units in compliance with a pre-established plan, the traditional control system objective. The Balanced Scorecard should be used as a communication, informing, and learning system, *not* a controlling system.

The four perspectives of the scorecard permit a balance between short- and long-term objectives, between outcomes desired and the performance drivers of those outcomes, and between hard objectives measures and softer, more subjective measures. While the multiplicity of measures on a Balanced Scorecard may seem confusing, properly constructed scorecards, as we will see, contain a unity of purpose since all the measures are directed toward achieving an integrated strategy.

Financial Perspective

The BSC retains the financial perspective since financial measures are valuable in summarizing the readily measurable economic consequences of actions already taken. Financial performance measures indicate whether a company's strategy, implementation, and execution are contributing to bottom-line improvement. Financial objectives typically relate to profitability—measured, for example, by operating income, return-on-capital-employed, or, more recently, economic value-added. Alternative financial objectives can be rapid sales growth or generation of cash flow. We will discuss, in Chapter 3, the linkages between a business's strategy and its objectives and measures for the financial perspective.

Customer Perspective

In the customer perspective of the Balanced Scorecard, managers identify the customer and market segments in which the business unit will compete and the measures of the business unit's performance in these targeted segments. This perspective typically includes several core or generic measures of the successful outcomes from a well-formulated and -implemented strategy. The core outcome measures include customer satisfaction, customer retention, new customer acquisition, customer profitability, and market and account share in targeted segments. But the customer perspective should also include specific measures of the value propositions that the company will deliver to customers in targeted market segments. The segment-specific drivers of core customer outcomes represent those factors that are critical for customers to switch to or remain loyal to their suppliers. For example, customers could value short lead times and on-time delivery. Or a constant stream of innovative products and services. Or a supplier able to anticipate their emerging needs and capable of developing new products and approaches to satisfy those needs. The customer perspective enables business unit managers to articulate the customer and market-based strategy that will deliver superior future financial returns. Chapter 4 presents an extensive discussion of the development of objectives and measures for the customer perspective.

Internal-Business-Process Perspective

In the internal-business-process perspective, executives identify the critical internal processes in which the organization must excel. These processes enable the business unit to:

- deliver the value propositions that will attract and retain customers in targeted market segments, and
- satisfy shareholder expectations of excellent financial returns.

The internal-business-process measures focus on the internal processes that will have the greatest impact on customer satisfaction and achieving an organization's financial objectives.

The internal-business-process perspective reveals two fundamental differences between the traditional and the BSC approaches to performance measurement. Traditional approaches attempt to monitor and improve existing business processes. They may go beyond financial measures of performance by incorporating quality and time-based metrics. But they still focus on improvement of existing processes. The scorecard approach, however, will usually identify entirely new processes at which an organization must excel to meet customer and financial objectives. For example, a company may realize that it must develop a process to anticipate customer needs or one to deliver new services that target customers value. The BSC internal-business-process objectives highlight the processes, several of which it may not be currently be performing at all, that are most critical for an organization's strategy to succeed.

The second departure of the BSC approach is to incorporate innovation processes into the internal-business-process perspective (see Figure 2-1). Traditional performance measurement systems focus on the processes of delivering today's products and services to today's customers. They attempt to control and improve existing operations that represent the *short wave* of value creation. This short wave of value creation begins with the receipt of an order from an existing customer for an existing product (or service)

Figure 2-1 The Internal-Business-Process Value-Chain Perspective

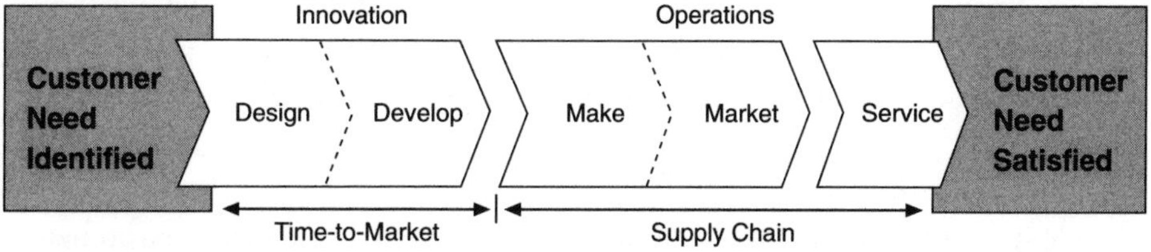

Business Processes

Innovation Process	Operations Process
▪ Product Design	▪ Manufacturing
▪ Product Development	▪ Marketing
	▪ Postsale Service

and ends with the delivery of the product to the customer. The organization creates value from producing, delivering, and servicing this product and the customer at a cost below the price it receives.

But the drivers of long-term financial success may require an organization to create entirely new products and services that will meet the emerging needs of current and future customers. The innovation process, the *long wave* of value creation, is for many companies a more powerful driver of future financial performance than the short-term operating cycle. For many companies, their ability to manage successfully a multiyear product-development process or to develop a capability to reach entirely new categories of customers may be more critical for future economic performance than managing existing operations efficiently, consistently, and responsively.

Managers, however, do not have to choose between these two vital internal processes. The internal-business-process perspective of the Balanced Scorecard incorporates objectives and measures for both the long-wave innovation cycle as well as the short-wave operations cycle. Chapter 5 contains many examples of how companies are formulating objectives and measures for the internal-business-process perspective.

Learning and Growth Perspective

The fourth perspective of the Balanced Scorecard, learning and growth, identifies the infrastructure that the organization must build to create long-term growth and improvement. The customer and internal-business-process perspectives identify the factors most critical for current and future success. Businesses are unlikely to be able to meet their long-term targets for customers and internal processes using today's technologies and capabilities. Also, intense global competition requires that companies continually improve their capabilities for delivering value to customers and shareholders.

Organizational learning and growth come from three principal sources: people, systems, and organizational procedures. The financial, customer, and internal-business-process objectives on the Balanced Scorecard typically will reveal large gaps between the existing capabilities of people, systems, and procedures and what will be required to achieve breakthrough performance. To close these gaps, businesses will have to invest in reskilling employees, enhancing information technology and systems, and aligning organizational procedures and routines. These objectives are articulated in the learning and growth perspective of the Balanced Scorecard. As in the customer perspective, employee-based measures include a mixture of generic outcome measures—employee satisfaction, retention, training, and skills—along with specific drivers of these generic measures, such as detailed, business-specific indexes of the particular skills required for the new competitive environment. Information systems capabilities can be measured by real-time availability of accurate, critical customer and internal process information to employees on the front lines of decision making and actions. Organizational procedures can examine alignment of employee incentives with overall organizational success factors, and measured rates of improvement in critical customer-based and internal processes. These issues are explored in further detail in Chapter 6.

Altogether, the Balanced Scorecard translates vision and strategy into objectives and measures across a balanced set of perspectives. The scorecard includes measures of desired outcomes as well as processes that will drive the desired outcomes for the future.

LINKING MULTIPLE SCORECARD MEASURES
TO A SINGLE STRATEGY

Many companies may already be using a mixture of financial and nonfinan-cial measures, even in senior management reviews and to communicate with boards of directors. Especially in recent years, the renewed focus on customers and process quality has caused many organizations to track and communicate measures on customer satisfaction and complaints, product and process defect levels, and missed delivery dates. In France, companies have developed and used, for more than two decades, the *Tableau de Bord,* a dashboard of key indicators of organizational success. The *Tableau de Bord* is designed to help employees "pilot" the organization by identifying key success factors, especially those that can be measured as physical variables.[8] Does a dashboard of financial and nonfinancial indicators supply a "Balanced Scorecard?"

Our experience is that the best Balanced Scorecards are more than collec-tions of critical indicators or key success factors. The multiple measures on a properly constructed Balanced Scorecard should consist of a linked series of objectives and measures that are both consistent and mutually reinforcing. The metaphor should be a flight simulator, not a dashboard of instrument dials. Like a flight simulator, the scorecard should incorporate the complex set of cause-and-effect relationships among the critical variables, including leads, lags, and feedback loops, that describe the trajectory, the flight plan, of the strategy. The linkages should incorporate both cause-and-effect relationships, and mixtures of outcome measures and performance drivers.

Cause-and-Effect Relationships

A strategy is a set of hypotheses about cause and effect. The measurement system should make the relationships (hypotheses) among objectives (and measures) in the various perspectives explicit so that they can be managed and validated. The chain of cause and effect should pervade all four perspectives of a Balanced Scorecard. For example, return-on-capital-employed may be a scorecard measure in the financial perspective. The driver of this measure could be repeat and expanded sales from existing customers, the result of a high degree of loyalty among those customers. So, customer loyalty is included on the scorecard (in the customer perspective) because it is expected to have a strong influence on ROCE. But how will the organization achieve customer loyalty? Analysis of customer preferences may reveal that on-time delivery of orders is highly valued by customers. Thus, improved OTD is expected to lead to higher customer loyalty, which, in turn, is expected to lead to higher financial performance. So both customer loyalty and OTD are incorporated into the customer perspective of the scorecard.

The process continues by asking what internal processes must the company excel at to achieve exceptional on-time delivery. To achieve improved OTD, the business may need to achieve short cycle times in operating processes and high-quality internal processes, both factors that could be scorecard measures in the internal perspective. And how do organizations improve the quality and reduce the cycle times of their internal processes? By training and improving the skills of their operating employees, an objective that would be a candidate for the learning and growth perspective. We can now see how an entire chain of cause-and-effect relationships can be established as a vertical vector through the four BSC perspectives:

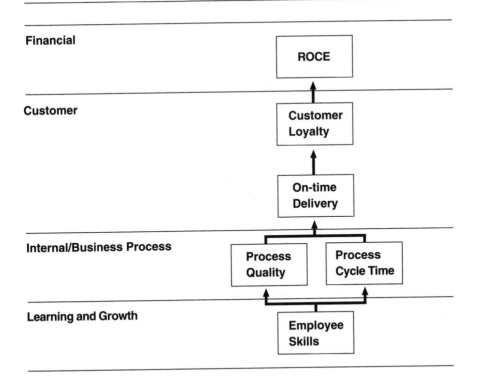

In a similar vein, recent work in the service profit chain has emphasized the causal relationships among employee satisfaction, customer satisfaction, customer loyalty, market share, and, eventually, financial performance.[9]

Thus, a properly constructed Balanced Scorecard should tell the story of the business unit's strategy. It should identify and make explicit the sequence of hypotheses about the cause-and-effect relationships between outcome measures and the performance drivers of those outcomes. Every measure selected for a Balanced Scorecard should be an element in a chain of cause-and-effect relationships that communicates the meaning of the business unit's strategy to the organization.

Performance Drivers

A good Balanced Scorecard should also have a mix of outcome measures and performance drivers. Outcome measures without performance drivers do not communicate how the outcomes are to be achieved. They also do not provide an early indication about whether the strategy is being implemented successfully. Conversely, performance drivers—such as cycle times and part-per-million (PPM) defect rates—without outcome measures may enable the business unit to achieve short-term operational improvements, but will fail to reveal whether the operational improvements have been translated into expanded business with existing and new customers, and, eventually, to enhanced financial performance. A good Balanced Scorecard should have an appropriate mix of outcomes (lagging indicators) and performance drivers (leading indicators) of the business unit's strategy.

Chapter 7 elaborates further on the theme that the Balanced Scorecard is not merely a collection of financial and nonfinancial measurements. The scorecard should be the translation of the business unit's strategy into a linked set of measures that define both the long-term strategic objectives, as well as the mechanisms for achieving those objectives.

SHOULD FINANCIAL MEASURES BE SCRAPPED?

Is the financial objective component in a Balanced Scorecard even relevant for driving the long-term performance of the organization? As noted, some critics see many business managers' short-term orientation arising from and inherent in attempting to achieve financial targets for measures like return-on-capital-employed, earnings-per-share, or even current share price. Several critics have advocated scrapping financial measures entirely to measure business unit performance. They argue that in today's technologically and customer-driven global competition, financial measures provide poor guidelines for success. They urge managers to focus on improving customer satisfaction, quality, cycle times, and employee skills and motivation. According to this theory, as companies make fundamental improvements in their operations, the financial numbers will take care of themselves.

Not all companies are able to translate improvements in quality and customer satisfaction into bottom-line financial results. Take the example of one electronics company, which, during the 1987–1990 period, had made remarkable improvements in its quality and on-time delivery performance. Outgoing defect rates dropped by a factor of 10, yields doubled, and missed delivery dates dropped from 30% to 4%. Yet these breakthrough improvements in quality, productivity, and customer service failed to deliver financial benefits. During the same three-year period, this former growth company produced flat financial performance, and disappointed shareholders saw the company's stock price drop by 70%.

How could such an anomalous outcome occur? Many quality and productivity improvement programs greatly expand the effective capacity of the organization. As companies, such as the electronics company described above, improve their quality and response times, they eliminate the need to build, inspect, and rework out-of-conformance products, and they no longer require people or systems to reschedule and expedite delayed orders. In general, once companies eliminate waste and defects, cease doing rework, rescheduling, engineering change orders, and expediting, and gain greater integration among suppliers, internal operations, and customers, they can produce the same quantity of output with much lower demands on resources. But in the short to intermediate term, commitments have already been made to most of the organization's resources, a situation often described as having high "fixed" costs. So reducing demands on resources creates unused capacity but few substantial reductions in spending.

But what about improvements in customer satisfaction, say from delivering zero-defect orders with perfect on-time delivery? If customers' sales are flat or declining, they may not be able to reward their better suppliers with increased business. The company described above was already the number one supplier to many of its customers. Customers may wish to retain one or two backup suppliers so that they are not completely dependent upon a single supplier. If customers are not able or willing to give increased business to a supplier, and if the supplier is reluctant to lay off employees (not unreasonable, since the employees were the source of the improvements in quality, productivity, and customer service), the operational improvements are not easily translated into higher profitability. Improved financial results are not an automatic outcome of operational improvement programs to improve quality and reduce cycle times.

Periodic financial statements and financial measures must continue to play an essential role in reminding executives that improved quality, response times, productivity, and new products are means to an end, not the end itself. Such improvements only benefit a company when they can be translated into improved sales, reduced operating expenses, or higher asset utilization. Not all long-term strategies are profitable strategies. IBM, Digital Equipment Corporation, and General Motors in the 1980s did not lack for long-term visions. These companies made huge investments in advanced manufacturing technologies, quality, and research and development. But their guiding vision and business model for success differed from what their markets were now rewarding. They did not recognize early enough that the failure of their financial measures to respond to their investment strategy was a powerful signal that they should reexamine the basic assumptions of their strategy. A failure to convert improved operational performance into improved financial performance should send executives back to the drawing board to rethink the company's strategy or its implementation plans.

Companies with greatly improved operating performance must identify how to increase sales to existing customers, how to market new products with attractive capabilities, and how to market the company's products and services to entirely new customers and market segments. Such new segments, previously inaccessible to a company, could become valued customers because of a company's improved capabilities in lower cost, superior performance, and higher quality, delivery, and customer service.

A comprehensive system of measurement and management must specify how improvements in operations, customer service, and new products and services link to improved financial performance, through higher sales, greater operating margins, faster asset turnover, and reduced operating expenses. The Balanced Scorecard must retain a strong emphasis on financial outcomes. Ultimately, causal paths from all the measures on a scorecard should be linked to financial objectives. The scorecard obtains the benefits from keeping financial measurements as ultimate outcomes, without the myopia and distortions that come from an exclusive focus on improving short-term financial measures.

FOUR PERSPECTIVES: ARE THEY SUFFICIENT?

The four perspectives of the Balanced Scorecard have been found to be robust across a wide variety of companies and industries. But the four perspectives should be considered a template, not a strait jacket. No mathematical theorem exists that four perspectives are both necessary and sufficient. We have yet to see companies using fewer than these four perspectives, but, depending on industry circumstances and a business unit's strategy, one or more additional perspectives may be needed. For example, some people have expressed concern that although the Balanced Scorecard explicitly recognizes the interests of shareholders and customers, it does not explicitly incorporate the interests of other important stakeholders, such as employees, suppliers, and the community. The employee perspective is certainly incorporated in virtually all scorecards within the learning and growth perspective. Similarly, if strong supplier relationships are part of the strategy leading to breakthrough customer and/or financial performance, the outcome and performance driver measures for supplier relationships should be incorporated within the organization's internal-business-process perspective. But we don't think that all stakeholders are automatically entitled to a position on a business unit's scorecard. The scorecard outcomes and performance drivers should measure those factors that create competitive advantage and breakthroughs for an organization.

Take the example of a chemicals company that wished to create an entirely new perspective to reflect environmental considerations. We challenged them:

> *Keeping the environment clean is important. Companies must comply with laws and regulations, but such compliance doesn't seem to be the basis for competitive advantage.*

The CEO and other senior executives responded immediately:

> *We don't agree. Our franchise is under severe pressure in many of the communities where we operate. Our strategy is to go well beyond what current laws and regulations require so that we can be seen in every community as not only a law-abiding corporate citizen but as the outstanding corporate citizen, measured both environmentally and by creating well-paying, safe, and productive jobs. If regulations get tightened, some of our competitors may lose their franchise, but we expect to have earned the right to continue operations.*

They insisted that outstanding environmental and community performance was a central part of that company's strategy and had to be an integral part of its scorecard.

Thus, all stakeholder interests, when they are vital for the success of the business unit's strategy, can be incorporated in a Balanced Scorecard. Stakeholder objectives, however, should not be appended to the scorecard via an isolated set of measures that managers must keep "in control." Other measurement and control systems can establish diagnostic and compliance requirements far more effectively than the Balanced Scorecard.[10] The measures that appear on the Balanced Scorecard should be fully integrated into the chain of causal event linkages that define and tell the story of the business unit's strategy.

ORGANIZATIONAL UNIT FOR A
BALANCED SCORECARD

Some companies operate within only a single industry. Indeed, some of the early applications of the Balanced Scorecard were for companies in particular niches of the semiconductor industry, like Advanced Micro Devices (AMD) and Analog Devices, or in a particular segment of the computer industry, like Apple Computer. These companies developed Balanced Scorecards that were also Corporate Scorecards (the term used at Analog Devices). Most corporations, however, are sufficiently diverse that constructing a corporate-level scorecard may be a difficult first task. Balanced Scorecards are best defined for strategic business units (SBUs). An ideal strategic business unit for a Balanced Scorecard conducts activities across an entire value chain: innovation, operations, marketing, distribution, selling, and service. Such an SBU has its own products and customers, marketing and distribution channels, and production facilities. And, most important, it has a well-defined strategy.

Once a Balanced Scorecard has been developed for an SBU, it becomes the basis for Balanced Scorecards for departments and functional units within the SBU. Mission and strategy statements for departments and functional units can be defined within the framework established by the business unit mission, strategy, and scorecard. Managers in departments and functional units can then develop their own scorecards that will be consistent with and help deliver the SBU mission and strategy. In this way, the SBU scorecard is cascaded down to local responsibility centers within the SBU, allowing all responsibility centers to work coherently toward the SBU objectives. The relevant question for whether a department or functional unit should have a Balanced Scorecard is whether that organizational unit has (or should have) a mission, a strategy, customers (internal or external), and internal processes that enable it to accomplish its mission and strategy. If it does, the unit is a valid candidate for a Balanced Scorecard.

If the organizational unit is defined too broadly, say beyond a strategic business unit, however, it may be difficult to define a coherent, integrated strategy. Instead, the scorecard objectives and measures may end up as an average or a blend of several different strategies. For example, originally we attempted to help an industrial gases company create a scorecard. Early on, it became clear that the company had three distinct business units, each defined by a unique distribution channel that had entirely different strategies and customers. It proved far simpler to construct scorecards for the individual SBUs, defined by their unique distribution channels.

Often, however, even corporations containing several, somewhat independent SBUs have started by developing a Balanced Scorecard at the corporate level. Such a corporate-level scorecard establishes a common framework, a corporate template, about themes and common visions that must be implemented in the scorecards developed at the individual SBUs. The corporate scorecard also establishes how the corporation adds value beyond the value created by the collection of SBUs operating as independent units. This value-creating role of the corporation is referred to by Goold and colleagues as the "parenting advantage."[11] Chapter 8 elaborates further on integrating SBU scorecards into the broader corporate framework.

STRATEGIC POSITIONING OR CORE COMPETENCIES/CAPABILITIES-DRIVEN?

In this book we will approach strategy as choosing the market and customer segments the business unit intends to serve, identifying the critical internal business processes that the unit must excel at to deliver the value propositions to customers in the targeted market segments, and selecting the individual and organizational capabilities required for the internal, customer, and financial objectives. This approach is consistent with the industry and competitive analysis articulated in several of Michael Porter's widely followed corporate strategy books.[12] We have seen this approach work well with dozens of organizations, as we will illustrate in subsequent chapters.

Alternatively, some companies compete by exploiting unique capabilities, resources, and core competencies.[13] For example, Honda leverages its capabilities for designing and building superb engines into market segments—motorcycles, automobiles, lawn mowers, utilities—where this capability gives it competitive advantage. Canon leverages its world-class capabilities in optics and miniaturization, developed initially for cameras, into other products, such as copying and facsimile machines and computer printers. Companies deploying a strategy based on core competencies or unique capabilities may wish to start their strategic planning process by identifying these critical competencies and capabilities for their internal-business-process perspective, and then, for the customer perspective, selecting customer and market segments where these competencies and capabilities are most critical for delivering customer value.

The Balanced Scorecard is primarily a mechanism for strategy implementation, not for strategy formulation.[14] It can accommodate either approach for formulating business unit strategy—starting from the customer perspective, or starting from excellent internal-business-process capabilities. For whatever approach that SBU senior executives use to formulate their strategy, the Balanced Scorecard will provide an invaluable mechanism for translating that strategy into specific objectives, measures, and targets, and monitoring the implementation of that strategy during subsequent periods.

APPENDIX:
LIMITATIONS OF FINANCIAL MEASUREMENTS OF BUSINESS PERFORMANCE

Several reports have expressed concern with an overemphasis on financial measures of corporate performance. The Harvard Business School Council on Competitiveness project identified the following systematic differences between investments made by U.S. corporations versus those made in Japan and Germany:

- The U.S. system is less supportive of long-term corporate investment because of the emphasis on improving short-term returns to influence current share prices.

- The U.S. system favors those forms of investment for which returns are most readily measurable; this leads to underinvestment in intangible assets—product and process innovation, employee skills, customer satisfaction—whose short-term returns are more difficult to measure.

- The U.S. system leads to overinvestment in assets that can be easily valued (such as through mergers and acquisitions) and to underinvestment in internal development projects whose returns are more difficult to value.

- The U.S. system allows companies with very strong asset bases (such as in natural resources, consumer goods companies with strong brand names, and film and broadcast companies) to operate inefficiently, without fully exploiting their undervalued assets, as long as short-term earnings are satisfactory. Realizing the value from these company's assets required expensive financial innovations involving hostile tender offers, leveraged buyouts, and issuance of junk bonds.[15]

Additional evidence comes from external investors expressing dissatisfaction with seeing only financial reports of past performance. They want information that will help them forecast the future performance of companies in which they have invested their capital (or in which they are contemplating investing). For example, Peter C. Lincoln, vice president of the U.S. Steel and Carnegie Pension Fund stated: "Nonfinancial performance measurement—such as measuring customer satisfaction or the speed at which new products move from the development stage—would be very helpful to investors and analysts. Companies should report this type of information to provide a complete picture of their operations."[16]

The concern with the overemphasis on financial performance measures has even permeated the leading U.S. professional association of public accountants. A high-level special committee on financial reporting of the American Institute of Certified Public Accountants reinforced our concerns with exclusive reliance on financial reporting for measuring business performance: "Users focus on the future while today's business reporting focuses on the past. Although information about the past is a useful indicator of future performance, users also need forward-looking information." The committee acknowledged the importance of reporting on how well companies are creating value for the future. The committee recommended linking business performance reporting to management's strategic vision: "Many users want to see a company through the eyes of management to help them understand management's perspective and predict where management will lead the company." It went on to say that nonfinancial measurement must play a key role: "Management should disclose the financial and nonfinancial measurements it uses in managing the business that quantify the effects of key activities and events."[17]

The committee concluded by recommending that companies adopt a more "balanced" and forward-looking approach:

To meet users' changing needs, business reporting must:

- *Provide more information about plans, opportunities, risks and uncertainties*

- *Focus more on the factors that create longer-term value, including nonfinancial measures indicating how key business processes are performing*

- *Better align information reported externally with the information reported internally to senior management to manage the business.*[18]

We discuss the opportunities for using the Balanced Scorecard for external reporting in Chapter 9.

NOTES

1. A. D. Chandler, *The Visible Hand: The Managerial Revolution in American Business* (Cambridge, Mass.: Harvard University Press, 1977), and H. T. Johnson and R. S. Kaplan, "Nineteenth-Century Cost Management Systems," Chap. 2 in *Relevance Lost: The Rise and Fall of Management Accounting* (Boston: Harvard Business School Press, 1987).
2. Johnson and Kaplan, "Controlling the Vertically Integrated Firm: The Du Pont Powder Company to 1914," Chap. 4, and "Controlling the Multidivisional Organization: General Motors in the 1920s," Chap. 5 in *Relevance Lost*.
3. Some of these criticisms appear in the appendix to this chapter.
4. "Implementing the Balanced Scorecard at FMC Corporation: An Interview with Larry D. Brady," *Harvard Business Review* (September–October 1993): 143–147.
5. This account is adapted from Joseph M. Juran, "Made in U.S.A.: A Renaissance in Quality," *Harvard Business Review* (July–August 1993): 45.
6. R. Simons, *Levers of Control: How Managers Use Innovative Control Systems to Drive Strategic Renewal* (Boston: Harvard Business School Press, 1995), 134.
7. P. Senge, *The Fifth Discipline: The Art and Practice of the Learning Organization* (New York: Currency Doubleday, 1990).
8. M. Lebas, "Managerial Accounting in France: Overview of Past Tradition and Current Practice," *European Accounting Review* 3, no. 3 (1994): 471–487.
9. J. Heskett, T. Jones, G. Loveman, E. Sasser, and L. Schlesinger, "Putting the Service Profit Chain to Work," *Harvard Business Review* (March–April 1994): 164–174.
10. Simons, *Levers of Control*.
11. M. Goold, A. Campbell, and M. Alexander, *Corporate-Level Strategy: Creating Value in the Multibusiness Company* (New York: John Wiley & Sons, 1994).

12. M. E. Porter, *Competitive Strategy: Techniques for Analyzing Industries and Competitors* (New York: Free Press, 1980) and *Competitive Advantage: Creating and Sustaining Superior Performance* (New York: Free Press, 1985).

13. C. K. Prahalad and G. Hamel, "The Core Competence of the Corporation," *Harvard Business Review* (May–June 1990): 79–91; R. Hayes, "Strategic Planning—Forward in Reverse," *Harvard Business Review* (November–December 1985): 111–119; and D. J. Collis and C. A. Montgomery, "Competing on Resources: Strategy in the 1990s," *Harvard Business Review* (July–August 1995): 118–128.

14. As many organizations start to develop Balanced Scorecards, however, they soon realize that they lack consensus about their business unit's strategy. In such cases, the development of Balanced Scorecard objectives and measures becomes the catalyst for a more precise strategy formulation process among the senior executives.

15. Michael E. Porter, "Capital Disadvantage: America's Failing Capital Investment System," *Harvard Business Review* (September–October 1992): 73.

16. The AICPA Special Committee on Financial Reporting, *Improving Business Reporting—A Customer Focus: Meeting the Information Needs of Investors and Creditors* (New York: American Institute of Certified Public Accountants, 1994), 9.

17. Ibid., 10.

18. Ibid., 30.

MEASURING BUSINESS STRATEGY

COMPANIES USING THE BALANCED SCORECARD as the corner-stone of a new strategic management system have two tasks: first, they must build the scorecard, and, second, they must use the scorecard. We have organized the book into these two tasks. Part One, Chapters 3 through 8, describes the construction of a Balanced Scorecard. Part Two, Chapters 9 through 12, explains how companies are using the Balanced Scorecard as an integrated strategic-management system.

Of course, the two tasks are not independent. As managers start to use their scorecard for key management processes, they will gain further insights about the scorecard itself—which measures are not working, which measures should be modified, and which new measures of strategic success have emerged that should be incorporated into the scorecard.

Chapters 3 through 6 cover the fundamentals for building objectives and measures in each of the four scorecard perspectives: financial, customer, internal business process, and learning and growth. In each chapter, we identify generic measures that show up in most organization's scorecards, such as the following:

Perspective	Generic Measures
Financial	Return on investment and economic value-added
Customer	Satisfaction, retention, market, and account share
Internal	Quality, response time, cost, and new product introductions
Learning and Growth	Employee satisfaction and information system availability

We stress, however, the importance of incorporating measures that are specifically derived from an organization's strategy. We show, with specific examples, how objectives and measures in each of the four perspectives have been derived to communicate and help implement the strategy.

Chapter 7 provides the integration of this strategic theme by illustrating the importance of linking the objectives and measures in the four perspectives into broad, interrelated strategic themes. The linkage of measures across the four perspectives clearly shows that the scorecard is not an ad hoc collection of two dozen or so measures that managers must juggle and trade-off against one another. Rather, in a good Balanced Scorecard, the measures should be linked to communicate a small number of broad strategic themes, such as grow the business, reduce risk, or increase productivity. In Chapter 7 the strategic measures developed in Chapters 3 through 6 are brought together to articulate what constitutes a good Balanced Scorecard.

Chapters 3 through 7 describe Balanced Scorecards for a single organizational unit—the strategic business unit (SBU). Chapter 8 extends the concept to developing a Balanced Scorecard for a corporation or sector that comprises several business units within the same organization. We apply the notion of corporate-level strategy to identify the broad themes that enable the whole (the corporation) to be more valuable than the sum of its parts (the operating divisions). We trace the implications of the corporate-level strategy to the Balanced Scorecards that will be developed for related but decentralized operating units and corporate-level functional departments. Chapter 8 also shows how Balanced Scorecards have been developed for organizational units in the government and not-for-profit sectors.

BALANCED SCORECARD COMPANIES

Throughout the book, we illustrate the innovative measurement practices from many companies. But the comprehensive use of the Balanced Scorecard is told through the experiences of five companies that we have followed closely for the past three years: Rockwater, Metro Bank, Pioneer Petroleum, National Insurance, and Kenyon Stores.

Rockwater is a several-hundred-million-dollar undersea construction company whose clients are major oil, gas, and offshore construction companies. Rockwater, headquartered in Aberdeen, Scotland, is an operating division of Brown & Root Energy Services which, in turn, is part of the Halliburton Corporation, a $4-billion worldwide construction company, headquartered in Dallas, Texas. Rockwater was formed in 1989 by merging two previously independent construction companies, one British and one Dutch. Rockwater's first president, Norman Chambers, used the Balanced Scorecard, starting in 1992, to unite the culture and operating philosophy of the two companies and to enable the new company to compete on the basis of quality, safety, and value-added relationships with customers, not low price. In 1994, Norman Chambers was promoted to president of Brown & Root Energy Services, where he continues to use the Balanced Scorecard as his strategic management system, now applying it at the group level and to each of the operating companies in the group.

Metro Bank is the retail banking division of a major bank with 8,000 employees, a 30% market share of the region's core deposit accounts, and about $1 billion in total revenue. The corporate parent is the surviving entity of a merger of two large and highly competitive banks in a major U.S. metropolitan area. The CEO of Metro Bank implemented the Balanced Scorecard, starting in 1993, to communicate and reinforce a new strategy for the merged retail bank, which would shift from its current focus and strengths in transaction-oriented services to offering a full range of financial products and services to targeted customer segments.

Pioneer Petroleum is the U.S. marketing and refining division of a large worldwide integrated petroleum company. Its CEO launched a scorecard process in 1993 to replace the division's extensive financial analysis and control approach with a new strategic performance-management process. The effort started with a divisionwide scorecard that identified targeted customer segments and broad themes, and then rolled out to developing scorecards for every business and service unit in the division.

National Insurance is the property and casualty division of one of the major, comprehensive U.S. insurance companies. In 1993, when it launched its scorecard project, National had 6,500 employees and $4 billion in revenues. But its operating results were so dismal, with losses measured in the hundreds of millions of dollars, that the parent corporation was considering closing down the company and exiting the property and casualty business entirely. Corporate, in a last ditch effort to save the division, brought in a new management team from outside. The team decided to shift the company from its generalist strategy, where it attempted to provide all underwriting services to all customers and market segments, to a specialist strategy. The team launched its scorecard program to clarify the new strategy and to develop and coordinate the necessary implementation programs. This program also expanded to develop a new strategic management system that succeeded in transforming National into a profitable insurer.

Kenyon Stores is a preeminent U.S. clothing retailer that operates 10 independent retail chains with more than 4,000 outlets and about $8 billion in annual sales. Historically, the individual chains operated independently with little central coordination or integration. Kenyon's CEO turned to the Balanced Scorecard in 1994 as part of his new strategy to leverage key corporate-level resources and direction to achieve an ambitious sales growth target of $20 billion by the year 2000, mainly from internal growth.

In addition to these five companies, we also draw upon the experience of Analog Devices and FMC Corporation, which were early adopters of the Balanced Scorecard.

Financial Perspective

BUILDING A BALANCED SCORECARD should encourage business units to link their financial objectives to corporate strategy. The financial objectives serve as the focus for the objectives and measures in all the other scorecard perspectives. Every measure selected should be part of a link of cause-and-effect relationships that culminate in improving financial performance. The scorecard should tell the story of the strategy, starting with the long-run financial objectives, and then linking them to the sequence of actions that must be taken with financial processes, customers, internal processes, and finally employees and systems to deliver the desired long-run economic performance. For most organizations, the financial themes of increasing revenues, improving cost and productivity, enhancing asset utilization, and reducing risk can provide the necessary linkages across all four scorecard perspectives.

Many corporations, however, use identical financial objectives for all their divisions and business units. For example, each business unit may be asked to achieve the same 16% return-on-capital-employed objective that has been established for the entire corporation. Alternatively, if the corporation is employing the economic value-added metric,[1] every business may be told to maximize its economic value-added each period. While this uniform approach is certainly feasible, consistent, and, in some sense, "fair" since all business unit managers will be evaluated by the same metric, it fails to recognize that different business units may follow quite different strategies. Thus, it would be unlikely for one financial metric, and especially a single target for a single financial metric, to be appropriate across a wide range of business units. So when they start developing the financial perspective for their Balanced Scorecard, business unit executives should determine appropriate financial metrics for their strategy. Financial objectives and measures must play a dual role: they define the financial performance expected from the strategy, and they serve as the ultimate targets for the objectives and measures of all the other scorecard perspectives.

LINKING FINANCIAL OBJECTIVES TO BUSINESS UNIT STRATEGY

Financial objectives can differ considerably at each stage of a business's life cycle. Business strategy theory suggests several different strategies that business units can follow, ranging from aggressive market share growth down to consolidation, exit, and liquidation.[2] For simplification purposes, we identify just three stages:[3]

- Growth
- Sustain
- Harvest

Growth businesses are at the early stages of their life cycle. They have products or services with significant growth potential. To capitalize on this potential, they may have to commit considerable resources to develop and enhance new products and services; construct and expand production facilities; build operating capabilities; invest in systems, infrastructure, and distribution networks that will support global relationships; and nurture and develop customer relationships. Businesses in the growth stage may actually operate with negative cash flows and low current returns on invested capital (whether one expenses investments in intangible assets or capitalizes them for internal purposes). The investments being made for the future may consume more cash than can currently be generated by the limited base of existing products, services, and customers. The overall financial objective for growth-stage businesses will be percentage growth rates in revenues, and sales growth rates in targeted markets, customer groups, and regions.

Probably the majority of business units in a company will be in the *sustain* stage, where they still attract investment and reinvestment, but are required to earn excellent returns on invested capital. These businesses are expected to maintain their existing market share and perhaps grow it somewhat from year to year. Investment projects will be directed more to relieving bottlenecks, expanding capacity, and enhancing continuous improvement, rather than the long payback and growth option investments that were made during the growth stage.

Most business units in the sustain stage will use a financial objective related to profitability. This objective can be expressed by using measures related to accounting income, such as operating income and gross margin. These measures take the capital invested in the business unit as given (or exogenous) and ask the managers to maximize the income that can be generated from the invested capital. Other, more autonomous business units, are asked not only to manage income flows but also the level of invested capital in the business unit. The measures used for these business units relate accounting income earned to the level of capital invested in the business unit; measures such as return-on-investment, return-on-capital-employed, and economic value-added are representative of those used to evaluate the performance of such business units.

Some business units will have reached a mature phase of their life cycle, where the company wants to *harvest* the investments made in the two earlier stages. These businesses no longer warrant significant investment—only enough to maintain equipment and capabilities, not to expand or build new capabilities. Any investment project must have very definite and short payback periods. The main goal is to maximize cash flow back to the corporation. The overall financial objectives for harvest-stage businesses would be operating cash flow (before depreciation) and reductions in working capital requirements.

Thus, the financial objectives for businesses in each of these three stages are quite different. Financial objectives in the growth stage will emphasize sales growth—in new markets and to new customers and from new products and services—maintaining adequate spending levels for product and process development, systems, employee capabilities, and establishment of new marketing, sales, and distribution channels. Financial objectives in the sustain stage will emphasize traditional financial measurements, such as ROCE, operating income, and gross margin. Investment projects for businesses in this category will be evaluated by standard, discounted cash flow, capital budgeting analyses. Some companies will employ newer financial metrics, such as economic value-added and shareholder value. These metrics all represent the classic financial objective—earn excellent returns on the capital provided to the business. And the financial objectives for the harvest businesses will stress cash flow. Any investments must have immediate and certain cash paybacks. Accounting measurements—such as return-on-investment, economic value-added, and operating income—are less relevant since the major investments have already been made in these business units. The goal is not to maximize return-on-investment, which may encourage managers to seek additional investment funds based on future return projections. Rather, the goal is to maximize the cash that can be returned to the company from all the investments made in the past. There will be virtually no spending for research or development or to expand capabilities because of the short time remaining in the economic life of business units in the harvest phase.

The development of a Balanced Scorecard, therefore, must start with an active dialogue between the CEO of the business unit and the CFO of the corporation about the specific financial category and objectives for the business unit. This dialogue will identify the role for the business unit in the company's portfolio. Of course, this dialogue requires that the company CEO and CFO have an explicit financial strategy for each business unit. The positioning of divisions in a financial category is not immutable. A normal progression, which could occur over decades, moves units from growth, to sustain, to harvest, and finally to exit.[4] But occasionally, a business even in a mature, harvest stage might unexpectedly find itself with a growth objective. A sudden technological, market, or regulatory change may take what had previously been a mature, commoditized product or service, and transform it into one with high-growth potential. Such a transformation would completely shift the financial and investment objectives for the business unit. That is why the financial objectives for all business units should be reviewed periodically, probably at least annually, to reaffirm or change the unit's financial strategy.

Risk Management

Effective financial management must address risk as well as return. Objectives relating to growth, profitability, and cash flow emphasize improving returns from investment. But businesses should balance expected returns with the management and control of risk. Thus, many businesses include an objective in their financial perspective that addresses the risk dimension of their strategy—for example, diversifying revenue sources away from a narrow set of customers, one or two lines of business, or particular geographical regions. In general, risk management is an overlay, an additional objective that should complement whatever expected return strategy the business unit has chosen.

Strategic Themes for the Financial Perspective

We have found that, for each of the three strategies of growth, sustain, and harvest, there are three financial themes that drive the business strategy:

- Revenue growth and mix
- Cost reduction/productivity improvement
- Asset utilization/investment strategy

Revenue growth and mix refer to expanding product and service offerings, reaching new customers and markets, changing the product and service mix toward higher-value-added offerings, and repricing products and services. The cost reduction and productivity objective refers to efforts to lower the direct costs of products and services, reduce indirect costs, and share common resources with other business units. For the asset utilization theme, managers attempt to reduce the working capital levels required to support a given volume and mix of business. They also strive to obtain greater utilization of their fixed asset base, by directing new business to resources currently not used to capacity, using scarce resources more efficiently, and disposing of assets that provide inadequate returns on their market value. All these actions enable the business unit to increase the returns earned on its financial and physical assets.

To view the selection of the drivers of aggregate financial objectives as cells in a 3 × 3 matrix across the three business strategies and the three financial themes, see Figure 3-1.

REVENUE GROWTH AND MIX

The most common revenue growth measure, both for growth- and harvest-stage business units, would be sales growth rates and market share for targeted regions, markets, and customers.

New Products

Growth-stage businesses will usually emphasize expansions of existing product lines or offering entirely new products and services. A common measure for this objective is the percentage of revenue from new products and services introduced within a specified period, say two to three years. This measure has been extensively used by innovative companies, like Hewlett-Packard (HP) and the 3M Corporation. Of course, like any good measure, this objective can be achieved in both good and less good ways. The preferred way is for the new product or new product extension to be a dramatic improvement on existing offerings so that it captures new customers and markets, not just replaces sales of existing products. But if too much pressure is placed on this measure alone (less of a danger with a Balanced Scorecard), a business unit could score well on this measure by making a continuing series of incremental improvements that replace existing products but none of which offers distinct advantages to customers. Or, alternatively, and more dysfunctionally (and, fortunately, much less likely), a business unit could simply cease selling a high-volume mature product, allowing recent product sales to represent a higher fraction of total

Figure 3-1 Measuring Strategic Financial Themes

		Strategic Themes		
		Revenue Growth and Mix	**Cost Reduction/ Productivity Improvement**	**Asset Utilization**
Business Unit Strategy	**Growth**	Sales growth rate by segment Percentage revenue from new product, services, and customers	Revenue/Employee	Investment (percentage of sales) R&D (percentage of sales)
	Sustain	Share of targeted customers and accounts Cross-selling Percentage revenues from new applications Customer and product line profitability	Cost versus competitors' Cost reduction rates Indirect expenses (percentage of sales)	Working capital ratios (cash-to-cash cycle) ROCE by key asset categories Asset utilization rates
	Harvest	Customer and product line profitability Percentage unprofitable customers	Unit costs (per unit of output, per transaction)	Payback Throughput

sales. To capture whether the new product or service represents a distinct improvement from existing offerings, some companies focus on the prices or gross margins from new products and services, anticipating that offerings with significantly more functionality and customer value will likely command a higher margin than mature existing products.

New Applications

Developing entirely new products can be very costly and time-consuming for companies, especially those in the pharmaceutical and agricultural chemical industries, with long product-development cycles, and whose products must pass through stringent governmental regulatory approval processes. Businesses in the sustain stage may find it easier to grow revenues by taking existing products and finding new applications for them—new diseases or ailments for which a drug is effective, or new crops for which a chemical offers comparable protection. Taking existing products to new applications requires that a company demonstrate effectiveness in the new application, but the basic chemistry does not have to be invented, its safety demonstrated, or its manufacturing process developed and debugged. If new product applications is an objective, the percentage of sales in new applications would be a useful BSC measure.

New Customers and Markets

Taking existing products and services to new customers and markets also can be a desirable route for revenue growth. Measures such as percentage of revenues from new customers, market segments, and geographic regions would emphasize the importance of investigating this source of revenue enhancement. Many industries have excellent information on the size of the total market and of relative market shares by participants. Increasing a unit's share of targeted market segments is a frequently used metric; it also enables the unit to assess whether its market share growth is from improved competitive offerings or just growth in the total size of the market. Gaining sales but losing share may indicate problems with the unit's strategy or the attractiveness of its products and services.

New Relationships

Some companies have attempted to realize synergies from their different strategic business units by having them cooperate to develop new products or to sell projects to customers. Whether the company strategy is to increase technology transfer across divisions or to increase sales to individual customers from multiple business units within the company, the objective can be translated into the amount of revenue generated from cooperative relationships across multiple business units.

For example, Rockwater was one of six engineering divisions within Brown & Root Energy Services. The other divisions all supplied engineering services of some type, typically to large oil and gas companies, with the services ranging across basic and applied engineering design, pipeline fabrication, pipeline installation (Rockwater), and pipeline maintenance and services. Historically, these divisions had operated as independent companies. When Norman Chambers was promoted from president of Rockwater to president of Brown & Root Energy Services, he asked that each company adopt, as a financial objective, an increase in the share of business won by collaboration. His long-term goal was to offer turnkey service to customers: from initial project design through long-term operations and maintenance of hydrocarbon pipeline facilities.

These examples mirror the experience of several businesses that are attempting to break away from undifferentiated commodity-like selling arrangements, driven principally by price, to offering products and services that satisfy particular customers' needs. The businesses may state that their strategy is to move to a more differentiated strategy. But if their financial measurements are only aggregate sales, profits, and ROCE, they may be achieving short-term financial targets but not succeeding in their strategy. They need to distinguish how much of their sales is coming from competitively priced offerings versus the sales made at a premium or through long-term relationships because of value-added features and services.

New Product and Service Mix

Extending this idea, businesses may choose to increase revenues by shifting their product and service mix. For example, a business may feel that it has a substantial cost advantage in selected segments, where it can win business away from competitors by offering significantly lower prices. If it is following this low-cost strategy, it should measure the growth of sales in the targeted segments. Alternatively, a business may choose a more differentiated strategy, deemphasizing low-price offerings and attempting to shift its product and service mix more toward premium priced items. This business could choose to measure the growth in sales and the percentage of total sales in the premium segment. Metro Bank, for example, adopted a strategy to increase the number of fee-based products it sold and tracked the success of this strategy with a measure of revenue growth from these products and services.

New Pricing Strategy

Finally, revenue growth, especially in mature, perhaps harvest-stage business units, may be realized by raising prices on products, services, and customers where revenues are not covering costs. Such situations are now much easier to detect as companies implement activity-based cost (ABC) systems that trace costs, profits, and even assets employed down to individual products, services, and customers. Some companies have discovered, especially for specialized, niche products or particularly demanding customers, that prices can be increased, or, equivalently, large discounts eliminated, without losing share, to cover the costs of features and services on currently unprofitable products and customers. Profitability by product, service, and customer, or the percentages of unprofitable products and customers, provide signals (not necessarily the only signals) on the opportunity for repricing, or the success and failure of past pricing strategies. For highly homogeneous products and services, a simple price index, such as net revenue per ton, price per call, or price per unit, will reveal the trends in pricing strategy for the company and the industry.

COST REDUCTION/PRODUCTIVITY IMPROVEMENT

In addition to establishing objectives for revenue growth and mix, a business may wish to improve its cost and productivity performance.

Increase Revenue Productivity

Business units in the growth stage are unlikely to be heavily focused on cost reduction. Efforts to reduce costs through dedicated automation and standardized processes may conflict with the flexibility required to customize new products and services for new markets. Therefore, the productivity objective for growth-stage businesses should focus on revenue enhancement—say revenue per employee—to encourage shifts to higher-value-added products and services and to enhance the capabilities of the organization's physical and personnel resources.

Reduce Unit Costs

For sustain-stage businesses, achieving competitive cost levels, improving operating margins, and monitoring indirect and support expense levels will contribute to higher profitability and return-on-investment ratios. Perhaps the simplest and clearest cost reduction objective is to reduce the unit cost of performing work or producing output. For firms with relatively homogeneous output, supplying a simple target for reducing cost per unit can suffice. A chemical company can establish targets for cost per gallon or cost per pound produced; a retail bank can aim for a lower cost per transaction (processing a deposit or a withdrawal) and a decreased cost per customer account sustained; and an insurance company can measure cost per premium processed or per claim paid. Since the cost of performing activities or producing outputs may use resources and activities from many different departments in an organization, an activity-based process-oriented costing system will likely be required for accurate measurement of the unit cost of processing transactions and producing output.

Improve Channel Mix

Some organizations have multiple channels by which customers can conduct transactions with them. For example, retail banking customers can transact manually with in-branch tellers, through automatic teller machines (ATMs), and electronically by phone and computer. The cost to the bank of processing transactions via these various channels is very different. For manufacturers, some ordering from suppliers can be done traditionally, with a purchasing person calling for bids from external suppliers, evaluating the bids, selecting the best one, and then negotiating terms of delivery. Alternatively, the manufacturer could establish long-term relationships with certified suppliers, provide electronic data interchange (EDI) between the manufacturing process and the supplier, with the supplier taking responsibility for providing the required goods on time and directly to the production process. The cost of an EDI transaction is much lower than a traditional purchase transaction performed manually. Thus, an especially promising method for reducing costs is to shift customers and suppliers from high-cost manually processed channels to low-cost electronic channels. If this cost-reduction strategy is deployed by a business unit, it can measure the percentage of business it transacts through the various channels, with a goal of shifting the mix from high- to low-cost channels. Thus, even without any efficiency improvements in the underlying processes (an unrealistically conservative assumption), just shifting to more efficient processing channels can significantly increase productivity and lower the cost of doing business.

Reduce Operating Expenses

Many organizations are now actively trying to lower their selling, general, and administrative expenses.[5] The success of these efforts can be measured by tracking the absolute amount of these expenses or their percentage to total costs or revenues. For example, if managers feel that their support spending is too high relative to competitors' and relative to the customer benefits being generated, they could set objectives to reduce, say, administrative expenses as a percentage of sales, or distribution or marketing and selling expenses. Objectives to reduce spending and expenses levels, however, should be balanced, on the scorecard, by other measures, say of customer responsiveness, quality, and performance, so that cost cutting does not interfere with achieving important customer and internal process objectives.

We admit, however, not being completely comfortable with this type of measurement since it implicitly assumes that these expenses are a "burden" on the organization that must be contained and eliminated over time. Ideally, organizations should attempt to measure the outputs produced from their indirect and support resources. They should try not just to reduce the spending and supply of these resources, but to increase their effectiveness—more customers, more sales, more transactions processed, more new products, better processes—as well as the efficiency of the work done by these resources—how much output and benefits these resources produce for a given level of input resources. These productivity-like measurements require that the organization analyze the work being performed by support resources, attempt to quantify the output produced, and then derive measures of the quantity and quality of the output produced as well as the ratio of outputs produced to inputs consumed. Activity-based cost analysis provides just such a linkage between spending on indirect, support, and administrative resources, and the activities and business processes performed by these resources and the outputs they produce and service. Viewed from this perspective, the somewhat artificial distinction, prevalent in many organizations today, between direct and indirect costs can be eliminated.

ASSET UTILIZATION/INVESTMENT STRATEGY

Objectives, such as return-on-capital employed, return-on-investment, and economic value-added, provide overall outcome measures of the success of financial strategies to increase revenues, reduce costs, and increase asset utilization. Companies may also wish to identify the specific drivers they will use to increase asset intensity.

Cash-to-Cash Cycle

Working capital, especially accounts receivable, inventory, and accounts payable, is an important element of capital for many manufacturing, retail, wholesale, and distribution companies. One measure of the efficiency of working capital management is the cash-to-cash cycle, measured as the sum of days cost-of-sales in inventory, days sales in accounts receivable, less days purchases in accounts payable (see Figure 3-2). The theory behind this measure is simple. The company purchases materials or products (and, for manufacturing companies, pays labor and conversion costs to produce finished goods). The length of time from when the purchases are made until they are sold represents the length of time capital is tied up in inventory. From this can be subtracted the length of time from purchasing materials and labor and conversion resources until cash payment must be made (the days purchases in accounts payable). The days sales in accounts receivable measures the length of time from when a sale is made until cash for it is received from customers. Thus the cash-to-cash cycle represents the time required for the company to convert cash payments to suppliers of inputs to cash receipts from customers. Some companies operate with negative cash-to-cash cycles; they pay suppliers after receiving cash from customers.

Figure 3-2 Cash-to-Cash Cycle

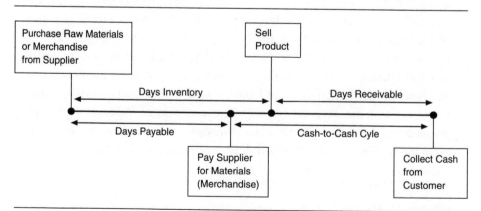

In effect, by matching inventories extremely closely to final sales, collecting quickly from customers, and negotiating favorable terms with suppliers, they are able to supply, not consume, capital from their day-to-day operating cycle. While many companies will find it difficult, if not impossible, to have zero or negative cash-to-cash cycles, the goal of reducing the cash cycle from current levels can be an excellent target for improving working capital efficiency.

Companies with long operating cycles, such as construction companies, find it equally important to manage working capital. Such companies need to track progress payments against cash expended for work completed to date. Rockwater, the undersea construction company, had a particular problem with accounts receivable. It often had to wait more than 100 days before the customer made its final project payment. One of Rockwater's principal financial objectives was to significantly reduce the length of this close-out cycle, an objective that, if reached, would produce a dramatic improvement for its return-on-capital-employed, another one of its financial objectives.[6]

Improve Asset Utilization

Other measures of asset utilization may focus on improving capital investment procedures, both to improve the productivity from capital investment projects and accelerate the capital investment process so that the cash returns from these investments are realized earlier; in effect, a reduction in the cash-to-cash cycle for investments in physical and intellectual capital.

Many of an organization's resources supply the infrastructure for accomplishing work: designing, producing, selling, and processing. These resources may require considerable capital investments. The investments certainly include physical capital, such as information systems, specialized equipment, distribution facilities, and other buildings and physical facilities. But the investments also include intellectual and human capital, such as skilled technologists, data bases, and market- and customer-knowledgeable personnel. Companies can increase the leverage from these infrastructure investments by sharing them across multiple business units. Apart from the potential revenue benefits from sharing knowledge and customers, cost reductions can be achieved by not replicating similar forms of physical and intellectual assets across multiple units. Thus, companies attempting to achieve some economy of scale or scope across investments in specialized physical and intellectual capital can set objectives to increase the percentage of system resources that are shared with other business units.

Particular focus can be placed on the utilization of scarce and expensive resources. Again, returning to Rockwater, one of its largest asset investments were unique vessels that supported underwater construction activities. Rockwater set an objective to increase the percentage of vessel utilization time to highlight the importance of eliminating nonproductive time for this expensive resource. The same philosophy led a large integrated oil company to choose a measure of refinery utilization as one of its financial objectives.

Return-on-investment in intellectual assets, such as research and development, employees, and systems, will also increase an organization's overall return-on-investment. We, however, defer discussion of objectives for these intellectual assets to Chapters 5 and 6, where we explicitly consider the objectives and measures for innovation, employees, and systems.

Risk Management Objectives and Measures

We have noted that, in addition to increasing returns—through growth, cost reduction, productivity, and asset utilization—most organizations are concerned with the risk and variability of their returns. When it is strategically important, these organizations will want to incorporate explicit risk management objectives into their financial perspective. Metro Bank chose a financial objective to increase the share of income arising from fee-based services not only for its revenue growth potential (as already mentioned) but also to reduce its current heavy reliance on income from core deposit and transaction-based products. Such income fluctuated widely with variations in interest rates. As the share of fee-based income increased, the bank believed that the year-to-year variability of its income stream would decrease. Thus, an objective to broaden revenue sources may serve both a growth and a risk management objective.

Risk is an essential part of the business of insurance companies, so National Insurance, a large property and casualty insurance company, included measures of loss exposure and reserve adequacy against maximum possible losses. A capital-intense company addressed its risk concerns by setting an objective that operating cash flow at the bottom of an economic cycle should still cover expenditures on physical capital maintenance and process and product improvement.

Some companies have recognized their generally poor record in forecasting actual operating results. Poor forecasts, especially when actual results were well below expected, led to unexpected borrowings and, therefore, higher risk to the businesses. These businesses chose an objective to reduce the percentage deviation between actual and projected results. Clearly, if this were the only measure in the financial perspective, managers would tend to issue conservative forecasts that they could easily fulfill. But since other financial objectives provided incentives to achieve stretch targets for revenue growth and return-on-assets, the forecast reliability objective could be balanced by growth and profitability objectives. Increasing backlogs of sales and orders was a risk-reducing objective chosen by one company that believed that a large and growing backlog made revenue and forecasts more reliable.

SUMMARY

Financial objectives represent the long-term goal of the organization: to provide superior returns based on the capital invested in the unit. Using the Balanced Scorecard does not conflict with this vital goal. Indeed, the Balanced Scorecard can make the financial objectives explicit, and customize financial objectives to business units in different stages of their growth and life cycle. Every scorecard we have seen uses traditional financial objectives relating to profitability, asset returns, and revenue enhancements. This evidence reinforces the strong links of the Balanced Scorecard to long-established business unit objectives.

Yet even staying within the financial perspective, the scorecard enables senior executives of business units to specify not only the metric by which the long-term success of the enterprise will be evaluated, but also the variables considered most important to create and to drive the long-term outcome objectives. The drivers in the financial perspective will be customized to the industry, the competitive environment, and the strategy of the business unit. We have suggested a classification scheme where businesses can choose financial objectives from themes relating to revenue growth, productivity improvement and cost reduction, asset utilization, and risk management.

Eventually, all objectives and measures in the other scorecard perspectives should be linked to achieving one or more objectives in the financial perspective, a theme we develop in Chapter 7. This linkage to financial objectives explicitly recognizes that the long-run goal for the business is to generate financial returns to investors, and all the strategies, programs, and initiatives should enable the business unit to achieve its financial objectives. Every measure selected for a scorecard should be part of a link of cause-and-effect relationships, ending in financial objectives, that represents a strategic theme for the business unit. Used this way, the scorecard is not a group of isolated, unconnected, or even conflicting objectives. The scorecard should tell the story of the strategy, starting with the long-run financial objectives, linking these to the sequence of actions that must be taken with financial processes, customers, internal processes, and finally employees and systems to deliver the desired long-term economic performance. For most organizations, the financial themes of increasing revenues, improving cost and productivity, enhancing asset utilization, and reducing risk can provide the necessary linkages across all four scorecard perspectives.

NOTES

1. See, for example, G. Bennett Stewart, *The Quest for Value* (New York: Harper Business, 1991) and G. B. Stewart, "EVA™: Fact and Fantasy," *Journal of Applied Corporate Finance* (Summer 1994): 71–84.
2. C. W. Hofer and D. E. Schendel, *Strategy Formulation: Analytical Concepts* (St. Paul: West Publishing, 1978); I. C. MacMillan, "Seizing Competitive Initiative," *Journal of Business Strategy* (Spring 1982): 43–57; and P. Haspeslagh, "Portfolio Planning: Uses and Limits," *Harvard Business Review* (January–February 1982): 58–73.
3. This treatment was influenced by Ernest H. Drew, "Scaling the Productivity of Investment," *Chief Executive* (July/August 1993).
4. Some businesses no longer fit the strategic objectives of the company or can no longer generate adequate cash or financial returns. These businesses must be maintained just sufficiently for the company to implement an "exit" strategy, either through sale or an orderly shutdown. In the exit stage, financial measurements must focus on sustaining existing value. The measurements for business in this stage must be derived from a clear understanding with the company CEO and CFO about what is required to prepare the business for an orderly and value-maximizing sale. Factors that might jeopardize the marketability of the unit, such as growth in liabilities and creating waste, scrap, pollution, or disappointed customers, can all be closely monitored.
5. S. L. Mintz, "Spotlight on SG&A," *CFO Magazine* (December 1994): 63–65.
6. We discuss how Rockwater addressed its long payment-cycle problem in Chapter 5, "Internal-Business-Process Perspective," since the solution required improving how project managers worked with customers. This example illustrates the importance of linking objectives across scorecard perspectives.

Chapter Four

Customer Perspective

IN THE CUSTOMER PERSPECTIVE of the Balanced Scorecard, companies identify the customer and market segments in which they have chosen to compete. These segments represent the sources that will deliver the revenue component of the company's financial objectives. The customer perspective enables companies to align their core customer outcome measures—satisfaction, loyalty, retention, acquisition, and profitability—to targeted customers and market segments. It also enables them to identify and measure, explicitly, the value propositions they will deliver to targeted customers and market segments. The value propositions represent the drivers, the lead indicators, for the core customer outcome measures.

In the past, companies could concentrate on their internal capabilities, emphasizing product performance and technology innovation. But companies that did not understand their customers' needs eventually found that competitors could make inroads by offering products or services better aligned to their customers' preferences. Thus, companies are now shifting their focus externally, to customers. Mission and vision statements routinely declare their goal to be "number one in delivering value to our customers," and to become "the number one supplier to our customers." Apart from the general impossibility of all companies being the number one supplier to their customers, one cannot quarrel with inspirational statements that focus all employees on satisfying customer needs. Clearly, if business units are to achieve long-run superior financial performance, they must create and deliver products and services that are valued by customers.

Beyond aspiring to satisfying and delighting customers, business unit managers must, in the customer perspective of the Balanced Scorecard, translate their mission and strategy statements into specific market- and customer-based objectives. Companies that try to be everything to everybody usually end up being nothing to anyone. Businesses must identify the market segments in their existing and potential customer populations and then select the segments in which they choose to compete. Identifying the value propositions that will be delivered to targeted segments becomes the key to developing objectives and measures for the customer perspective. Thus, the customer perspective of the scorecard translates an organization's mission and strategy into specific objectives about targeted customers and market segments that can be communicated throughout the organization.

MARKET SEGMENTATION

In general, existing and potential customers are not homogeneous. They have different preferences and value the attributes of the product or service differently. A strategy formulation process, using in-depth market research, should reveal the different market or customer segments, and their preferences along dimensions like price, quality, functionality, image, reputation, relationship, and service. The company's strategy can then be defined by those customer and market segments that it chooses to target. The Balanced Scorecard, as a description of a company's strategy, should identify the customer objectives in each targeted segment.

Some managers object to choosing targeted customer segments; they have never seen a customer they didn't like, and want to be able to satisfy all customers' preferences. But this approach runs the risk of doing nothing well for anybody. The essence of strategy is not just choosing what to do; it also requires choosing what not to do.[1]

In building its Balanced Scorecard, Rockwater managers interviewed many of its current and potential customers. They found that some customers wanted to continue business as usual. These customers developed internally all the specifications for their bids, put the detailed bidding document out to tender, and chose, from among all qualified suppliers, the one submitting the lowest bid. As one of these customers said during an interview:

We don't have the resources or time for doing anything fancy with our suppliers. Our business has become ruthlessly competitive, with price and margin reductions in recent years, and the need for us to cut costs wherever we can. We can't afford to choose anyone but the lowest-price supplier.

Historically, Rockwater competed by attempting to be the selected low-price bidder for such customers.

But the interviews also revealed that several large and important customers, Chevron, BP, and Amerada Hess, for example, were looking for more than low price from their most valued supplier of undersea construction services. They said:

We have to cut costs wherever we can. But we are looking to our suppliers to help us in this goal. If it's cheaper and more effective for them to take over some of our engineering functions, we should let them do that, and reduce our internal engineering staffs accordingly. Also, our comparative advantage is finding oil and gas reserves, refining them, and bringing them to the market. We don't have any special capabilities in undersea construction. We want suppliers that can suggest new ways of doing business, and that can develop improved technologies for this task. Our best suppliers of engineering services will anticipate our needs, and suggest creative ways to meet these needs through new technologies, new project management approaches, and new financing methods.

These companies acknowledged that rapidly changing technology and an increasingly competitive marketplace for their final products had motivated them to look to their suppliers for innovative ways to lower their costs. While price would still be a factor, an ability to offer innovative and more cost-effective approaches would be a strong influence on supplier selection. Rockwater, although wanting to retain some business with its price-sensitive customers, chose a strategy to increase its market share with value-seeking customers. Consequently, its core customer measures of market share, and customer retention, acquisition, and satisfaction focused on customers where it had established value-adding relationships. To communicate that strategy and evaluate its success, Rockwater chose to measure the percentage of its revenue generated from value-added customer relationships.

Similarly, Metro Bank had competed, historically, by offering low-price, efficient, and high-quality service to all of its retail banking customers. A squeeze on operating profits and margins, and changes in technology and competitive conditions led the bank to a strategic review. Metro concluded that it did not want to attract business just on the basis of being the lowest-priced provider of commodity-like transaction services. It wanted to target customers who would be attracted by knowledgeable financial advisers providing a broad range of financial products and services, in defect-free transactions, and who would expect a reasonable, but not necessarily the lowest, price for those transactions.

As another example of market segmentation, Pioneer Petroleum, a major U.S. refiner and retail marketer of gasoline and automobile lubricants, began the development of its customer strategy with a market research program. The findings identified five customer segments.

1. Road Warriors: 16% of buyers

Higher-income middle-aged men who drive 25,000–50,000 miles a year . . . buy premium gasoline with a credit card . . . purchase sandwiches and drinks from the convenience store . . . will sometimes wash their cars at the carwash.

2. True Blues: 16% of buyers

Usually men and women with moderate to high incomes who are loyal to a brand and sometimes to a particular station . . . frequently buy premium gasoline and pay in cash.

3. Generation F3: 27% of buyers

Fuel, Food, and Fast: Upwardly mobile men and women—half under 25 years of age—who are constantly on the go . . . drive a lot and snack heavily from the convenience store.

4. Homebodies: 21% of buyers

Usually housewives who shuttle their children around during the day and use whatever gasoline station is based in town or along their route of travel.

5. Price Shoppers: 20% of buyers

Generally aren't loyal to either a brand or a particular station, and rarely buy the premium line . . . frequently on tight budgets.

Pioneer concluded that oil companies had been fighting over the Price Shoppers for years. Pioneer's executives now realized that these customers numbered only 20% of all gasoline buyers, and were the 20% with the lowest profit margins. Pioneer shifted its focus to the most profitable 59% of gasoline buyers (Road Warriors, True Blues, and Generation F3), with specific value propositions designed to attract and retain business from these three segments.

Once a business has identified and targeted its market segments, it can address the objectives and measures for its targeted segments. We have found that companies generally select two sets of measures for their customer perspective. The first set represents generic measures that virtually all companies want to use. Because these measures, such as customer satisfaction, market share, and customer retention, appear in so many balanced scorecards, we refer to them as the *core measurement group*. The second set of measures represents the performance drivers—differentiators—of the customer outcomes. They answer the question, What must the company deliver to its customers to achieve high degrees of satisfaction, retention, acquisition, and, eventually, market share? The performance-driver measures capture the value propositions that the company will attempt to deliver to its targeted customer and market segments.

Customer Core Measurement Group

The core measurement group of customer outcomes is generic across all kinds of organizations. The core measurement group includes measures of:

- Market share
- Customer retention
- Customer acquisition
- Customer satisfaction
- Customer profitability

These core measures can be grouped in a causal chain of relationships (see Figure 4-1).

These five measures may appear to be generic across all types of organizations. For maximum impact, however, the measures should be customized to the targeted customer groups from whom the business unit expects its greatest growth and profitability to be derived.

MARKET AND ACCOUNT SHARE

Measuring market share is straightforward once the targeted customer group or market segment has been specified. Industry groups, trade associations, government statistics, and other public sources can often provide estimates of the total market size. Rockwater's market-share measure was the percentage of business it received from Tier 1 customers, those with whom it had long-term partnering relationships. Such a measure illustrates how the Balanced Scorecard should be used to motivate and monitor a business unit's strategy. Using only financial measures, Rockwater may have been able, in the short run, to achieve sales growth, profitability, and return-on-capital targets by increasing business that it won purely on competitive pricing. In this case, however, the measure of market share with Tier 1 customers would signal that Rockwater was not implementing its strategy

Figure 4-1 The Customer Perspective—Core Measures

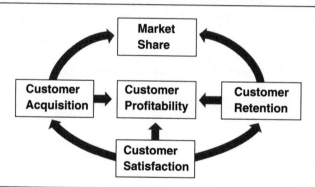

Market Share	Reflects the proportion of business in a given market (in terms of number of customers, dollars spent, or unit volume sold) that a business unit sells.
Customer Acquisition	Measures, in absolute or relative terms, the rate at which a business unit attracts or wins new customers or business.
Customer Retention	Tracks, in absolute or relative terms, the rate at which a business unit retains or maintains ongoing relationships with its customers.
Customer Satisfaction	Assesses the satisfaction level of customers along specific performance criteria within the value proposition.
Customer Profitability	Measures the net profit of a customer, or a segment, after allowing for the unique expenses required to support that customer.

effectively. It was not increasing its share of business based on value-adding relationships with customers. The measure of market share with targeted customers would be *balancing* the pure financial signals to indicate that an immediate review of the strategy implementation was likely required.

When companies have targeted particular customers or market segments, they can also use a second market-share measure: the account share of those customers' business (some refer to this as the share of the "customers' wallet"). The overall market share measure based on business with these companies could be affected by the total amount of business these companies offer in a given period. That is, the share of business with these targeted customers could decrease because the customers are giving less business to all their suppliers. Companies can measure, customer by customer (if small in number, like Rockwater), or segment by segment (when selling to mass markets, like Metro Bank and Pioneer Petroleum), how much of the customers' and market segments' business they are receiving. A financial institution, like Metro Bank, can measure its "share of wallet" by its percentage of a targeted customer's total financial transactions or accounts. A beverage food company could measure its share of targeted customers' total purchases of beverages (share of stomach), an apparel retailer its share of customers' total clothing purchases (share of closet), and a construction company its share of its targeted customers' total construction business. Such a measure provides a strong focus to the company when trying to dominate its targeted customers' purchases of products or services in categories that it offers.

CUSTOMER RETENTION

Clearly, a desirable way for maintaining or increasing market share in targeted customer segments is to start by retaining existing customers in those segments. The insights from research on the service profit chain has demonstrated the importance of customer retention.[2] Companies that can readily identify all of their customers—for example, industrial companies, distributors and wholesalers, newspaper and magazine publishers, computer on-line service companies, banks, credit card companies, and long-distance telephone suppliers—can readily measure customer retention from period to period. Beyond just keeping customers, many companies will want to measure customer loyalty by the percentage growth of business with existing customers.

CUSTOMER ACQUISITION

In general, companies seeking to grow their business will have an objective to increase their customer base in targeted segments. The customer acquisition measure tracks, in absolute or relative terms, the rate at which a business unit attracts or wins new customers or business. Customer acquisition could be measured by either the number of new customers or the total sales to new customers in these segments. Companies such as those in the credit and charge card business, magazine subscriptions, cellular telephone service, cable television, and banking and other financial services solicit new customers through broad, often expensive, marketing efforts. These companies could examine the number of customer responses to solicitations, and the conversion rate—number of actual new customers divided by number of prospective inquiries. They could measure solicitation cost per new customer acquired, and the ratio of new customer revenues per sales call or per dollar of solicitation expense.

CUSTOMER SATISFACTION

Both customer retention and customer acquisition are driven by meeting customers' needs. Customer satisfaction measures provide feedback on how well the company is doing. The importance of customer satisfaction probably cannot be overemphasized. Recent research has indicated that just scoring adequately on customer satisfaction is not sufficient for achieving high degrees of loyalty, retention, and profitability. Only when customers rate their buying experience as completely or extremely satisfied can a company count on their repeat purchasing behavior.[3]

Some companies are fortunate to have customers that voluntarily supply ratings to all their suppliers. For example, Hewlett-Packard provides ratings and rankings of vendors in various supplier categories. Ford gives recognition and awards to its most valued suppliers. The treasurer's offices of several multinational companies give report cards to all banks with whom they have relationships, providing detailed feedback on how well each bank is performing in supplying capital, financial services, and financial advice. And part of Rockwater's relationship with Tier 1 customers consists of receiving monthly feedback along performance dimensions specified by the customer in advance as being critical for its particular project.

Companies, however, cannot count on having all their targeted customers proactively supplying feedback on performance. Many companies, including British Airways, Hewlett-Packard, Xerox, Procter & Gamble, Motorola, PepsiCo, Boeing, and 3M, conduct systematic customer satisfaction surveys. Writing a customer survey may seem simple, but getting valid responses from a high percentage of customers usually requires specialized expertise. Three techniques can be generally employed: mail surveys, telephone interviews, and personal interviews. These techniques range in cost from low to high, but response rates and valuable insights also range from low to high across them. Customer satisfaction surveys have now become one of the most active areas for market research firms, with current billings of nearly $200 million and annual growth of 25%. This specialized service can mobilize expertise in psychology, market research, statistics, and interviewing techniques, as well as considerable numbers of personnel and the computing power capable of providing comprehensive indicators of customer satisfaction.

CUSTOMER PROFITABILITY

Succeeding in the first four core customer measures of share, retention, acquisition, and satisfaction, however, does not guarantee that a company has profitable customers. Obviously, one way to have extremely satisfied customers (and angry competitors) is to sell products and services at very low prices. Since customer satisfaction and high market share are themselves only a means to achieving higher financial returns, companies will probably wish to measure not only the extent of business they do with customers, but also the profitability of this business, particularly in targeted customer segments. Activity-based cost systems permit companies to measure individual and aggregate customer profitability.[4] Companies should want more than satisfied and happy customers; they should want profitable customers. A financial measure, like customer profitability, helps keep customer-focused organizations from becoming customer-obsessed. Not all customer demands can be satisfied in ways that are profitable to an organization. Particularly difficult or demanding services may require that the unit either decline the business or else seek price increases that will compensate it for the resources that must be deployed to satisfy that customer's demand. Or, if the customer or the nature of the demands is particularly important to the organization, and repricing is not a viable option, the business unit still receives a signal from the ABC system about unprofitable relationships. Such a signal enables it to see where key processes that deliver the product or service to the customer can be reengineered or redesigned so that customers' demands can be met and the company can still be profitable.

The customer profitability measure may reveal that certain targeted customers are unprofitable. This is particularly likely to occur with newly acquired customers, where the considerable acquisition effort has yet to be offset from the margins earned by selling products and services to the customers. In these cases, lifetime profitability becomes the basis for retaining or discouraging currently unprofitable customers. Newly acquired customers, even if currently unprofitable, are still valuable because of their growth potential. But unprofitable customers that have been with the company for many years will likely require explicit action (or other rationales, like credibility and learning opportunities) to turn them into assets.

Figure 4-2 presents a simple way to combine considerations of targeted market segments and customer profitability.

Customers in the two main diagonal cells in Figure 4-2 are easy to handle. A company certainly wants to retain its profitable customers in targeted segments, and should have little future interest in unprofitable customers in untargeted segments. The customers in the two off-diagonal cells create more interesting managerial situations. Unprofitable customers in targeted segments (the upper righthand cell) represent opportunities to transform them into profitable customers. As discussed, newly acquired customers may require little action other than watching to see whether increased business in the future makes them profitable. Longer-standing customers that are unprofitable may require repricing of services or products that they use extensively, or developing improved ways of producing and delivering these products and services. Profitable customers in untargeted segments (the lower lefthand cell) may certainly be retained, but need to be monitored to assess that new demands for services or features, or changes in the volume and mix of products and services they purchase do not cause them to become unprofitable. By using both market segment and

Figure 4-2   Targeted Segments and Customer Profitability

Customers	Profitable	Unprofitable
Targeted Segment	Retain	Transform
Untargeted Segment	Monitor	Eliminate

profitability measures to view customers, managers get valuable feedback on the effectiveness of their market segmentation strategies.

Beyond the Core: Measuring Customer Value Propositions

Customer value propositions represent the attributes that supplying companies provide, through their products and services, to create loyalty and satisfaction in targeted customer segments. The value proposition is the key concept for understanding the drivers of the core measurements of satisfaction, acquisition, retention, and market and account share.

While value propositions vary across industries, and across different market segments within industries, we have observed a common set of attributes that organizes the value propositions in all of the industries where we have constructed scorecards. These attributes can be organized into three categories (see Figure 4-3).

- Product/service attributes
- Customer relationship
- Image and reputation

PRODUCT AND SERVICE ATTRIBUTES

Product and service attributes encompass the functionality of the product/service, its price, and its quality. For example, one can view the two customer segments identified by Rockwater as illustrative of the classic choice between customers that want a reliable low-cost producer versus those customers that want a differentiated supplier, capable of offering unique products, features, and services. Rockwater's Tier 2 customers did not want frills and customization. They wanted the basic product, delivered reliably and on-time, with no defects, and at the lowest possible price. Its Tier 1 customers, on the other hand, were willing to pay a price premium for particular features or services that they perceived as highly valuable for achieving their competitive strategic vision. Similarly, Metro Bank identified several market segments in its customer base. One segment just sought the lowest-priced supplier of standard banking products like checking accounts. Another segment, however, looked to the bank as a one-stop source of financial products and services, and were willing to pay a reasonable, but not necessarily the lowest, price for conducting financial transactions. Both segments, however, wanted high-quality service (zero defects) in transactions with the bank.

CUSTOMER RELATIONSHIP

The customer relationship dimension includes the delivery of the product/service to the customer, including the response and delivery time dimension, and how the customer feels about purchasing from the company. For example, Metro Bank identified for its customer relationship objective that it should build and maintain high expectations about how the bank treated its customers. Metro defined three key elements of an excellent relationship with its customers.

Figure 4-3 The Customer Value Proposition

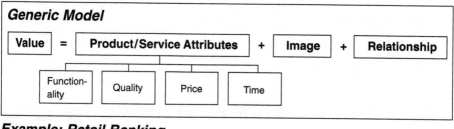

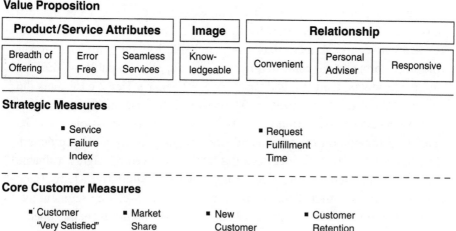

1. Knowledgeable People: Differentiate ourselves through employees capable of recognizing customer needs and possessing the knowledge to proactively satisfy them.

2. Convenient Access: Give customers access to banking services or information 24 hours a day.

3. Responsive: Service customers expediently. The timeliness of the response should meet or exceed the customer's perceived sense of urgency.

A retail chain like Nordstrom emphasizes the extraordinary level of service its salespersons are prepared to give its targeted and valued customers. The success of Intuit, a relatively small software company that dominates its market segment of personal-computer-based financial-management software, can be attributed to users' passionate approval of the transparency and ease of use of its products. The relationship dimension also encompasses long-term commitments, such as when the supplying company links its information systems with customers'—electronic data interchange—to facilitate a broad range of activities across the selling/buying relationship: shared designs of products, linked production schedules, and electronic ordering, invoicing, and payment. The relationship could encompass qualification as a preferred supplier so that incoming items are delivered directly to workstations on the factory floor, bypassing receiving, inspection, handling, and storage. Some companies have even turned over their purchasing function to qualified suppliers, providing supplier representatives with office space and storage facilities on-site, and allowing the supplier to manage completely the flow of materials to arrive in the exact mix and quantity just-in-time to workstations. Such relationships are another dimension of choosing suppliers on a basis other than the one that quotes the lowest unit price.

IMAGE AND REPUTATION

The image and reputation dimension reflects the intangible factors that attract a customer to a company. Some companies are able, through advertising and delivered quality of product and service, to generate customer loyalty well beyond the tangible aspects of the product and service. Consumer preferences for certain brands of athletic shoes, designer clothing, theme parks ("I'm going to Disneyworld"), cigarettes ("The Marlboro

Man"), soft drinks ("the Pepsi generation"), and even chickens (Perdue) connote the power of image and reputation for targeted consumer segments. Metro Bank was attempting to build a reputation as a knowledgeable, friendly financial adviser capable of supplying a full line of banking products and services. Pioneer Petroleum, trying to differentiate its product in what is basically a commodity business, used advertising to communicate certain nonobvious features of its product, like purity that helped keep engines "clean" and free of sludge. Several investment banking firms convey an image of personalized, high-quality financial advice and service, and the "Big 6" accounting firms attempt to establish a reputation for quality and integrity that distinguishes them from smaller, more regional competitors.

The image and reputation dimension enables a company to proactively define itself for its customers. Rockwater, for example, wanted to outgrow an image dating back to the boom years of the early 1970s in which underwater engineering construction companies were viewed as a collection of guys, equipped with wet suits, scuba gear, and welding guns, jumping off barges into the North Sea. The construction of the Balanced Scorecard and the establishment of customer-based objectives and explicit feedback about the value propositions it delivered to customers were intended to convey a new professionalism about the way the company would do business. It would be part of the process by which Rockwater communicated to Tier 1 customers that it was now a technologically sophisticated, trusted, and valued partner capable of engaging in long-term supplier-customer relationships.

Kenyon Stores, a large clothing retailer, developed an image of who its targeted customers were.

- Range: 20–40-year-old female (target: 29 years)
- College educated
- Works full-time in professional executive position
- Innovatively fashionable
- Self-confident, great sense of humor

It then communicated this targeted customer image externally through a variety of advertising and in-store promotional material.

By communicating a clear image to potential customers, the store enables its existing and future customers to imagine themselves fitting an image associated with purchasing clothes at Kenyon. The company creates for its customers, an image of who they can be, in addition to selling them fashionable clothing of high quality at reasonable prices. Thus companies attempting to exploit the image and reputation attribute define their ideal customer and attempt to influence customer buying behavior by the image associated with purchasing from them.

We can illustrate the development of customer value propositions across product and service attributes, relationship, and image and reputation with case studies of Kenyon, Rockwater, and Pioneer Petroleum.

KENYON STORES: DIRECT SELLING TO MASS MARKET

Kenyon Stores started the development of its customer objective by defining a customer strategy:

1. Kenyon must increase its customer share of wardrobe.

2. Increased share of wardrobe will be achieved by customer loyalty: We want the customer to visit us throughout the year and come to Kenyon for the complete range of her lifestyle needs.

3. To create this loyalty:

   - Our merchandise must define our customer, her needs and aspirational image.

   - Our brand must satisfy the customer's aspirational and lifestyle goals.

   - Our shopping experience must promote customer loyalty.

4. We must do a superb job of defining who our customers are and their buying behavior.

Kenyon used customer loyalty and customer feedback scores for its core customer outcome measures. The performance drivers for these measures were derived from the strategy statement. These drivers represented objectives and measures in the three elements of value propositions.

Product Attributes

Kenyon identified three objectives as key product attributes for its consumer value proposition: price, fashion, and quality. The price objective was stated as:

Provide fashion and quality that the customers perceive as high-value and consider to be fairly priced.

The measures for this objective were the average unit retail price that the retailer wanted to maintain (i.e., no price discounting) and the number of transactions per store.

The fashion and design objective was to:

Provide fashionable merchandise that satisfies our customer's aspirational and wardrobe needs within the Kenyon brand.

This, clearly, is not an easy objective to translate into specific operational measures. The company selected the average annual growth in purchases of "strategic merchandise" defined as key merchandise items that best exemplified the Kenyon image. A second measure selected was MMU, retailer jargon for maintained mark-up. MMU represents the actual margin realized by the retailer over purchase price, net of all discounts. Improving MMU would be an outcome (lagging) indicator of the store's ability to sustain good margins because of well-received merchandise design and fashion.

The quality objective,

Ensure the highest quality and consistency of fit both within a style and across all product categories

was measured by the return rate of merchandise, an indication of the satisfaction of consumers with the quality of the product, and the fairness of the price paid.

Relationship: The Shopping Experience

The shopping experience dimension was considered extremely important. Key attributes were availability of merchandise and the in-store shopping experience. Availability was defined as having the customers' first choice items in stock. It was measured by the responses on a "What do you think?" card solicited from each customer, asking about satisfaction with the availability of size and color. The in-store shopping experience dimension was captured by an explicit vision of the six elements of the "perfect shopping experience":

1. Great looking stores with fashion impact
2. Customer welcomed by attractive associates, fashionably dressed, with a smile on their faces
3. Clear communication of special sales
4. Associates with good product knowledge
5. Personal name recognition by attending associate
6. A sincere thanks and an invitation to return soon

The goal was to deliver the six elements every time the customer entered a store. "Mystery shopper" audits would measure how well an individual store was achieving this objective in its daily operations.

Brand and Image

Kenyon, as described, had constructed a very specific definition of its "ideal shopper." The ideal shopper image communicated to all employees the fashion expectations of their customers. The brand image objective for Kenyon was stated as:

We will build Kenyon into a dominant national brand by clearly understanding our target customer and differentiating ourselves in meeting her needs.

The success of developing this dominant brand image was measured by *market share in key merchandise items* and by the *premium price earned on branded items*. The success of communicating an attractive brand image would be measured by the higher price Kenyon could command over nonbranded or generic items of comparable characteristics and quality.

The mechanism of how Kenyon would deliver on the objectives and measures developed for its value proposition to targeted customers (see

Figure 4-4) was defined in the internal-business-process perspective, to be discussed in the next chapter.

ROCKWATER: DIRECT SELLING TO INDIVIDUAL CUSTOMERS

Rockwater used two of the core outcome measures in its customer perspective: an annual customer ranking survey versus competition, and market and account share with key (Tier 1) customers. To address its price-sensitive Tier 2 customers, Rockwater developed a price index for competitive bids. Rockwater still wanted to retain some business from Tier 2 customers to help manage capacity utilization and to provide order backlogs that would lead to greater predictability of financial results.

To measure the value proposition it was delivering to its Tier 1 customers, Rockwater developed a "customized" customer satisfaction index that reflected attributes related to product and service offerings and the relationship between the Rockwater project team and the customer. Rockwater identified 16 attributes associated with a project engagement (see Figure 4-5). Each customer, on each project, selected a subset of these 16 attributes felt to be most important for that project. The attributes could be weighted to reflect relative priorities and importance on particular categories. Then,

Figure 4-4 The Customer Value Proposition—Kenyon Stores

Value Proposition

Product Attributes			Image	Relationship	
Price Benefits	Fashion and Design	Quality	Brand Image	Availability	Shopping Experience

Strategic Measures

- Average Unit Retail Price
- Mark-up
- Return Rate
- Market Share (key item)
- Out-of-Stock (%) (key items)
- Mystery Shopper

- Transactions per Store
- Target Item Growth Rate
- Premium on Brand Label

Core Customer Measures

- Customer Loyalty (annual purchase growth)
- Customer Satisfaction (survey)

as shown in Figure 4-6, in the monthly customer satisfaction feedback, the Rockwater project team received a score, from 1 to 10, on each selected attribute, from which a weighted customer satisfaction score could be calculated. Thus, Rockwater stayed attuned to the specific objectives each customer wanted to emphasize on each project.

Rockwater, in addition to getting a monthly customer satisfaction score on each project with a Tier 1 customer, totaled the scores received on all projects for the 16 attributes. The mean score for each attribute signaled areas where the project teams were all performing well, and the attributes where, across the board, the company was falling short of its best customers' expectations.

PIONEER PETROLEUM: INDIRECT SELLING TO MASS MARKET

One of the most interesting customer perspectives is illustrated by Pioneer Petroleum. Pioneer is representative of the many organizations that sell to

Figure 4-5 The Customer Value Proposition (Tier I)—Rockwater

Product Attributes				Image	Relationship
Functionality	Quality	Price	Timeliness	Professional Management	Relationship

- Safety
- Engineering Service

- Minimum Revision of Submitted Procedures
- Quality and Awareness of Performance
- Standard of Equipment Provided
- Quality of Personnel
- Production Quality

- Hours Worked
- Value for Money
- Innovativeness to Reduce Cost

- Meeting Schedule
- Timely Submission of Procedures

- Honesty and Openness of Contractor
- Flexibility
- Contractual Responsiveness
- Team Rapport/ Spirit

retailers, distributors, and wholesalers. Such companies actually have two distinct groups of customers they must satisfy. The first group is their immediate customers—the organizations that purchase the products or services and then resell them to their customers. And it is the customers' customers—often the ultimate consumer—that represent the second group of Pioneer customers. For such organizations, we have found it useful to split the customer perspective into two segments: the immediate customers and the ultimate consumer. For example, producers of consumer packaged goods, like Procter & Gamble, Coca-Cola, and Pillsbury, must understand and work well with their retailers, wholesalers, and distributors. But they also work very diligently to understand the tastes and preferences of the final purchaser of their products, the consumer.

Pioneer's dealers (the immediate customers) were independent business people, not employees of the company. The dealers had their own financial objectives, primarily profitability, and looked to their supplier (Pioneer) to provide them with training and business management skills. Dealers wanted

Figure 4-6 The Customer Satisfaction Measure—Rockwater

Criteria	Customer						Average Satisfaction
	A	B	C	D	E	F	
1. Safety	9	8	8	10		8	8.6
2. Meeting Schedule	9	6	7				7.3
3. Ratio of Hours Worked/Breakdown	9	5	4				6.0
4. Timely Submission of Procedure	9	4	5				6.0
5. Minimum Revision of Submitted Procedures	9	5	6				6.7
6. Honesty and Openness of Contractor	4	7	7	10	9		8.3
7. Flexibility	9	4	7		9		7.3
8. Contractual Responsiveness	8	5	7				6.7
9. Engineering Service	8	7	7				7.3
10. Quality Awareness and Performance	10	6	8		8	7	7.8
11. Value for Money	7	6	6	10	9	7	7.2
12. Standard of Equipment Provided	9	7	7			8	7.8
13. Quality of Personnel	10	7	7	10		8	8.5
14. Innovativeness w/Drive to Reduce Costs					7		7.0
15. Production Quality				10			10.0
16. Team Rapport/Spirit			7				7.0
Satisfaction Index	8.8	5.9	6.6	10.0	8.4	7.6	7.9

Pioneer to provide them with a broad range of nongasoline services, such as car washes, lubrication facilities and supplies, and convenience stores, and to provide a strong brand image to Pioneer-brand gasoline that would differentiate their operations from those of competitive stations.

Pioneer defined, for its customer perspective, core outcome objectives relating to dealer satisfaction, retention, and new acquisition. Pioneer then proceeded to identify measures of the value proposition for its targeted dealers that would be the performance drivers of these core outcomes. The product and service attributes encompassed objectives for new products and services (functionality) and dealer profitability (price, quality, functionality). The relationship dimension emphasized how Pioneer could contribute to management skill development of dealers and their employees, and image and reputation were measured by brand promotion (see Figure 4-7).

For its consumer perspective, Pioneer had learned from its market research (described earlier in this chapter) that consumers in its targeted segments bought from a branded gasoline dealer because they expected

Figure 4-7 The Customer Value Proposition—Pioneer Petroleum

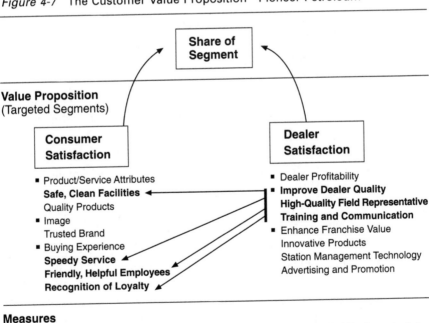

the stations to be safe and clean and staffed with employees who were friendly and helpful. A second large segment valued speed of service highly. Pioneer measured consumer satisfaction (its core outcome measure) through a "mystery shopper" program, independent third parties who purchased products at the retail outlet and evaluated the experience relative to the strategic objectives of clean-friendly-fast. Performance drivers of the consumer satisfaction outcome measure included measures of clean and safe, friendly employees, and rapid service.

Because of the commodity nature of Pioneer's product (gasoline), consumers did not place great value on specific product attributes when choosing among competing retailers. Targeted consumers' preferences (once the highly price-sensitive segment was eliminated as a targeted group) emphasized the nature of the relationship when making the purchase. Pioneer, however, did survey consumers on their perception of product quality and brand image, enabling it to include one measure each from the product attribute and reputation and image categories. Pioneer's value proposition for targeted consumers is shown in Figure 4-7.

The scorecard process at Pioneer did not develop the dealer and consumer objectives. These had already been determined through normal market research, though the scorecard did help focus and articulate these objectives for senior management. But, the scorecard did provide a mechanism to clarify and communicate the targeted dealer and consumer segments and the associated value propositions throughout the organization. The scorecard objectives and measures in the customer perspective were the foundation of a broad-based communication program to more than 5,000 employees. And by showing the linkages from better performance for customers and consumers, everyone could understand the story of the strategy; how what they did contributed to accomplishing overall business-unit objectives, leading ultimately to dramatically improved financial performance.

TIME, QUALITY, AND PRICE

The case studies of Kenyon, Rockwater, and Pioneer Petroleum show how objectives can be established for the value propositions delivered to targeted customers. While each organization should develop its own set of value propositions that it wishes to capture in the customer perspective of its Balanced Scorecard, we have found that virtually all value propositions typically incorporate measures related to the response time, quality, and price of customer-based processes. The appendix to this chapter presents a brief discussion of representative measures that can capture the time, quality, and price dimensions of its customer relationships.

SUMMARY

At the conclusion of formulating the customer perspective, managers should have a clear idea of their targeted customer and business segments, and selected a set of core outcome measurements—share, retention, acquisition, satisfaction, and profitability—for these targeted segments. These outcome measures represent the targets for companies' marketing, operational, logistics, and product and service development processes. But, these outcome measures have some of the defects of traditional financial measures. They are lagging measures—employees will not know how well they are doing with customer satisfaction or customer retention until it is too late to affect the outcome. Also, the measures do not communicate what employees should be doing in their day-to-day activities to achieve the desired outcomes.

Managers must also identify what customers in targeted segments value and choose the value proposition they will deliver to these customers. They can then select objectives and measures from among three classes of attributes that, if satisfied, will enable the company to retain and expand its business with these targeted customers. The three classes of attributes are:

- Product and service attributes: functionality, quality, and price
- Customer relationship: quality of purchasing experience and personal relationships
- Image and reputation

By selecting specific objectives and measures across these three classes, managers can focus their organization on delivering a superior value proposition to their targeted customer segments.

APPENDIX:
PERFORMANCE DRIVERS FOR CUSTOMER SATISFACTION

We discuss here representative measures that companies can use to develop time, quality, and price metrics for the customer perspective of their Balanced Scorecard.

TIME

Time has become a major competitive weapon in today's competition. Being able to respond rapidly and reliably to a customer's request is often the critical skill for obtaining and retaining valuable customers' business. For example, Hertz introduced its #1 Card, enabling busy travelers to be taken directly to their rented car where the completed paperwork has previously been placed, the trunk opened for luggage, and the car already air-conditioned in summer or heated in winter. The traveler only has to show his or her driver's license for identification upon departing the parking lot. Banks accelerate approval of mortgage and loan applications, reducing waiting times from weeks to minutes. Japanese auto manufacturers can deliver a newly ordered customized car to a consumer's driveway in less time (one week) than it takes the purchaser to obtain a valid parking sticker from government authorities. Including time-based customer measures signals the importance of achieving and continually reducing lead times for meeting targeted customers' expectations.

Other customers may be more concerned with the reliability of lead times than with just obtaining the shortest lead times. For example, many shippers still prefer to use trucks rather than rail, not because trucks are cheaper or even faster for long-distance moves. But since many railroads cannot deliver reliably on time, within a one-day receiving window, the shippers (and their customers) prefer a more expensive, even longer, transport medium that can guarantee arrival within a desired time interval. Such reliability is especially important for manufacturers who operate without inventories under a just-in-time discipline. Honda and Toyota want deliveries to their assembly plants to arrive within a one-hour time window. Observers have noted delivery trucks driving around outside an automobile assembler's facility until the production process is ready for the items being delivered. At the upper end of the receiving time window, a late delivery will shut down an entire production facility that operates with zero inventories of raw materials and purchased parts. For service companies, think about the frustration of a consumer who has taken time off from work to be at home, only to find that delivery or installation is not made at the scheduled time. If reliable delivery is vital for important customer segments, a measure of on-time delivery will be a useful performance driver for customer satisfaction and retention. The OTD measure should be based on the customer's expectation. Telling Honda or Toyota that your definition of "on time" is

± 1 day, when their production process can tolerate a window no wider than ± 1 hour, will not likely win you much business from these demanding companies.

Hospitals and medical practices that have purchased or leased expensive diagnostic equipment demand high reliability and up-time from this equipment. One manufacturer developed two customer-based metrics for such customers: equipment up-time percentage and mean-time response to a service call. The focus on these objectives led the company to install fault detection circuitry in the equipment that could automatically page for a service call, in anticipation of an equipment failure.

Lead time is important not only for existing products and services. Several customers value suppliers that can offer a continual stream of new products and services. For such market segments, a short lead time for introducing new products and services could be a valued performance driver for customer satisfaction. This objective could be measured as the elapsed time from when a new customer demand has been identified to the time when the new product or service has been delivered to the customer. We explore this time-to-market measure when discussing the innovation process in the internal-business-process perspective (Chapter 5).

QUALITY

Quality was a critical competitive dimension during the 1980s and remains important to this day. By the mid-1990s, however, quality has shifted from a strategic advantage to a competitive necessity. Many organizations that could not reliably deliver defect-free products or services have ceased to be serious competitors. Because of all the attention devoted to improving quality during the past 15 years, it may offer limited opportunities for competitive advantage. It has become a hygiene factor; customers take for granted that their suppliers will execute according to product and service specifications. Nevertheless, for certain industries, regions, or market segments, excellent quality may still offer opportunities for companies to distinguish themselves from their competitors. In this case, customer-perceived quality measures would be highly appropriate to include in the BSC's customer perspective.

Quality measures for manufactured goods could be measured by incidence of defects, say part-per-million defect rates, as measured by customers. Motorola's famed 6σ program strives to reduce defects to fewer than

10 PPM. Frequently, third-party evaluations provide feedback on quality. The J. D. Power organization provides information and rankings on defects and perceived quality in automobiles and airlines. The Department of Transportation provides information on the frequency of late arrivals and lost baggage by airline.

Other readily available quality measures include returns by customers, warranty claims, and field service requests. Service companies have a particular problem not faced by manufacturers. When a manufacturer's product or piece of equipment fails to work or satisfy the customer, the customer will usually return the product or call the company asking for repairs to be made. In contrast, when a quality failure occurs in a service company, the customer has nothing to return and usually no one responsive to complain to. The customer's response is to cease patronizing the organization. The service organization may eventually note a decline in business and market share, but such a signal is delayed and almost impossible to reverse. The organization will typically not even know the identity of customers who tried the service, were poorly treated, and then decided never to use that organization's services again. For this reason, several service firms offer service guarantees.[5] This offer, to immediately refund not only the purchase price but generally a premium above the purchase price, provides several valuable benefits to a company. First, a guarantee allows it to retain a customer who otherwise might be lost forever. Second, an organization receives a signal about the incidence of defective service, enabling it to initiate a program of corrective action. And, finally, knowledge of the existence of the service guarantee provides strong motivation and incentives for the people delivering customer service to avoid defects that would trigger a request for the guarantee. Thus, companies that have service guarantee programs will likely want to include the incidence and cost of service guarantees as measures in their customer's perspective.

Quality can also refer to performance along the time dimension. The on-time delivery measure, previously discussed, is actually a measure of the quality of the company's performance to its promised delivery date.

PRICE

With all the emphasis on time, responsiveness and quality, one might wonder whether customers still care about price. One can be assured that whether a business unit is following a low-cost or a differentiated strategy, customers will *always* be concerned with the price they pay for the product or service. In market segments where price is a major influence on the purchasing decision, units can track their net selling price (after discounts and allowances) with that of competitors. If the product or service is sold after a competitive bidding process, the percentage of bids won, especially in targeted segments, would provide an indication of the unit's price competitiveness.

Even price-sensitive customers, however, may favor suppliers that offer not low prices, but low costs to acquire and use the product or service. At first glance, one may think we are playing with semantics by distinguishing between low price and low cost, but real and important differences exist between them. Take a manufacturing company that is sourcing a key purchased part from a supplier. The low-price supplier may turn out to be an extremely high-cost supplier. The low-price supplier may only deliver in large quantities, thereby requiring extensive storage space, receiving, and handling resources, plus the cost of capital associated with buying and paying for the parts well in advance of when they are used. The low-price supplier may also not be a certified supplier; that is, the quality of the parts received is not guaranteed to conform to the buyer's specifications. Therefore, the buying company has to inspect the incoming items, return those found to be defective, and arrange for replacement parts to arrive (which themselves have to inspected). The low-price supplier may also not have a stellar on-time delivery capability. Its failure to deliver reliably at scheduled times causes the buying company to order well in advance of need and hold protective stock in case delivery is not when expected. Late deliveries cause higher costs for expediting orders and rescheduling the plant around the missing items. And low-price suppliers may not be electronically connected to their customers, thereby imposing higher costs on customers when they order and pay for the purchased parts.

In contrast, a low-cost supplier may have a slightly higher purchase price but delivers defect-free products, directly to the workstation, just-in-time, as they are needed. The low-cost supplier also enables customers to order and pay electronically. The buying company incurs virtually no costs for ordering, receiving, inspecting, storing, handling, expediting, rescheduling, rework, and paying for parts purchased from this low-cost supplier. Some companies, as mentioned in the chapter, allow certain suppliers to replace their purchasing function, not taking ownership of parts until they are released, just-in-time, directly to a workstation. Suppliers should strive to organize their production and business processes so that they can be their customers' lowest-cost supplier. They may choose to compete along the cost (to the customer) dimension, not just by offering low prices and discounts. Such a measure requires that the supplier set an objective to minimize its customers' total costs for acquiring parts.

Companies in several industries have the opportunity to do even better than become their customers' lowest-cost supplier. If the customer is an organization that resells purchased items to its own customers and consumers, like a distributor, wholesaler, or retailer, the supplier can strive to become its customers' most profitable supplier. Using activity-based costing techniques, the supplier can work with its customers to build an ABC model that enables the customer to calculate the profitability by supplier. For example, Maplehurst, a frozen bakery goods company, works directly with its customers—in-store bakeries in supermarkets—to calculate the profitability by different classes of products: purchased bread, cakes, and muffins; in-store prepared goods; and in-store heated frozen bakery products (Maplehurst's product line). Maplehurst has been able to demonstrate to customers that the frozen (and subsequently in-store heated) goods are among the most profitable in the product line, a discovery that invariably leads to increased business for Maplehurst.

The current battle between national branded beverages, such as Coca-Cola and Pepsi-Cola, versus retail-branded private labels, like President's Choice and Safeway Select, is being fought on both sides by calculations for the retail grocery store about which product is more profitable for the store to stock and sell. The calculation is more complex than the traditional gross margin (net selling price less purchase price) used by most distributors, wholesalers, and retailers to calculate their profitability by product line or supplier. For example, the national-branded beverage companies deliver their product directly to the store and have their delivery people stock the product on the shelves. The retail-branded beverage companies deliver their product to warehouses and require the store to spend its resources for receiving, handling, storing, delivery, and merchandising. But the national brands also tend to occupy some of the most visible and valuable space in the stores, whereas the retail-branded products occupy normal shelf space. So care must be taken to correctly and fully account for all costs when comparing the profitability of alternative suppliers.

The benefits, to the excellent supplier, from a customer's profitability calculation are enormous. What more powerful message can a company deliver to its customers than a demonstration that it is the most profitable supplier the customer has? Thus, a company supplying customers that stock and re-sell their products or services, can drive customer satisfaction, loyalty, and retention by measuring its customers' profitability and striving to become a highly profitable supplier. Of course, the supplier must also balance this measure by calculating its own profitability of supplying each of its customers. Decreasing its own profitability to increase its customers' may lead to satisfied and loyal customers but not happy shareholders and bankers.

NOTES

1. See discussion of boundary systems in R. Simons, *Levers of Control: How Managers Use Innovative Control Systems to Drive Strategic Renewal* (Boston: Harvard Business School Press, 1995), 47–55, 156.
2. J. Heskett, T. Jones, G. Loveman, E. Sasser, and L. Schlesinger, "Putting the Service Profit Chain to Work," *Harvard Business Review* (March–April 1994): 164–174.
3. T. O. Jones and W. E. Sasser, "Why Satisfied Customers Defect," *Harvard Business Review* (November–December 1995): 88–99.
4. R. Cooper and R. S. Kaplan, "Profit Priorities from Activity-Based Costing," *Harvard Business Review* (May–June 1991): 130–135.
5. C. Hart, "The Power of Unconditional Service Guarantees," *Harvard Business Review* (July–August 1988): 54–62; and J. Heskett, E. Sasser, and C. Hart, *Service Breakthroughs: Changing the Rules of the Game* (New York: Free Press, 1990).

Chapter Five

Internal-Business-Process Perspective

FOR THE INTERNAL-BUSINESS-PROCESS PERSPECTIVE, managers identify the processes that are most critical for achieving customer and shareholder objectives. Companies typically develop their objectives and measures for this perspective after formulating objectives and measures for the financial and customer perspectives. This sequence enables companies to focus their internal-business-process metrics on those processes that will deliver the objectives established for customers and shareholders.[1]

Most organizations' existing performance measurement systems focus on improving existing operating processes. For the Balanced Scorecard, we recommend that managers define a complete internal-process value chain that starts with the innovation process—identifying current and future customers' needs and developing new solutions for these needs—proceeds through the operations process—delivering existing products and services to existing customers—and ends with postsale service—offering services after the sale that add to the value customers receive from a company's product and service offerings.

The process of deriving objectives and measures for the internal-business-process perspective represents one of the sharpest distinctions between the Balanced Scorecard and traditional performance measurement systems. Traditional performance measurement systems focus on controlling and improving existing responsibility centers and departments. The limitations of relying exclusively on financial measurements and monthly variance reports for controlling such departmental operations are, of course, well known.[2] Fortunately, most organizations today have moved well beyond using variance analysis of financial results as their primary method for evaluation and control. They are supplementing financial measurements with measures of quality, yield, throughput, and cycle time.[3] These more comprehensive performance measurement systems are certainly an improvement over exclusive reliance on monthly variance reports, but they still attempt to improve performance of individual departments rather than of integrated business processes. So more recent trends encourage companies to measure performance of business processes like order fulfillment, procurement, and production planning and control that span several organizational departments. Typically, cost, quality, throughput, and time measures would be defined and measured for these processes.[4]

For most companies today, having multiple measurements for cross-functional and integrated business processes represents a significant improvement over their existing performance measurement systems. Indeed, this is the goal we set for ourselves when we launched, back in 1990, a one-year performance measurement project with a dozen companies. This project, building on the experience of Analog Devices and other companies, led to our formulation of the Balanced Scorecard as a new corporate measurement system.[5]

Subsequent work with innovating companies has revealed to us the limitations of even these improved performance-measurement systems. We believe that simply using financial and nonfinancial performance measures for existing business processes will not lead companies to make major improvements in their economic performance. Merely slapping performance measures on existing or even reengineered processes can drive local improvements, but are unlikely to produce ambitious objectives for customers and shareholders.

All companies are now attempting to improve quality, reduce cycle times, increase yields, maximize throughput, and lower costs for their business processes. Therefore, an exclusive focus on improving the cycle time, throughput, quality, and cost of existing processes may not lead to unique competencies. Unless one can outperform competitors across the board on all business processes, in quality, time, productivity, and cost, such improvements will facilitate survival, but will not lead to distinctive and sustainable competitive advantages.[6]

In the Balanced Scorecard, the objectives and measures for the internal-business-process perspective are derived from explicit strategies to meet shareholder and targeted customer expectations. This sequential, top-down process will usually reveal entirely new business processes at which an organization must excel.

Rockwater's experience provides two vivid examples of why entirely new business processes may be required if companies are to achieve their financial and customer objectives. Recall, from Chapter 3, that Rockwater was plagued by long closeout cycles at the end of many of its construction projects. Some customers delayed their final payment by more than 100 days, leading to high accounts receivable and low return-on-capital-employed. Rockwater executives specified, as one of their financial objectives, to reduce the length of this closeout cycle so that ROCE would improve. In constructing the Rockwater scorecard, managers linked this financial objective to an internal process to collect end-of-project payments faster. A simplistic analysis would have directed attention to the existing accounts receivable process and attempted to identify the problems in that process, which led to 110-day collection periods. But the root cause of 110-day collection periods was not to be found in the accounts receivable department. No amount of quality improvement or reengineering of the accounts receivable process would do much to reduce the long closeout cycles. Customers were delaying paying their bills not because they were unaware of the invoice or because they needed more reminders and coaxing from accounts receivable clerks to pay their bill. The customers were not paying on time because, from their point of view, the project had yet to be successfully completed.

Anyone who has been involved with contractors, particularly in home construction or renovation projects, has learned that the contractor's definition of when a project has been successfully completed often differs considerably from the customer's definition of a successful completion. Thus, although Rockwater's engineers had completed the last scheduled weld on the pipeline, and had already moved on to their next project, the customer may have been less than completely satisfied with the results. One of the few ways that customers have of communicating the difference in opinion they have with contractors about the definition of project completion is to withhold the final payment until the additional work is done so that both parties agree that the project is indeed completed.

The solution for Rockwater's long closeout cycle did not lie with additional training, education, or even technology in the accounts receivable department. The solution had to come from greatly improved communication between Rockwater's on-site project manager and the customer's representative. Such communication would reveal, much earlier, any concerns that the customer had about the work already performed and the progress of the project. Ideally, if communication occurred on a continual basis throughout the project, with the customer kept satisfied during every stage, the final payment should be made promptly. So Rockwater identified, as an entirely new internal process, that project managers should continually be communicating with the customer about the progress and expected completion of the project, and asking the customer for prompt payment at every scheduled milestone, especially the final payment upon project completion. The process stressed that project engineers needed to focus on the commercial success of a project, not just technical success. This new internal process for project engineers and managers was revealed and derived from the financial objective to increase return-on-capital-employed.

A second example of a new internal process arose from Rockwater's customer objective to become a preferred supplier to its Tier 1 customers. Rockwater executives recognized that if they were to win business from Tier 1 customers, they would have to offer services that those customers valued. The problem was how to determine what those services were. Rather than take a large one-time survey of customers, Rockwater executives wanted their managers, as part of their day-to-day activities, to continually learn about customers' evolving needs. The services could include innovative technologies for operating in hostile undersea environments, increased concern about management of safety, new project financing methods, or enhanced project-management methodologies. Rockwater established an internal process objective, to be able to anticipate and influence its customers' future needs. This was an entirely new process for the company. In the past, Rockwater responded reactively—waiting for a customer's request for tender, and then preparing a work plan and a bid price. In the future, it would act proactively, by influencing the content of their customers' requests for tenders.

Thus, the process of linking internal-business-process objectives to financial and customer objectives revealed to Rockwater executives two entirely new internal processes at which they must excel:

1. Manage existing project relationships to facilitate a fast closeout cycle

2. Anticipate and influence customers' future requests

Establishing objectives and measures for these processes could only have been derived from a top-down procedure that translated strategy into operational objectives. With such a procedure, managers identified, for the internal-business-process perspective, new procedures that would lead to breakthrough performance for customers and shareholders.

THE INTERNAL-BUSINESS-PROCESS VALUE CHAIN

Each business has a unique set of processes for creating value for customers and producing financial results. We have found, however, that a generic value-chain model provides a template that companies can customize in preparing their internal-business-process perspective (see Figure 5-1). This model encompasses three principal business processes:

- Innovation
- Operations
- Postsale service

In the innovation process, the business unit researches the emerging or latent needs of customers, and then creates the products or services that will meet these needs. The operations process, the second major step in the generic internal value chain, is where existing products and services are produced and delivered to customers. This process has historically been the focus of most organizations' performance measurement systems.

Figure 5-1 The Internal-Business-Process Perspective—The Generic Value-Chain Model

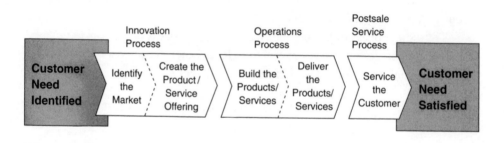

Operational excellence and cost reduction in manufacturing and service delivery processes are still important goals. The generic value chain in Figure 5-1 shows, however, that such operational excellence may be only one component, and perhaps not the most decisive component, in an entire internal value chain for achieving financial and customer objectives.

The third major step in the internal value chain is service to the customer after the original sale or delivery of a product or service. Some companies have explicit strategies to offer superior postsale service. For example, companies that sell sophisticated equipment or systems may offer training programs for customers' employees to help them use the equipment or system more effectively and efficiently. They may also offer rapid response to actual or potential failures and downtime. One distributor of industrial chemicals developed a capability to maintain detailed documentation and disposal services for used chemicals, freeing its customers from an expensive task, fraught with liability, and subject to intense governmental scrutiny by such agencies as the Environmental Protection Agency and the Occupational Safety and Health Administration. All these activities add value to targeted customers' use of the company's product and service offerings.

The Innovation Process

Some formulations of a business unit's value chain treat research and development as a support process, not a primary element in the value creation process. In fact, in our early writings on the Balanced Scorecard, we also separated the innovation process from the internal-business-process perspective. As we worked with companies, however, we came to realize that innovation was a critical *internal* process. Being effective, efficient, and timely in innovation processes is, for many companies, even more important than excellence in the day-to-day operating processes that have been the traditional focus of the internal value chain literature. The relative importance of the innovation cycle over the operating cycle is especially noticeable for companies with long design and development cycles, such as pharmaceutical, agricultural chemicals, software, and high-tech electronics. Once products reach the manufacturing stage in these companies, operating gross margins may be quite high. The opportunities for substantial cost reduction may also be limited. Most of the costs occur and are designed in during the research and development stages. The importance of the innovation process led us to modify our "geography" of the Balanced

Scorecard so that the innovation process could be recognized as an integral part of the internal-business-process perspective.

Think of the innovation process as the long wave of value creation in which companies first identify and nurture new markets, new customers, and the emerging and latent needs of existing customers. Then, continuing in this long wave of value creation and growth, companies design and develop the new products and services that enable them to reach the new markets and customers and to satisfy customers' newly identified needs. The operations process, in contrast, represents the short wave of value creation, in which companies deliver existing products and services to existing customers.

The innovation process (see Figure 5-2) consists of two components. In the first, managers undertake market research to identify the size of the market, the nature of customers' preferences, and price points for the targeted product or service. As organizations deploy their internal processes to meet specific customer needs, having accurate, valid information on market size and customer preferences becomes a vital task to perform well. In addition to surveying existing and potential customers, this segment could also include imagining entirely new opportunities and markets for products and services that the organization could supply. Hamel and Prahalad describe this process as searching for the "white spaces . . . , the opportunities that reside between or around existing product-based business definitions." They urge companies not to satisfy or delight customers but to amaze them, by finding answers to two crucial questions:

Figure 5-2　The Internal-Business-Process Perspective—The Innovation Process

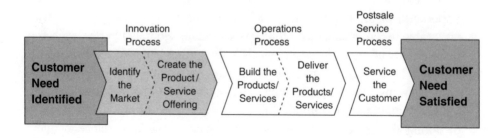

1. What range of benefits will customers value in tomorrow's products?

2. How might we, through innovation, preempt competitors in delivering those benefits to the marketplace?[7]

Clearly, Rockwater wanted to encourage its personnel to spend more time talking with customers to learn about their emerging needs, and to think of innovative solutions to these needs. Measures for this customer and market research component could be the number of entirely new products and services developed, success in developing specific products and services to targeted customer groups, or just the preparation of market research on emerging and future customer preferences.

Information on markets and customers provides the input for the actual product/service design and development processes, the second step in the innovation process.[8] During this step, the organization's research and development group:

- performs basic research to develop radically new products and services for delivering value to customers,

- performs applied research to exploit existing technology for the next generation of products and services, and

- makes focused development efforts to bring new products and services to market.

Historically, little attention has been devoted to developing performance measures for product design and development processes. Such inattention could have been caused by several factors. Decades ago, when most organizations' performance measurement systems were designed, the focus was on manufacturing and operational processes, not research and development. This was a rational focus since far more money was being spent on production processes than on R&D processes, and the key to success was efficient manufacture of high-volume products. Today, however, many organizations gain competitive advantage from a continued stream of innovative products and services so that the R&D process has become a more important element of the business' value chain. The success of this process should be motivated and evaluated by specific objectives and measures.

The increased importance of the research and development process has also led organizations to spend more money on R&D processes. In fact, some businesses spend more in their research, design, and development processes than they do to support their production and operating processes. For example, one automotive component supplier discovered that 10% of its expenses was for design and development activities, whereas its production direct labor expenses were only 9% of expenses. Yet direct labor was tightly controlled with standard costs and an extensive system of variance analysis, whereas design and development groups had hardly any financial system monitoring their rate of expenditure or measuring their output. Many companies' performance measurement systems remain anchored to operational efficiencies rather than to the effectiveness and efficiency of research and development processes.

Of course, the relationship between inputs expended (on salaries, equipment, and materials) during R&D processes and the outputs achieved (innovative products and services) is much weaker and more uncertain than in manufacturing processes, where standards can be established relatively easily for the conversion of labor, materials, and equipment resources into finished goods. A typical product development process in the electronics industry could have two years of product development followed by five years of sales. So the first success indicator of a product's development process may not appear for three years (the first year after the initial year of sales). Manufacturing processes with cycle times measured in time intervals ranging from minutes to several days are more amenable to the use of standards, yields, and a variety of productivity measures for evaluation and control. But difficulty in measuring the conversion of inputs to outputs in R&D should not prevent organizations from specifying objectives and measures for such a critical organizational process. Companies should not fall into the trap of "if you can't measure what you want, want what you can measure."

MEASURES FOR BASIC AND APPLIED RESEARCH

Advanced Micro Devices, a leading semiconductor manufacturer, competes in an industry with extremely rapid technological change. AMD focused many measures of its Balanced Scorecard on the innovation process. Among the measures it used were:

1. Percentage of sales from new products
2. Percentage of sales from proprietary products[9]

3. New product introduction versus competitors'; also new product introduction versus plan

4. Manufacturing process capabilities (density of chips that could be produced on a silicon wafer)

5. Time to develop next generation of products

These measures communicated the importance that the company placed on an effective innovation process.

Analog Devices, also in the semiconductor business, uses a measure of the return to R&D: the ratio of operating profit before taxes over a five-year period to total development cost. This metric can be measured in aggregate for all new products that have been introduced, as well as applied on a product-by-product basis. Using, as a performance measure, the ratio of operating profit to development cost signals to design and development engineers that the goal of the R&D activity is not just technically sophisticated and innovative devices, but devices that have a market potential that will more than repay their development costs.

MEASURES FOR PRODUCT DEVELOPMENT

Despite the inherent uncertainty in many product development activities, consistent patterns can be found that can be exploited in a measurement process. For example, pharmaceutical product development goes through a sequential process, starting with screening large numbers of compounds, then investigating promising ones in more detail, moving from laboratory to animal testing, shifting from animal testing to human testing, and then traversing complex governmental review and certification processes. Each stage can be characterized by measures, such as yields (number of compounds that successfully pass to the next stage divided by number of compounds that entered that stage), cycle time (how long do compounds stay in the stage), and cost (how much was spent processing compounds in the stage). Managers can establish objectives to increase yields and reduce both cycle times and cost at each stage of the development process.

An electronics company did a root cause analysis of the high time and cost of its new-product development process. The analysis revealed that the number one cause for long time-to-market of new devices was products that failed to function properly the first time they were designed, and hence had to be redesigned and retested, often several times. Therefore, while the company retained time-to-market as a critical outcome measure for the product development process, it added a performance driver measure—the percentage of products for which the first design of a device fully met the customer's functional specification. Another performance driver was the number of times the design needed to be modified, even slightly, before it was released for production. The company estimated that each design error cost $185K. With an average of two errors per product introduced, and with 110 new products introduced each year, the total amount spent on design errors was about $40 million, an amount that represented more than 5% of revenue. And added to this calculation must be the value of sales lost from late market introduction of new products caused by the time delays in redesigning the products to eliminate the errors.

Hewlett-Packard engineers developed a metric called break-even time (BET) to measure the effectiveness of its product development cycle.[10] BET measures the time from the beginning of product development work until the product has been introduced and has generated enough profit to pay back the investment originally made in its development (see Figure 5-3). BET brings together in a single measure three critical elements in an effective and efficient product-development process. First, for the company to break even on its R&D process, its investment in the product development process must be recovered. So BET incorporates not only the outcome from the product development process but also the cost of the process. It provides incentives to make the product development process more efficient. Second, BET stresses profitability. Marketing managers, manufacturing personnel, and design engineers are encouraged to work together to develop a product that meets real customer needs, including offering the product in an effective sales channel at an attractive price, and at a cost that enables the company to earn profits that will repay the product-development investment cost. And third, BET is denominated in time: it encourages the launch of new products faster than the competition so that higher sales can be earned faster to repay the product development investment.

While BET is an attractive measure, it functions better as a measure to signal desired behavior than as an outcome measure. Excellent break-even times can be achieved by choosing only incremental rather than breakthrough projects. Also, the measure is difficult to average across multiple projects to produce an aggregated BET metric—one project with an extremely long BET can distort an aggregate index. And finally, the actual value of a project's break-even time is not revealed until long after the product development process has been completed. Marv Patterson, vice president of engineering for Hewlett-Packard concluded: "It is a very good metric for describing the desired behavior a company is trying to foster within its product development process. Furthermore, it is widely used within HP to assess the viability of individual projects before they are fully staffed."

Hewlett-Packard's experience with the BET metric highlights that pressures to reduce cycle time and spending, and to increase yield, in the product development process must be balanced by measures of the innovativeness of the products produced. Otherwise, product designers and developers may emphasize incremental product improvements that can be achieved easily, quickly, and predictably, rather than radical breakthrough products. Measures such as gross margin from new products may help differentiate truly innovative products from those that are straightforward line extensions of existing products and technologies. Another measure can be derived from the time profile of sales from new product introductions. Incremental prod-

Figure 5-3 The Break-Even Time Metric

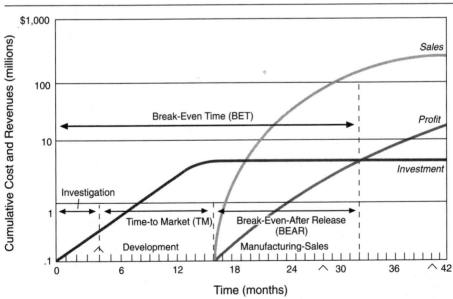

Source: Adapted from Charles H. House and Raymond L. Price, "The Return Map: Tracking Product Teams," *Harvard Business Review* (January–February 1991): 95. Reprinted with permission.

ucts, representing simple line extensions, will likely have only a few years of product life, with sales in year five a small fraction of sales in year one or two. Products or services that represent radical innovation should enjoy longer life cycles, and higher ratios of sales several years in the future to initial sales.

The Operations Process

The operations process (see Figure 5-4) represents the short wave of value creation in organizations. It starts with receipt of a customer order and finishes with delivery of the product or service to the customer. This process stresses efficient, consistent, and timely delivery of existing products and services to existing customers.

Existing operations tend to be repetitive so that scientific management techniques can be readily applied to control and improve customer order receipt and processing, and vendor, production, and delivery processes. Traditionally, these operating processes have been monitored and controlled by financial measures, such as standard costs, budgets, and variances. Over time, however, excessive focus on such narrow financial measures as labor efficiency, machine efficiency, and purchase price variances led to highly dysfunctional actions: keeping labor and machines busy building inventory not related to current customer orders, and switching from supplier to supplier to chase cheaper purchase prices (but ignoring the costs of large-volume orders, poor quality, uncertain delivery times, and disconnected ordering, receiving, invoicing, and collection processes between lower-

Figure 5-4   The Internal-Business-Process Perspective—The Operations Process

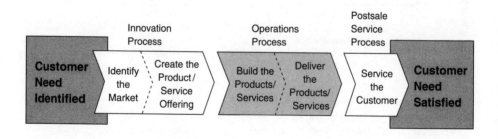

priced suppliers and the customer). By now the defects associated with using traditional cost accounting measures in today's short cycle time, and a high-quality, customer-focused environment have been amply documented.[11]

The influence, in recent years, of the total quality management and time-based competition practices of leading Japanese manufacturers has led many companies to supplement their traditional cost and financial measurements with measurements of quality and cycle time.[12] Measurements of operating processes' quality, cycle time, and cost have been developed extensively during the past 15 years. Some aspects of these measurements will likely be included as critical performance measures in any organization's internal-business-process perspective. Because these measurements tend to be generic, and do not arise uniquely from the scorecard approach, we defer to the appendix of this chapter, the discussion of the time, quality, and cost performance measurements of operating processes.

In addition to these measurements, managers may wish to measure additional characteristics of their processes, and product and service offerings. Such additional measures could include measurement of flexibility, and of the specific characteristics of products or services that create value for customers. For example, companies may offer unique products and service performance (as can be measured by accuracy, size, speed, clarity, or energy consumption) that enable them to earn high margins on sales to targeted market segments. Companies that can identify the differentiating characteristics of their products and services will certainly want the focus and attention that measurement on the Balanced Scorecard can command. Thus critical product and service performance attributes (beyond response time, quality, and cost) can certainly be incorporated into the operating process component of the Balanced Scorecard's internal-business-process perspective.

Postsale Service

The final stage in the internal value chain is postsale service (see Figure 5-5). Postsale service includes warranty and repair activities, treatment of defects and returns, and the processing of payments, such as credit card administration. Companies that sell sophisticated equipment or systems, like Otis Elevator and General Electric Medical Systems (a manufacturer of electronic imaging equipment including computer-assisted tomography

[CAT] scanners and magnetic resonance imagers [MRI]), know that any downtime on their equipment is extremely expensive and inconvenient to their customers. Both these companies enhance the value of their equipment by offering rapid, reliable service to customers to minimize such disruptions. They even imbed electronic technology in their equipment that senses and transmits signals to company service personnel when the equipment shows signs of imminent failure. This technology enables repair people to show up on-site to perform preventive maintenance and repair, often surprising customers who had yet to notice any degradation in equipment performance. Newly established automobile dealerships, like Acura and Saturn, have deservedly earned superb reputations by offering dramatically improved customer service for warranty work, periodic maintenance, and repairs. A major element in the value proposition these car companies deliver to their customers is responsive, friendly, and reliable warranty and service work. And several department stores offer generous terms under which customers can exchange or return merchandise.

Companies attempting to meet their targeted customers' expectations for superior postsale service can measure their performance by applying some of the same time, quality, and cost metrics, described for operating processes (see appendix to this chapter), to their postsale service processes. Thus, cycle times—from customer request to ultimate resolution of the problem—can measure the speed of response to failures. Cost metrics can evaluate the efficiency—the cost of resources used—for postsale service processes. And first-pass yields can measure what percentage of customer requests are

Figure 5-5 The Internal-Business-Process Perspective—The Postsale Service Process

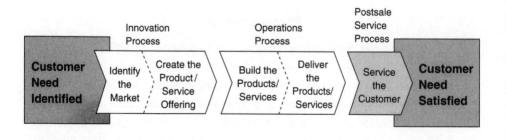

handled with a single service call, rather than requiring multiple calls to resolve the problem.

Another aspect of postsale service is the invoicing and collection process. The Rockwater objective presented earlier in this chapter, to reduce the length of the time between project completion and final cash payment by the customer, is an excellent example of bringing focus and discipline to a critical postsale-service process. Companies with extensive sales on credit or on company-specific credit cards will likely need to apply cost, quality, and cycle time measurements to their billings, collection, and dispute resolution processes.

And companies that deal with hazardous or environmentally sensitive chemicals and materials may introduce critical performance measures associated with the safe disposal of waste and by-products from the production process. Recognizing that excellent community relations may be a strategic objective for continuing to enjoy a franchise to operate, companies set objectives, under postsale service, for excellent environmental performance. Measures such as waste and scrap produced during production processes may be more significant for their impact on the environment, than for their slight increase in production costs.

SPECIFIC INTERNAL-BUSINESS-PROCESS PERSPECTIVES

Kenyon Stores

Kenyon Stores (introduced in the previous chapter) is a multibillion dollar retailer of clothing. Kenyon's senior executives had established an aggressive goal for sales growth of 150% over five years. They intended to achieve this ambitious goal by providing:

1. a premium brand image;
2. great fashion, design, and quality merchandise at an attractive price; and
3. quick, efficient service and excellent product availability.

Kenyon had established specific customer objectives and measures (see Chapter 4) for product attributes, customer relationships, and image and brand. To deliver on its customer objectives, Kenyon identified five critical internal-business processes:

1. Brand management
2. Fashion leadership
3. Sourcing leadership
4. Merchandise availability
5. Memorable shopping experience

The first two of these, brand management and fashion leadership, can be considered part of Kenyon's innovation process—identifying and influencing customer needs, and developing the fashion merchandise to fulfill those needs. The last three processes relate to the operations process—getting the correct merchandise to the point of sale and providing the customer with "a perfect shopping experience."

BRAND MANAGEMENT

Within the brand management process, Kenyon identified four subobjectives:

1. Brand Concept Definition: Build Kenyon into a dominant national brand with an increased share of wardrobe for the target customer.
2. Category Dominance: Continue the growth of casual pants and jeans as the dominant category within Kenyon's product mix.
3. Positioning Strategy: Expand the Kenyon image from successful private label to mature brand that is clearly defined by the customer.
4. Store Concept Definition: Develop successful merchandise assortment and marketing program.

These subobjectives were directed at building a concept and loyalty among targeted customers. The measures selected for these subobjectives were:

1. Market share in selected categories (e.g., casual pants and jeans)
2. Brand recognition (from market research)
3. New accounts opened per year

These measures were intended to reflect Kenyon's success in implementing its brand management strategy.

FASHION LEADERSHIP

Fashion leadership was defined as providing targeted customer segments with fashionable merchandise that supported the brand and influenced customers' buying habits.

Fashion leadership focused on effectively using information to choose fashions that would meet customers' expectations in key clothing categories. This objective communicated the importance of early identification of fashion trends and rapid dissemination of this information so that key items could be introduced into stores ahead of the competition. The measure selected was the number of key items in which Kenyon was first or second to market. A second fashion definition measure was the percentage of sales from items newly introduced in the store. The definition of items that would be included in this measure would change year to year to reflect the new categories or accessories that would be emphasized each year.

SOURCING LEADERSHIP

As a retailer, Kenyon knew that its own excellent performance was critically dependent on the performance of its key suppliers. These suppliers would need to manufacture goods quickly, responsively, and at low cost for Kenyon to achieve its ambitious objectives. Sourcing leadership stressed development and management of the supplier base so that desired volumes and mix of high-quality merchandise could be rapidly produced and delivered. Kenyon's in-store personnel examined all incoming shipments of merchandise. They recorded the percentage of items that could not be offered to customers because of quality-related defects. The scorecard measured the overall percentage of quality-related returns, and could trace those returns back to individual vendors.

A second sourcing leadership measure came from a newly created vendor scorecard that evaluated suppliers along dimensions of quality, price, lead time, and input into fashion decisions.

MERCHANDISE AVAILABILITY

Merchandise availability related to a "perfect inventory" objective in which customer satisfaction, sales, and gross margin would be achieved by buying the right quantities of merchandise in the right colors and sizes, and stocking the right stores with the appropriate assortment in advance of customer demands. The first element of this objective, for an excellent buying process, was measured by stores' out-of-stock percentage on selected key items. Balancing this measure, to avoid excess inventory, was a measure of inventory turns on the selected key items.

The second element, getting the right product to the right store, used two measures. One was the total amount of markdowns. The second product allocation measure was the percentage of merchandise that had to be transferred between stores.

MEMORABLE SHOPPING EXPERIENCE

A measure for Kenyon's memorable shopping-experience objective has already been described in Chapter 4: a rating along the six elements of a "perfect shopping experience." This measure occupied a position in both the customer and the internal-business-process perspective. In addition to this customized measure, Kenyon solicited feedback from customers; a score on customers' satisfaction with their shopping experiences was included in this subobjective.

The complete set of internal-business-process perspective objectives and measures, and their link to customer perspective objectives, is shown in Figure 5-6.

Metro Bank

Metro Bank's internal perspective (see Figure 5-7) follows the same sequencing of value chain objectives that we described for Kenyon. Metro's ability, in its innovation process, to identify and sell into profitable market segments was measured by its profitability in targeted market segments. This measure was implemented via an extensive activity-based costing system that could produce monthly profit and loss statements for each of the 3 million accounts at the bank. The ability to create new products for targeted customers was measured by the percentage of revenue from new products. And the ability to deliver the product through desired distribution channels was measured by the percentage of transactions conducted through various channels (ATM, teller, computer-mediated).

A key internal-perspective objective was for salespersons to increase their productivity, both by selling to more customers in targeted segments, and by increasing the depth of relationship the bank had with its targeted customers. This productivity objective was reflected in the three strategic measures shown under the Cross-Sell strategic theme in Figure 5-7.

The delivery of products and services to customers was measured by two aggregate indices:

- "Trailway to Trolls"
- Internal customer satisfaction

The "Trailway to Trolls" measure (trolls are grumpy customers; see appendix) was an index composed of up to 100 different service delivery failures that could produce customer dissatisfaction. The components in the "Trailways to Trolls" index were publicized to personnel in all the bank's branches and offices so that every employee was aware of the defects that should

Figure 5-6   The Internal Scorecard and Linkages—Kenyon Stores

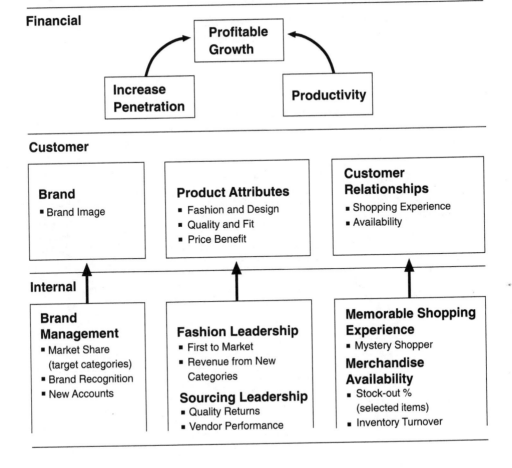

be avoided. The internal customer satisfaction index was constructed by monthly surveys of randomly selected customers in the bank's targeted segments.

Collectively, Metro Bank's internal perspective measured the bank's ability to identify profitable market segments, develop new products and services for these segments, sell existing and new products to customers in these segments, and to service these customers in an efficient and timely manner, without service defects.

Pioneer Petroleum

Our third example illustrates the internal-business-process perspective for Pioneer Petroleum. Recall, from Chapter 4, that Pioneer had to meet objectives from two types of customers: its immediate customers, the gasoline dealers; and its consumers who ultimately purchased Pioneer's products at retail outlets. Pioneer's internal perspective had to incorporate objectives

Figure 5-7 The Internal Scorecard—Metro Bank

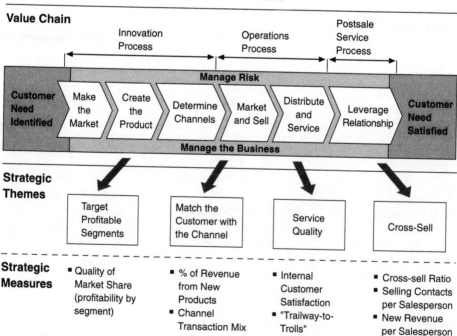

Value Chain			
	Innovation Process	Operations Process	Postsale Service Process

Manage Risk

| Customer Need Identified | Make the Market | Create the Product | Determine Channels | Market and Sell | Distribute and Service | Leverage Relationship | Customer Need Satisfied |

Manage the Business

Strategic Themes			
Target Profitable Segments	Match the Customer with the Channel	Service Quality	Cross-Sell

Strategic Measures			
▪ Quality of Market Share (profitability by segment)	▪ % of Revenue from New Products ▪ Channel Transaction Mix	▪ Internal Customer Satisfaction ▪ "Trailway-to-Trolls"	▪ Cross-sell Ratio ▪ Selling Contacts per Salesperson ▪ New Revenue per Salesperson

and measures that would meet the expectations of both the gasoline retailers and the automobile drivers.

For its gasoline retailers (see righthand column of Figure 5-8), Pioneer had established a customer goal of dealer satisfaction. The internal-business-process objectives to achieve this outcome included:

- Develop new products and services
- Develop the dealer

Figure 5-8 The Internal Scorecard and Linkages—Pioneer Petroleum

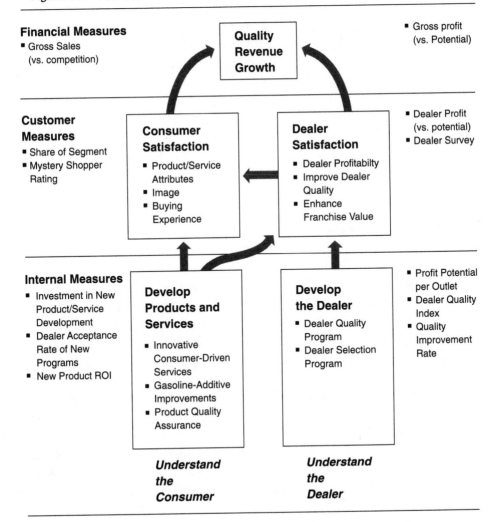

The objective to develop new products and services actually drove both dealer and consumer satisfaction objectives. Pioneer could be a more attractive supplier to dealers by offering them differentiated products and services so that they did not have to compete for consumers solely on the basis of price. Pioneer's new products and services were also attractive to consumers in its three targeted market segments, those who were looking for gas stations that offered a full array of products and services. The measure for this objective was nongasoline revenues, which included dealer revenues from convenience stores and service bays. This measure was also benchmarked against top operators in the industry. Both total revenues from nongasoline sources as well as sales per square foot were calculated.

The objective to develop the dealer was accomplished by two measures. Pioneer established a tool kit for its marketing representatives. The tool kit helped the reps make more focused and effective calls with franchisees and also provided a template for the marketing representatives to evaluate the performance of individual dealers along seven dimensions:

1. Financial management
2. Service bays
3. Personnel management
4. Car wash operation
5. Convenience stores
6. Gasoline purchasing
7. Better buying experience

These ratings gave feedback to the individual dealers about their opportunities for improvement. The ratings were aggregated into an index that Pioneer monitored to determine whether it was successfully upgrading the quality and performance of its franchised dealers. Pioneer also used key dealer retention as a measure of whether it was retaining the loyalty of high-volume, profitable dealers.

For its end-use consumers, Pioneer, in addition to the objective of developing new products and services, identified an objective to promote the brand image. This was measured by Pioneer's share of market in key geographic areas among its three targeted consumer-market segments: Road Warriors, True Blues, and Generation F3s (see descriptions on page 66). To assess whether its franchised dealers were delivering a superior buying experience to targeted consumers, Pioneer employed a mystery shopping rating, in which an independent third party shopped at each station monthly (and local competitors quarterly). The mystery shopper made a gasoline and snack purchase and then calculated a dealer quality score that could be compared to the station's previous performance and to competitive stations. The score was particularly weighted toward five key areas:

1. Facility exterior
2. Service islands
3. Sales area
4. Personnel
5. Restrooms

The mystery shopper rating provided information and incentives for franchised dealers to offer the value proposition that would attract consumers in Pioneer's three targeted segments.

SUMMARY

In the internal-business-process perspective, managers identify the critical processes at which they must excel if they are to meet the objectives of shareholders and of targeted customer segments. Conventional performance measurement systems focus only on monitoring and improving cost, quality, and time-based measures of existing business processes. In contrast, the approach of the Balanced Scorecard enables the demands for internal process performance to be derived from the expectations of specific external constituencies.

One recent development has been to incorporate the innovation process as a vital component of the internal-business-process perspective. The innovation process highlights the importance of, first, identifying the characteristics of market segments that the organization wishes to satisfy with its future products and services, and, then, designing and developing the products and services that will satisfy those targeted segments. This approach enables the organization to put considerable weight on research, design, and development processes that yield new products, services, and markets.

The operations process remains important and organizations should identify the cost, quality, time, and performance characteristics (see appendix) that will enable it to deliver superior products and services to its targeted current customers. And the postsale service process enables companies to feature, when appropriate, important aspects of service that occur after the purchased product or service has been delivered to the customer.

APPENDIX:
OPERATIONS PROCESS—TIME, QUALITY, AND COST MEASUREMENTS

Process Time Measurement

The value proposition being delivered to targeted customers often includes short response times as a critical performance attribute (see discussion in Chapter 4) Many customers value highly short lead times, measured as the time elapsed from when they place an order until the time when they receive the desired product or service. They also value reliable lead times, as measured by on-time delivery. Manufacturing companies generally have two ways of offering short and reliable lead times to customers. One is to have efficient, reliable, defect-free, short-cycle order fulfillment and production processes that can respond rapidly to customer orders. The other is to produce and hold large stocks of inventory of all products so that any customer request can be met by shipments from existing finished-goods inventory. The first way enables the company to be a low-cost and timely supplier. The second way usually leads to very high production, inventory carrying, and obsolescence costs, as well as an inability to respond quickly to orders for nonstocked items (because the manufacturing processes are typically busy building inventories for normally stocked items). Since many manufacturing companies are attempting to shift from the second way of satisfying customer orders (producing large batches for just-in-case inventory) to the first way (producing small orders, just-in-time), reducing cycle or throughput times of internal processes becomes a critical internal-process objective. Cycle or throughput times can be measured many different ways. The start of the cycle can correspond to the time when:

1. customer order is received
2. customer order, or production batch, is scheduled
3. raw materials are ordered for the order or production batch
4. raw materials are received
5. production on the order or batch is initiated

Similarly the end of the cycle can correspond to the time when:

1. production of the order or the batch has been completed
2. order or batch is in finished goods inventory, available to be shipped
3. order is shipped
4. order is received by the customer

The choice of starting and ending points is determined by the scope of the operating process for which cycle time reductions are being sought. The broadest definition, corresponding to an order fulfillment cycle, would start the cycle with receipt of a customer order and would stop when the customer has received the order. A narrower definition, aimed at improving the flow of physical material within a factory, could correspond to the time between when a batch is started into production and when it has been fully processed. Whatever definition is used, an organization would continually measure cycle times and set targets for employees to reduce total cycle times.

A metric used by many organizations attempting to move to just-in-time production flow processes is manufacturing cycle effectiveness (MCE), defined as:

$$\text{MCE} = \frac{\text{Processing Time}}{\text{Throughput Time}}$$

This ratio is less than 1 because:

$$\frac{\text{Throughput}}{\text{Time}} = \frac{\text{Processing}}{\text{Time}} + \frac{\text{Inspection}}{\text{Time}} + \frac{\text{Movement}}{\text{Time}} + \frac{\text{Waiting/Storage}}{\text{Time}}$$

For many operations, processing time, the time when the product is actually being worked on (machined or assembled) is less than 5% of throughput time; that is when total throughput time may be six weeks (30 working days), only one to two days of actual processing time may be required. During the remaining time, the part or product is being inspected, moved around the factory, or is simply waiting: in storage, on the factory floor, or just before or just after a processing operation until the next operation can be scheduled, the machine set up, and the part fixtured into place. In an ideal JIT production flow process, the throughput time for a part just equals its processing time. In this ideal situation, the MCE ratio equals 1, a goal that, like zero defects, may never be attainable but is worth moving toward.

The theory behind the MCE ratio is that all time, other than processing time—time used for inspection, reworking defective items, moving items from one process to the next, and just having items wait until processed at the next stage—is waste or non-value-added time. This time is wasted because the physical form of the product is not being enhanced to meet a customer's need. And the product is being delayed for delivery to the customer, with no value added during the delay. As the MCE ratio approaches 1, the organization knows that the amount of time wasted moving, inspecting, repairing, and storing products is decreasing, and its ability to respond rapidly to customer orders is improving.

APPLYING PROCESS TIME MEASUREMENTS IN SERVICE INDUSTRIES

While just-in-time production processes and the manufacturing cycle effectiveness (MCE) ratio were developed for manufacturing operations, they are just as applicable to service companies. If anything, eliminating waste time in a service delivery process is even more important than in manufacturing companies, since consumers are increasingly intolerant of being forced to wait in line for service delivery.

Take an example from the banking industry. Many of us are familiar with the process of gaining approval for a mortgage on a house that we wish to purchase. The process starts by showing up at a local bank branch, and filling out an extensive application form that includes employment history, salary, assets and liabilities, as well as a description of the house. After completing the application, the employee thanks us for choosing her bank, and then says that we can expect to hear whether or not the mortgage application has been approved in three to four weeks.

One bank vice president, very familiar with the normal cycle time of 26 days to process such requests, asked employees to keep track of how much time was spent actually processing the application during these 26 days. The answer turned out to be about 15 minutes of work, spread across 26 days, an MCE ratio of 0.0004 (0.25 hours/[26 days × 24 hours per day]). The vice president set a target to reengineer the approval process so that it would only take 15 minutes from completion of the application to a yes/no decision. This target corresponded to an MCE of 1.0. Bank personnel would continue to do all the value-added processing work but would eliminate all the non-value-added waiting times. At first, all the employees involved in the mortgage approval process claimed this was an impossible target. Among other tasks, credit references had to be requested and confirmed, a process that took at least a week or two. Further study revealed that credit references could be accessed on-line for almost all possible customers. Much of the analytic work and approval routines could also be automated. A reengineered mortgage-approval process, supported by enhanced information technology, was designed that yielded a yes/no decision within 15 minutes. Thus, after customers filled out the mortgage application, they were directed to a cafeteria for a cup of coffee and by the time they returned, a decision was available.[13] A 15-minute one-stop mortgage approval process turned out to be highly attractive to a broad market segment of customers.

Similar studies in other service industries yielded similar conclusions; long cycle times for customer service during which actual processing time was remarkably low. Automobile rental companies and a few hotel chains have now automated, for targeted customer segments, all aspects of check-in and check-out, enabling valued customers to skip waiting in line when initially accessing the service and upon completion of the service delivery process. Thus, companies attempting to deliver products and services on demand to targeted customers can set objectives to have MCE ratios approach 1, thereby producing dramatically shortened lead times for customer orders.

PROCESS QUALITY MEASUREMENT

Almost all organizations today have quality initiatives and quality programs in place. Measurement is a central part of any such program, so organizations are already familiar with a variety of process quality measurements:

- Process part-per-million defect rates
- Yields (ratio of good items produced to good items entering the process)
- Waste
- Scrap
- Rework

- Returns
- Percentage of processes under statistical process control

Service organizations, especially, should identify the defects in their internal processes that could adversely affect costs, responsiveness, or customer satisfaction. They can then develop customized measures of quality shortfalls. Metro Bank, as one of its measures of service quality, developed an index called "Trailway to Trolls" (trolls are unhappy customers) to indicate the defects in its internal processes that lead to customer dissatisfaction. The index included such items as:

- Long waiting times
- Inaccurate information
- Access denied or delayed
- Request or transaction not fulfilled
- Financial loss for customer
- Customer not treated as valued
- Ineffective communication

A particularly demanding quality measure, analogous to the MCE ratio described earlier is first-pass yields. Two real stories illustrate the importance of this metric.

National Motors

Several years ago, one of the authors visited a major automobile company, which we call National Motors (to protect the guilty). The plant superintendent was conducting a tour for the visitor, emphasizing the transformation of the plant to a total quality and just-in-time environment. To illustrate the success of the total quality initiative, a banner at the end of the production line declared that the plant had achieved a perfect score of 155 at the final inspection point of finished products. The superintendent then showed the already impressed visitor to the incoming materials receipt area, where the tracks formerly used for freight car deliveries of raw materials and purchased parts had been ripped out. They had been replaced by loading docks where truckload deliveries were made several times per day. On the way through the plant, however, the visitor noticed many tall racks containing what appeared to be large quantities of inventory. He asked, naively, why was there a need to store inventory? If materials and parts deliveries were being made just-in-time and moved immediately into linked production processes that could pass intermediate goods from one process to the next without delays, where did all the inventory he saw come from? He was told, quickly and somewhat condescendingly, that he was not looking at inventory. That was the rework area! The plant had achieved its perfect quality score by inspecting items after every production process, and putting to one side any items that failed the quality test. This plant was still operating the expensive way: by inspecting quality in, not designing it in.

National Electric

About 1980, the defense electronics division of National Electric was experiencing significant quality problems in its printed circuit-board production and assembly process. It sent a team of engineers to a similar Japanese company to compare the two firms' production processes. Early in its visit to the Japanese company, National Electric's team was asked how many of a batch of 100 printed circuit boards made it all the way through their entire production process. The National team leader responded indignantly, "They all do. These are expensive boards. We don't lose any." The Japanese inquirer apologized for the poor translation of his question. He meant to ask, "How many boards make it through the entire production process the first time, without any rework having to be done to them?" The National Electric engineers huddled for several minutes and then were forced to admit that they had no idea. It was not a statistic that they had collected or ever considered collecting. They were too busy attempting to minimize adverse labor and machine efficiency variances to contemplate additional production measures, especially a nonfinancial one. Nevertheless, their interest piqued by the question, they asked their Japanese hosts what their percentage was. The Japanese responded that they were currently at 96% first-pass yields. Twelve months ago, they were only at 90% but had been working hard to increase this percentage, with a goal of eventually reaching 100% first-pass yields.

When the engineers returned to their U.S. plant, they asked their plant manager and plant controller the same question. Neither knew the answer. A special study was performed and several weeks later the answer emerged: 16%! Everyone agreed they would not be in this business for long without a significant improvement in this percentage. Within six months, TQM efforts had raised the percentage to 60%, and this increase in first-pass yields enabled the operating work force to be reduced by 25%: from 400 to 300 employees. In effect, 100 people had been employed at the plant to produce defective products, then to inspect and detect them, and finally to repair them until they were acceptable finished goods. Once the plant decided that it was not in business to make and repair defective goods, the 100 people formerly employed in this activity were no longer needed.

These stories reveal the power of using first-pass yields as a quality measure. The success of a quality program should not be measured by the quality of outgoing items after they have survived numerous inspections and rework processes. It must be measured by reductions in percentage of items, at each stage of a production process, that do not conform to customer-based specifications.

PROCESS COST MEASUREMENT

Amidst all the attention to process time and process quality measurements, one might lose sight of the cost dimension of processes. Traditional cost accounting systems measure the expenses and efficiencies of individual tasks, operations, or departments. But these systems fail to measure costs at the process level. Typically, processes like order fulfillment, purchasing, or production planning and control use resources and activities from several responsibility centers. Not until the advent of activity-based cost systems could managers obtain cost measurement of their business processes.[14]

For example, an early ABC application in the late 1980s occurred with a branded manufacturer of personal care products. The study focused on manufacturing costs, but the ABC analysis revealed that one of the principal contributors to manufacturing costs and complexity was the production of small lots of new products. As new flavors and varieties of products were designed in the company's R&D activity, small lots had to be manufactured for initial testing. This often required stopping a high-volume production run already in process to set up for the R&D production lot and then resetting up for the high-volume run. After the new product variant was launched into test markets, feedback from consumers was used to redesign the product, leading to a demand for even more small-lot runs. In the past, the cost of changeovers for the small runs of R&D production lots, and for testing the reformulations, had been treated as part of manufacturing overhead and allocated to existing products using traditional (and arbitrary) cost allocation procedures. As part of the ABC study, all the production costs, both volume-related and batch- or lot-related (including the round-trip cost of setups when a large volume run was interrupted by an R&D test lot) plus production runs for test marketing, and for reformulating products, were assigned to a newly defined activity, launching new products. The analysis revealed that the company was spending a very high amount per product launch, far more than it had ever imagined. Previously, the company had managed total spending for the R&D group but had neither traced such spending to the outputs produced (number of new products created and launched), nor had it included the costs incurred outside of the R&D department, such as the high manufacturing costs for the small R&D lots. Once they understood the total costs associated with launching new products, the managers were more receptive to suggestions to reorganize the new product formulation and to initiate procedures to obtain a far more efficient and effective process. They also had a much better analytic understanding of the costs associated with simple line extensions that could be compared with the benefits from these extensions.

In general, ABC analysis will enable organizations to obtain process cost measurements that, along with quality and cycle time measurement, will provide three important parameters to characterize important internal-business processes. As companies use either continuous improvement (such as TQM) or discontinuous improvement (such as reengineering or business process redesign) of important internal-business processes, the three sets of measurements—on cost, quality, and time—will provide data on whether the goals of these improvement programs are being achieved.

NOTES

1. Alternatively, organizations whose strategy is derived from a resource-based view (RBV) of the firm (see, for example, D. Collis and C. Montgomery, "Competing on Resources: Strategy in the 1990s," *Harvard Business Review* [July–August 1995]: 118–128) may wish to establish objectives and measures for the internal-business-process perspective before addressing the customer perspective, or even the financial one. The RBV approach to business strategy attempts to leverage certain critical core capabilities (or competencies) to achieve sustainable competitive advantage. This approach can be implemented by translating the critical capabilities into specific objectives and measures for the core internal processes. These internal-business-process measures can

then be linked to the customer perspective by identifying objectives and measures for the markets and customer segments that the company expects to succeed in with its core capabilities.

2. R. S. Kaplan, "Yesterday's Accounting Undermines Production," *Harvard Business Review* (July–August 1984): 95–101; H. T. Johnson and R. S. Kaplan, *Relevance Lost: The Rise and Fall of Management Accounting* (Boston: Harvard Business School Press, 1987); R. Howell, J. Brown, S. Soucy, and A. Seed, *Management Accounting in the New Manufacturing Environment* (Montvale, N.J.: National Association of Accountants and CAM-I, 1987); and R. S. Kaplan, "Limitations of Cost Accounting in Advanced Manufacturing Environments," in *Measures for Manufacturing Excellence Accounting,* ed. R. S. Kaplan (Boston: Harvard Business School Press, 1990), 15–38.

3. See discussion in A. Nanni, J. Miller, and T. Vollmann, "What Shall We Account For?" *Management Accounting* (January 1988): 42–48; John Lessner, "Performance Measurement in a Just-in-Time Environment: Can Traditional Performance Measurements Still Be Used?" *Journal of Cost Management* (Fall 1989): 22–28; Kelvin Cross and Richard Lynch, "Accounting for Competitive Performance," *Journal of Cost Management* (Spring 1989): 20–28; and A. Nanni, R. Dixon, and T. Vollmann, "Strategic Control and Performance Measurement," *Journal of Cost Management* (Summer 1990): 33–42.

4. While any measurement across departmental and organizational lines is a nontrivial task, it should not be that difficult to derive quality, yield, throughput, and cycle time measures for most business processes. Cost measurement is more difficult since direct physical measurement of *cost* is not possible. Activity-based costing provides a valuable role in facilitating the *cost* measurement of business processes.

5. R. S. Kaplan, "Analog Devices: The Half-Life System," 9-190-061 (Boston: Harvard Business School, 1990) and R. S. Kaplan and D. P. Norton, "The Balanced Scorecard: Measures That Drive Performance," *Harvard Business Review* (January–February 1992): 71–79.

6. Robin Cooper, in *When Lean Enterprises Collide: Competing through Confrontation* (Boston: Harvard Business School Press, 1995), argues that many Japanese companies do indeed attempt to compete by outperforming all rivals on cost, quality, functionality, and time-to-market of new products, rather than competing in targeted customer and market segments, or with subsets of company capabilities.

7. Gary Hamel and C. K. Prahalad, *Competing for the Future: Breakthrough Strategies for Seizing Control of Your Industry and Creating the Markets of Tomorrow* (Boston: Harvard Business School Press, 1994), 84, 100, 101.

8. By performing market research prior to designing the product or service, the organization can use approaches like target costing and value engineering during the actual design process so that customers' desired quality, functional-

ity, and price combinations can be incorporated at a cost for which the company can earn its desired profit. Intensive consideration of quality, functionality, and cost during the design stage is especially important in industries where up to 80% of a product's cost is determined during the design stage. See Cooper, *When Lean Enterprises Collide;* also Robin Cooper and W. Bruce Chew, "Control Tomorrow's Costs Through Today's Designs," *Harvard Business Review* (January–February 1996): 88–97.

9. For pharmaceutical and agricultural chemicals companies, the sales of proprietary products would represent sales of products still under patent protection versus sales of generic products that could be manufactured by competitors.

10. Charles H. House and Raymond L. Price, "The Return Map: Tracking Product Teams," *Harvard Business Review* (January–February 1991): 92–100; also Marvin L. Patterson, "Designing Metrics," chap. 3 in *Accelerating Innovation: Improving the Process of Product Development* (New York: Van Nostrand Reinhold, 1993).

11. See Lessner, "Performance Measurement in a Just-in-Time Environment"; R. Kaplan, "Limitation of Cost Accounting in Advanced Manufacturing Environments," chap. 1 in *Measures for Manufacturing Excellence;* and Eliyahu Goldratt and Jeff Cox, *The Goal: A Process of Ongoing Improvement* (Croton-on-Hudson, N.Y.: North River Press, 1986).

12. A representative sample of references includes C. Berliner and J. Brimson, "CMS Performance Measurement," Chap. 6 in *Cost Management for Today's Advanced Manufacturing: The CAM-I Conceptual Design,* ed. C. Berliner and J. A. Brimson (Boston: Harvard Business School Press, 1988); C. J. McNair, W. Mosconi, and T. Norris, *Meeting the Technology Challenge: Cost Accounting in a JIT Environment* (Montvale, N.J.: Institute of Management Accountants, 1988); R. S. Kaplan, "Management Accounting for Advanced Technological Environments," *Science* (25 August 1989): 819–823; and R. Lynch and K. Cross, *Measure Up! Yardsticks for Continuous Improvement* (Cambridge, Mass.: Basil Blackwell, 1991).

13. Some aspects of the application could not be verified within 15 minutes. An approval decision was made contingent on the information supplied on the application being valid, including employment history, salary, and market value of purchased house. This information would be confirmed during the next several days. But the analytic work and the credit record could be accomplished within the 15-minute processing window.

14. See G. Cokins, A. Stratton, and J. Helbling, *An ABC Manager's Primer* (Montvale, N. J.: Institute of Management Accountants, 1993) and R. Cooper, R. Kaplan, L. Maisel, E. Morrissey, and R. Oehm, *Implementing Activity-Based Cost Management* (Montvale, N. J.: Institute of Management Accountants, 1993).

Learning and Growth Perspective

THE FOURTH AND FINAL PERSPECTIVE on the Balanced Scorecard develops objectives and measures to drive organizational learning and growth. The objectives established in the financial, customer, and internal-business-process perspectives identify where the organization must excel to achieve breakthrough performance. The objectives in the learning and growth perspective provide the infrastructure to enable ambitious objectives in the other three perspectives to be achieved. Objectives in the learning and growth perspective are the drivers for achieving excellent outcomes in the first three scorecard perspectives.

Managers in several organizations have noted that when they were evaluated solely on short-term financial performance, they often found it difficult to sustain investments to enhance the capability of their people, systems, and organizational processes. Expenditures on such investments are treated as period expenses by the financial accounting model so that cutbacks in these investments are an easy way to produce incremental short-term earnings. The adverse long-term consequences of consistent failure to enhance employee, systems, and organizational capabilities will not show up in the short run, and when they do, these managers reason, it may be on somebody else's "watch."

The Balanced Scorecard stresses the importance of investing for the future, and not just in traditional areas for investment, such as new equipment and new product research and development. Equipment and R&D investments are certainly important but they are unlikely to be sufficient by themselves. Organizations must also invest in their infrastructure—people, systems, and procedures—if they are to achieve ambitious long-term financial growth objectives.

Our experience in building Balanced Scorecards across a wide variety of service and manufacturing organizations has revealed three principal categories for the learning and growth perspective:

1. Employee capabilities
2. Information systems capabilities
3. Motivation, empowerment, and alignment

EMPLOYEE CAPABILITIES

One of the most dramatic changes in management thinking during the past 15 years has been the shift in the role of organizational employees. In fact, nothing better exemplifies the revolutionary transformation from industrial age thinking to information age thinking than the new management philosophy of how employees contribute to the organization. The emergence of giant industrial enterprises a century ago and the influence of the scientific management movement left a legacy where companies hired employees to perform well-specified and narrowly defined work. Organizational elites— the industrial engineers and managers—specified in detail the routine and repetitive tasks of individual workers, and established standards and monitoring systems to ensure that workers performed these tasks just as designed. Workers were hired to do physical work, not to think.

Today, almost all routine work has been automated: computer-controlled manufacturing operations have replaced workers for routine machining, processing, and assembly operations; and service companies are, increasingly, giving their customers direct access to transactions processing through advanced information systems and communications. In addition, doing the same job over and over, at the same level of efficiency and productivity, is no longer sufficient for organizational success. For an organization just to maintain its existing relative performance, it must continually improve. And, if it wants to grow beyond today's financial and customer performance, adhering to standard operating procedures established by organizational elites is not enough. Ideas for improving processes and performance for customers must increasingly come from front-line employees who are closest to internal processes and an organization's customers. Standards for

Wesin Hotch.

how internal processes and customer responses were performed in the past provide a baseline from which improvements must continually be made. They cannot be a standard for current and future performance.

This shift requires major reskilling of employees so that their minds and creative abilities can be mobilized for achieving organizational objectives. Take an example from Metro Bank. In the past, the bank had emphasized efficient processing of customer transactions for their demand and time deposit accounts. Recall, from Chapter 4, that the senior executives of Metro Bank had set, as a key financial objective, to market and sell effectively a much broader array of financial products and services. A customer walked into a Metro branch bank. She told the bank employee that she had changed jobs and wanted to know how to have payroll checks from her new employer deposited directly into her checking account. The employee duly and correctly informed the customer that she should go to her human resources department and sign a form authorizing the direct deposit of the payroll check. The customer left with her "need" satisfied.

The bank, however, had lost a major opportunity. This request could have provided the occasion for the bank employee to get a more complete personal financial profile of the customer, including:

- Own or rent a house/apartment?
- Automobiles: how many, how old?
- Credit and charge cards: how many, which?
- Annual income
- Household assets and liabilities
- Insurance
- Children: how many, how old?

Such a profile would have allowed the bank employee to suggest a much wider array of financial products and services—credit card, consolidating personal loan, home equity loan, investments, mutual funds, insurance policies, home mortgage, car loans, savings plans for college, and student loan programs, for example—in addition to the particular financial service that brought the customer into the bank: the direct deposit of a payroll check.

Before the financial profile could have been used effectively, however, the bank employee would have to have been trained in all the bank's product and service offerings, and would need the skills to match particular products and services to the needs of the individual customer. Metro Bank executives recognized that a multiyear program would be required for their front-line employees to obtain these capabilities to transform them from routine processors of customer requests into proactive, trusted, and valued financial counselors.

CORE EMPLOYEE MEASUREMENT GROUP

We have found most companies use employee objectives drawn from a common core of three outcome measurements (see Figure 6-1). These core outcome measurements are then supplemented with situation-specific drivers of the outcomes. The three core employee measurements are

1. Employee satisfaction
2. Employee retention
3. Employee productivity

Figure 6-1 The Learning and Growth Measurement Framework

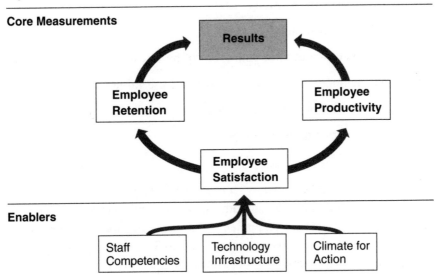

Within this core, the employee satisfaction objective is generally considered the driver of the other two measures, employee retention and employee productivity.

Measuring Employee Satisfaction

The employee satisfaction objective recognizes that employee morale and overall job satisfaction are now considered highly important by most organizations. Satisfied employees are a precondition for increasing productivity, responsiveness, quality, and customer service. Rockwater noticed early in its scorecard implementation process that employees who scored highest in the satisfaction surveys tended to have the most satisfied customers. So, for companies to achieve a high level of customer satisfaction, they may need to have the customers served by satisfied employees.

Employee morale is especially important for many service businesses where, frequently, the lowest-paid and lowest-skilled employees interact directly with customers. Companies typically measure employee satisfaction with an annual survey, or a rolling survey in which a specified percentage of randomly chosen employees is surveyed each month. Elements in an employee satisfaction survey could include:

- Involvement with decisions
- Recognition for doing a good job
- Access to sufficient information to do the job well
- Active encouragement to be creative and use initiative
- Support level from staff functions
- Overall satisfaction with company

Employees would be asked to score their feelings on a 1 to 3 or a 1 to 5 scale, anchored at the low end with "Discontented" and at the high end with "Very (or Extremely) Satisfied." An aggregate index of employee satisfaction could then be posted on the Balanced Scorecard, with executives having a drill-down capability to determine satisfaction by division, department, location, and supervisor.

Measuring Employee Retention

Employee retention captures an objective to retain those employees in whom the organization has a long-term interest. The theory underlying this measure is that the organization is making long-term investments in its employees so that any unwanted departures represents a loss in the intellectual capital of the business. Long-term, loyal employees carry the values of the organization, knowledge of organizational processes, and, we hope, sensitivity to the needs of customers. Employee retention is generally measured by percentage of key staff turnover.

Measuring Employee Productivity

Employee productivity is an outcome measure of the aggregate impact from enhancing employee skills and morale, innovation, improving internal processes, and satisfying customers. The goal is to relate the output produced by employees to the number of employees used to produce that output. There are many ways in which employee productivity has been measured.

The simplest productivity measure is revenue per employee. This measure represents how much output can be generated per employee. As employees and the organization become more effective in selling a higher volume and a higher value-added set of products and services, revenue per employee should increase.

Revenue per employee, while a simple and easy-to-understand productivity measure, has some limitations, particularly if there is too much pressure to achieve an ambitious target. For example, one problem is that the costs associated with the revenue are not included. So revenue per employee can increase while profits decrease when additional business is accepted at below the incremental costs of providing the goods or services associated with this business. Also, any time a ratio is used to measure an objective, managers have two ways of achieving targets. The first, and usually preferred, way is to increase the numerator—in this case, increasing output (revenues) without increasing the denominator (the number of employees). The second, and usually less preferred, method is to decrease the denominator—in this case, downsizing the organization, which might yield short-term benefits but risks sacrificing long-term capabilities. Another way of increasing the revenue per employee ratio through denominator decreases is to outsource functions. This enables the organization to support the same level of output (revenue) but with fewer internal employees. Whether outsourcing is a sensible element in the organization's long-term strategy must be determined by a comparison of the capabilities of the internally supplied service (cost, quality, and responsiveness) versus those of the external supplier. But the revenue per employee metric is not likely to be relevant to this decision.

One way to avoid the incentive to outsource to achieve a higher revenue per employee statistic is to measure value-added per employee, subtracting externally purchased materials, supplies, and services from revenues in the numerator of this ratio. Another modification, to control for the substitution of more productive but higher paid employees, is to measure the denominator by employee compensation rather than number of employees. The ratio of output produced to employee compensation measures the return on compensation, rather than return to number of employees.

So, like many other measures, revenue per employee is a useful diagnostic indicator as long as the internal structure of the business does not change too radically, as it would if the organization substitutes capital or external suppliers for internal labor. If a revenue-per-employee measure is used to motivate higher productivity of individual employees, it must be balanced with other measures of economic success so that the targets for the measure are not achieved in dysfunctional ways.

SITUATION-SPECIFIC DRIVERS OF LEARNING AND GROWTH

Once companies have chosen measures for the core employee measurement group—satisfaction, retention, and productivity—they should then identify the situation-specific, unique drivers in the learning and growth perspective. We have found that the drivers tend to be drawn from three critical enablers (see Figure 6-2): reskilling the work force, information systems capabilities, and motivation, empowerment, and alignment.

RESKILLING THE WORK FORCE

Many organizations building Balanced Scorecards are undergoing radical change. Their employees must take on dramatically new responsibilities if the business is to achieve its customer and internal-business-process objectives. The example, earlier in this chapter, illustrates how front-line employees in Metro Bank must be retrained. They must shift from merely reacting to customer requests to proactively anticipating customers' needs and marketing an expanded set of products and services to them. This transformation is representative of the change in roles and responsibilities that many organizations now need from their employees.

We can view the demand for reskilling employees along two dimensions: level of reskilling required and percentage of work force requiring reskilling (see Figure 6-3). When the degree of employee reskilling is low (the lower half of Figure 6-3), normal training and education will be sufficient to maintain employee capabilities. In this case, employee reskilling will not be of sufficient priority to merit a place on the organizational Balanced Scorecard.

Companies in the upper half of Figure 6-3, however, need to significantly reskill their employees if they are to achieve their internal-business-process, customer, and long-run financial objectives. We have seen several organizations, in different industries, develop a new measure, the strategic job coverage ratio, for its reskilling objective. This ratio tracks the number of employees qualified for specific strategic jobs relative to anticipated organizational needs. The qualifications for a given position are defined so that employees in this position can deliver key capabilities for achieving particular customer and internal-business-process objectives. Figure 6-4 illustrates the sequence of steps followed by one company in developing its strategic job coverage ratio.

Usually, the ratio reveals a significant gap between future needs and present competencies, as measured along dimensions of skills, knowledge, and attitudes. This gap provides the motivation for strategic initiatives designed to close this human resource staffing gap.

For the organizations needing massive reskilling (the upper righthand quadrant of Figure 6-3), another measure could be the length of time required to take existing employees to the new, required levels of competency. If

Figure 6-2 Situation-Specific Drivers of Learning and Growth

Staff Competencies	Technology Infrastructure	Climate for Action
Strategic skills	Strategic technologies	Key decision cycle
Training levels	Strategic databases	Strategic focus
Skill leverage	Experience capture	Staff empowerment
	Proprietary software	Personal alignment
	Patents, copyrights	Morale
		Teaming

the massive reskilling objective is to be met, the organization itself must be skillful in reducing the cycle time required per employee to achieve the reskilling.

INFORMATION SYSTEMS CAPABILITIES

Employee motivation and skills may be necessary to achieve stretch targets for customer and internal-business-process objectives. But they are unlikely to be sufficient. If employees are to be effective in today's competitive environment, they need excellent information—on customers, on internal processes, and of the financial consequences of their decisions.

Front-line employees need accurate and timely information about each customer's total relationship with the organization. This could likely include, as Metro Bank has done, an estimate, derived from an activity-based cost analysis, of the profitability of each customer. Front-line employees should also be informed about which segment an individual customer

Figure 6-3 Learning and Growth Measurement—Reskilling

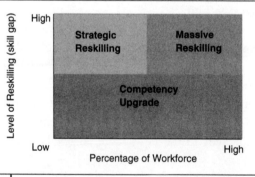

The Reskilling Scenarios	The key strategic theme is the need to reskill or upgrade the skills of the work force in order to achieve the vision.
Strategic Reskilling	A focused portion of the work force requires a high level of new, strategic skills.
Massive Reskilling	A large proportion of the work force requires massive skill renovation.
Competency Upgrade	Some portion of the work force, small or large, requires an upgrade of core skills.

Figure 6-4   The Strategic Job Coverage Ratio—Measurement Concept

1 The value chain can be used to identify the critical job families of the future

Process	Activities	Strategic Job Families
Make the Market	▪ Identify segments ▪ Economic value ▪ Listen to customer	Customer Consultant ▪ Generalist ▪ Specialist
Create the Offering	▪ Design the product ▪ Sourcing the product ▪ Develop and package	Customer Service
Market and Sell	▪ Promote ▪ Advise clients	Operations

2 Overall market development strategy identifies the timing of requirements

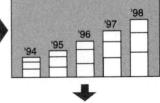

Measure
Strategic Job Coverage (percentage of job requirements met)

	'94	'95	'96	'97
Level I	85%	60%	30%	10%
Level II	–	80%	50%	30%
Level III	–	–	75%	50%
Level IV				

3 Each job family has a competency profile

Competency	Customer Consultant		Customer Service	Operations
	Generalist	Specialist		
Knowledge				
▪ Industry	x		x	
▪ Company	x		x	
▪ Financial	x			
▪ Product		x		x
▪ Systems			x	x
Skills				
▪ Selling	x	x	x	x
▪ Advisory	x	x	x	x
▪ Financial Analyst		x	x	x
▪ Service Level	x	x	x	
Orientation				
▪ Style	x			
▪ Culture	x		x	
▪ Background		x		x

5 Competency development strategy builds a pipeline for job development

Level I	Certified (master)
Level II	Senior (journeyman)
Level III	(craftsman)
Level IV	Junior (apprentice)

4 Inventory assessment determines which employees are currently qualified or capable of reskilling occupies so that they can judge how much effort should be expended not only to satisfy the customer on the existing relationship or transaction, but also on learning about and attempting to satisfy emerging needs from that customer.

Employees in the operations side of the business need rapid, timely, and accurate feedback on the product just produced or the service just delivered. Only by having such feedback can employees be expected to sustain improvement programs where they systematically eliminate defects and drive excess cost, time, and waste out of the production system. Excellent information systems are a requirement for employees to improve processes, either continuously, via TQM efforts, or discontinuously, through process redesign and reengineering projects. Several companies have defined a strategic information coverage ratio. This ratio, analogous to the strategic job coverage ratio introduced in the preceding section, assesses the current availability of information relative to anticipated needs. Measures of strategic information availability could be percentage of processes with real-time quality, cycle time, and cost feedback available and percentage of customer-facing employees having on-line access to information about customers.

MOTIVATION, EMPOWERMENT, AND ALIGNMENT

Even skilled employees, provided with superb access to information, will not contribute to organizational success if they are not motivated to act in the best interests of an organization or if they are not given freedom to make decisions and take actions. Thus the third of the enablers for the learning and growth objectives focuses on the organizational climate for employee motivation and initiative.

Measures of Suggestions Made and Implemented

One can measure the outcome of having motivated, empowered employees in several ways. One simple, and widely used, measure is the number of suggestions per employee. This measure captures the ongoing participation of employees in improving the organization's performance. Such a measure can be reinforced by a complementary measure, number of suggestions implemented, which tracks the quality of the suggestions being made, as well as communicating to the work force that its suggestions are valued and taken seriously.

For example, senior management in one company was disappointed in the level and quality of employee participation in suggesting improvement opportunities. They deployed an initiative that:

- published successful suggestions to increase the visibility and credibility of the process,
- illustrated the benefits and improvements that had been achieved through employee suggestions, and
- communicated a new reward structure for implemented suggestions.

This initiative led to dramatic increases in both the number of suggestions submitted and the number implemented.

Rockwater used numbers of suggestions as one of its early scorecard measures but was disappointed in the measured results. An investigation revealed that employees felt that their suggestions were not being acted upon. Senior executives then directed project managers to follow up and provide feedback to employees on every submitted suggestion. This feedback and implementation of many of the submitted suggestions led to an increased number of suggestions. The sum total of implementing these suggestions led to savings that Rockwater executives estimated at several hundred thousand dollars per year.

Measures of Improvement

The tangible outcome from successfully implemented employee suggestions does not have to be restricted to expense savings. Organizations can also look for improvements, say in quality, time, or performance, for specific internal and customer processes. The half-life metric (see Figure 6-5), developed by Art Schneiderman when he was vice president of quality improvement and productivity at Analog Devices, measures the length of time required for process performance to improve by 50%.[1] The half-life metric can be applied to any process metric (such as cost, quality, or time) that the organization wants to reduce to zero. Examples of such metrics are late deliveries, number of defects, scrap, and absenteeism. The metric can even be applied to the "waste" time in process cycle times and new product-development times.

The half-life metric assumes that when TQM teams are successfully applying formal quality improvement processes, they should be able to reduce defects at a constant rate (see table below). For example, suppose the organization has identified on-time delivery as a critical customer objective. Currently, the business unit may be missing promised delivery dates on 30% of orders. If its goal is to reduce the missed delivery percentage to 1% over a four-year (48-month) period, a 30-fold improvement, it can reach (actually exceed) this target by a continuous improvement process that reduces missed deliveries by 50% every nine months, as shown below:

Month	Missed Delivery %
0	30
9	15
18	7.5
27	3.8
36	1.9
45	1.0

Figure 6-5 The Half-Life Metric

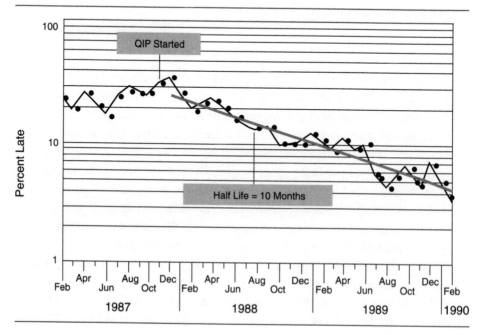

By establishing the rate at which defects are expected to be eliminated from the system, managers can validate whether they are on a trajectory that will yield the desired performance over the specified time period. While the Chinese proverb tells us that a voyage of a 1,000 miles starts with a single step, a continuous improvement metric, like the half-life, tells us whether we are stepping in the correct direction, and at a rate that will enable us to reach our ambitious target in the requisite time period.

To use the half-life metric as an outcome measure for employee suggestions and involvement in process improvement, a company should:

- identify the process metrics where it wants process improvements,
- estimate the half-lives expected for these processes, and
- construct an index that will report the percentage of processes that are improving at the rate specified by the estimated half-lives.

Measuring the number of suggestions successfully implemented and the rate of improvements actually occurring in critical processes are good outcome measures for the organizational and individual alignment objective. These measures indicate that employees are actively participating in organizational improvement activities.

Measures of Individual and Organizational Alignment

The performance drivers for individual and organizational alignment focus on whether departments and individuals have their goals aligned with the company objectives articulated in the Balanced Scorecard. One organization described an evolving process by which senior management implemented a process for introducing the scorecard to lower levels of the organization (see Figure 6-6). The rollout process had two principal objectives:

1. Individual and organizational subunit goals, and reward, and recognition systems aligned with achieving business objectives
2. Team-based measures of performance

The measurements for the rollout procedure evolved over the course of the implementation process. In the first phase, senior management established the context and framework for the Balanced Scorecard. It engaged managers to develop measures for their areas of responsibility and develop an implementation plan for cascading the scorecard approach downward within their organizations. The initial measure for accomplishing this implementation phase was percentage of top managers exposed to BSC. After the introductory phase had been completed, the Balanced Scorecard was communicated throughout the organization, along with specific implementation plans. The organizational alignment measure shifted to percentage of staff employees exposed to BSC. In the third phase, senior management and executives were to define specific targets for the financial and nonfinancial measures on the scorecard, and to link their incentive pay to achieving these targets. They introduced a new measure, percentage of top managers with personal goals aligned to BSC, to reflect the outcome from this process.

Figure 6-6 Personal Goals Alignment—Measurement Concept

1. Top-Down Management Rollout

- Establish context for BSC as a means to communicate shared objects
- Build understanding and acceptance of the BSC
- Engage managers to adapt the measures to fit their area of responsibility
- Engage managers to track performance to establish a baseline of information for establishing targets
- Engage managers to develop and execute an implementation plan for cascading the BSC down within their organizations

2. Employee Rollout

- Communicate context, organizational strategies, and initiatives
- Introduce the BSC—What is it; How is it being used; What's the implementation plan; What's been accomplished; What are the next steps?

3. Profit Plan/Target Setting

- Implement top-down process for defining financial targets
- Implement bottom-up process for establishing targets for nonfinancial measures

4. Personal Goals Alignment

- Each employee establishes a strategy-aligned goal by identifying an activity which they perform (and/or a measure) which will impact a measurement on the scorecard
- Personal goals established through negotiation process with management

Measurement Approach

Measure Evolves through Implementation
1. Percent of top managers exposed to BSC
2. Percent of staff exposed to BSC
3. Percent of top managers with personal goals aligned to BSC
4. Percent of staff with personal goals aligned to BSC and percent of employees who achieved personal goals

And, in the final implementation phase, all individuals were to have their activities and goals linked to scorecard objectives and measures. The alignment outcome measures for this phase became percentage of employees with personal goals aligned to BSC and percentage of employees who achieved personal goals.

Another organization tracked how many of the 20 business units that reported directly to the senior executives had been aligned with BSC objectives. The executives established a schedule of in-depth meetings with the 20 business units to gain agreement on the following:

- How the major activities of the business unit align to the scorecard
- Development of measures for these activities to indicate success
- Communication of the BSC alignment of business unit managers to their staffs
- Alignment of individual performance goals to the scorecard

The organizational alignment measure was the percentage of business units that had successfully completed this alignment process.

Organizations can measure not only outcomes but also short-term, intermediate indicators about their attempts to communicate and align individuals with organizational objectives. One company conducted a periodic climate survey to assess employees' motivation and drive to achieve the BSC objectives. A step before assessing motivation is determining awareness. Some organizations, especially in the early stages of the scorecard implementation process, measured percentage of employees who recognized and understood the new company vision.

One organization, a consumer goods company that used extensive market research to gain feedback on its advertising, promotion, and merchandising programs, used its expertise to gauge the reactions and buy-in of employees to its new strategy. The company treated the introduction of the Balanced Scorecard as a new product launch and surveyed employees every six months to estimate the market penetration of the program in different parts of the organization. The survey classified employee responses into one of four levels of awareness:

Awareness Level	Typical Response
I. Brand Awareness	"I have heard about the new strategy and the Balanced Scorecard, but it hasn't affected me yet."

Awareness Level	Typical Response
II. Customer	"I have started to do things differently based on what I learned from the Balanced Scorecard."
III. Brand Preference	"The new things I am trying are working. I can see them helping me, our customers, and the company."
IV. Brand Loyalty	"I'm a believer. I'm convinced that the new strategy is the right way to go. I'm an active missionary, trying to get others on the bandwagon."

This survey (see Figure 6-7) helped managers measure progress in gaining awareness and commitment to the objectives and measures for the Balanced Scorecard, and identify areas that needed additional effort and attention.

Measures of Team Performance

Many organizations today recognize that meeting ambitious targets for customers and shareholders requires superb internal business processes. Managers in these organizations often believe that their stretch targets for

Figure 6-7 "Mindshare Campaign" Measurements for Understanding the New Vision/Strategy

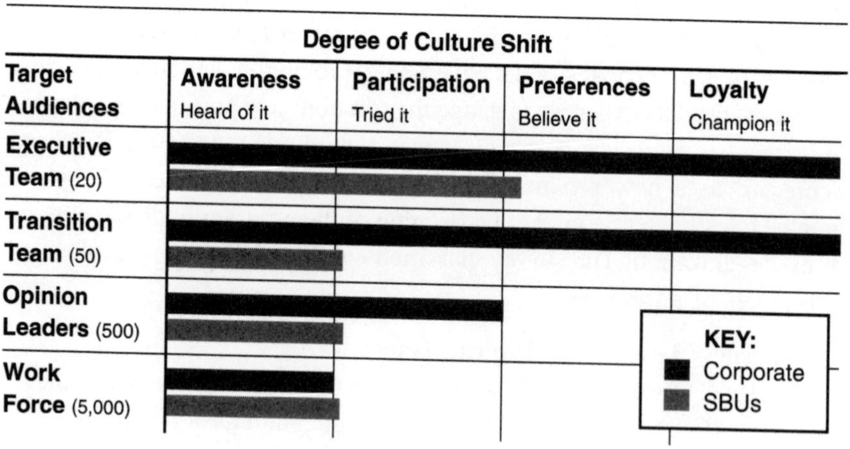

Target Audiences	Degree of Culture Shift			
	Awareness Heard of it	Participation Tried it	Preferences Believe it	Loyalty Champion it
Executive Team (20)				
Transition Team (50)				
Opinion Leaders (500)				
Work Force (5,000)				

KEY:
■ Corporate
■ SBUs

internal-business-process performance cannot be achieved just by individuals working harder, smarter, and more informed, by themselves. Increasingly, organizations are turning to teams to accomplish important business processes—product development, customer service, and internal operations. These organizations want objectives and measures to motivate and monitor the success of team building and team performance. National Insurance, as part of its turnaround strategy to become a specialist property and casualty insurer, organized all its work processes around teams. In its learning and growth perspective, National developed six measures of team building and team performance:

1. Internal Survey on Teaming: Survey of employees to determine if business units are supporting and creating opportunities for one another.

2. Gain-Sharing Level: Tracks the degree to which the organization is entering team-based relationships with other business units, organizations, or customers.

3. Number of Integrated Engagements: The number of projects on which more than one business unit participated.

4. Loss Control Utilization: The percentage of new policies written in which the loss control unit was consulted.

5. Percentage of Business Plans Developed by Teams: The proportion of business units that develop their plan with the assistance of headquarters-support resources.

6. Percentage of Teams with Shared Incentives: The number of teams where team members share common objectives and incentives.

These measures communicated clearly the corporate objective for individuals to work effectively in teams, and for teams in different parts of the organization to provide mutual assistance and support.

The teaming concept can be extended even further by coupling it to gain-sharing plans. Gain sharing distributes rewards to all team members when the team achieves a common goal. One organization proposed three measures of gain-sharing activity:

1. Percentage of all projects with customer gain sharing

2. Percentage of projects in which potential gains were achieved

3. Percentage of projects with individual team incentives linked to project success

MISSING MEASUREMENTS

Unlike some of the specific measures developed for individual companies that we have described previously for the financial, customer, and internal-business-process perspectives, we can supply many fewer examples of company-specific measures for the learning and growth perspective. We have found that many companies already have excellent starts on specific measures for their financial, customer, innovation, and operating process objectives. But when it comes to specific measures concerning employee skills, strategic information availability, and organizational alignment, companies have devoted virtually no effort for measuring either the outcomes or the drivers of these capabilities. This gap is disappointing since one of the most important goals for adopting the scorecard measurement and management framework is to promote the growth of individual and organizational capabilities.

We return to this missing measurement theme in Chapter 10 when we discuss the management process implications of the Balanced Scorecard. For now, we note that the absence of specific measures is an unusually reliable indication that the company is not linking its strategic objectives to activities for reskilling employees, supplying information, and aligning individuals, teams, and organizational units to the company's strategy and long-run objectives. Frequently, the advocates for employee training and reskilling, for employee empowerment, for information systems, and for motivating the work force take these programs as ends in themselves. The programs are justified as being inherently virtuous, but not as means to help the organization accomplish specific long-run economic and customer objectives. Resources and initiatives are committed to these programs, but the programs have not been held specifically and measurably accountable to achieving strategic objectives. This gap leads to frustration; senior executives wonder how long they are expected to continue to make heavy investments in employees and systems without measurable outcomes, while human resource and information system advocates wonder why their efforts are not considered more central and more strategic to the organization.

We believe that the absence, at this time, of more explicit, company-specific measures for learning and growth objectives is not an inherent limitation or weakness of incorporating this perspective in the Balanced Scorecard. Rather, it reflects the limited progress that most organizations have made in linking employees, information systems, and organizational alignment with their strategic objectives. We expect that as companies implement management processes based on the measurement framework of the Balanced Scorecard that we will soon see many more examples of creative, customized measures for the learning and growth perspective. Also, we demonstrate in the next chapter how the Balanced Scorecard, by providing a mechanism for explicating the causal relationships among measures in the four perspectives, enables measures in the learning and growth perspective to be linked explicitly to achieving outcomes in the other three scorecard perspectives.

Rather than ignore the learning and growth perspective until companies develop these customized measures, we prefer to use the generic measures identified in this chapter—strategic job coverage, strategic information availability, percentage of processes achieving targeted rates of improvement, and percentage of key employees aligned to strategic BSC objectives. These generic measures do identify gaps in organizational capabilities, and also serve as markers until managers and employees can develop more customized and specific measures.

MEASUREMENTS AS MARKERS

An additional approach, suggested by Michael Beer, based on his strategic human-resource-management research, is to substitute text when measurements are undeveloped or unavailable.[2] Suppose an organization has set an objective to upgrade the skills of employees so that they can better implement and improve the strategy. Currently, exactly what this objective means is too uncertain to be measured with any accuracy or credibility, or at a reasonable cost. But each time, perhaps quarterly, that managers conduct a strategic review of this human-resource-development process, key managers write a one- to two-page memorandum describing, as best they can, the actions taken during the most recent period, the outcomes achieved, and the current state of the organization's human resource capabilities. This memorandum substitutes text for measurements as the basis for active dialogue and debate about the initiatives being performed and the outcomes being achieved. While not the same as measurement, and not a long-term substitute for measurement, the text is a marker that serves many of the same objectives as a formal measurement system. It motivates action in intended directions since key managers know that each strategic review period, they must report on programs and outcomes. It provides a tangible basis for periodic accountability, review, feedback, and learning. And the report serves as a signal that a gap in measurement exists. The signal reminds executives of the need to continue to quantify strategic objectives, and to develop a system of measurement that provides a more tangible basis for communicating and evaluating objectives for developing capabilities of employees, information systems, and organizational units.

SUMMARY

Ultimately, the ability to meet ambitious targets for financial, customer, and internal-business-process objectives depends on the organizational capabilities for learning and growth. The enablers for learning and growth come primarily from three sources: employees, systems, and organizational alignment. Strategies for superior performance will generally require significant investments in people, systems, and processes that build organizational capabilities. Consequently, objectives and measures for these enablers of superior performance in the future should be an integral part of any organization's Balanced Scorecard.

A core group of three employee-based measures—satisfaction, productivity, and retention—provide outcome measures from investments in employees, systems, and organizational alignment. The drivers of these outcomes are, to date, somewhat generic and less developed than those of the other three balanced scorecard perspectives. These drivers include summary indices of strategic job coverage, strategic information availability, and degree of personal, team, and departmental alignment with strategic objectives. The absence of company-specific measures indicates the opportunity for future development of customized employee, systems, and organizational metrics that can be more closely linked to a business unit's strategy.

NOTES

1. A. Schneiderman, "Setting Quality Goals," *Quality Progress* (April 1988), 51–57; see also R. Kaplan, "Analog Devices, Inc.: The Half-Life System," 9-190-061 (Boston: Harvard Business School, 1990).
2. M. Beer, R. Eisenstat, and R. Biggadike, "Developing an Organization Capable of Strategy Implementation and Reformulation," in *Organizational Learning and Competitive Advantage,* ed. B. Moingon and A. Edmonson (London: Sage, 1996).

Chapter Seven

Linking Balanced Scorecard Measures to Your Strategy

IN THE PREVIOUS FOUR CHAPTERS, we established the foundations for building a Balanced Scorecard. We described the construction of financial and nonfinancial measures, grouped into four perspectives: financial, customer, internal business process, and learning and growth. What makes for a successful Balanced Scorecard? Is it just having a mixture of financial and nonfinancial measures, grouped into four distinct perspectives?

The objective of any measurement system should be to motivate all managers and employees to implement successfully the business unit's strategy. Those companies that can translate their strategy into their measurement system are far better able to execute their strategy because they can communicate their objectives and their targets. This communication focuses managers and employees on the critical drivers, enabling them to align investments, initiatives, and actions with accomplishing strategic goals. Thus, a successful Balanced Scorecard is one that communicates a strategy through an integrated set of financial and nonfinancial measurements.

Why is it important to build a scorecard that communicates a business unit's strategy?

- The scorecard describes the organization's vision of the future to the entire organization. It creates shared understanding.

- The scorecard creates a holistic model of the strategy that allows all employees to see how they contribute to organizational success. Without such linkage, individuals and departments can optimize their local performance but not contribute to achieving strategic objectives.

- The scorecard focuses change efforts. If the right objectives and measures are identified, successful implementation will likely occur. If not, investments and initiatives will be wasted.

How can you tell when the scorecard is telling the story of the strategy? One test of whether a Balanced Scorecard truly communicates both the outcomes and the performance drivers of a business unit's strategy is its sensitivity and transparency. A scorecard should not only be derived from the organization's strategy; it should also be transparent back to the strategy. Observers should be able to look at the scorecard and see behind it, into the strategy that underlies the scorecard objectives and measures.

As an example, one division president reported to his company's president when he turned in his first Balanced Scorecard:

> In the past, if you had lost my strategic planning document on an airplane and a competitor found it, I would have been angry but I would have gotten over it. In reality, it wouldn't have been that big a loss. Or if I had left my monthly operating review somewhere and a competitor obtained a copy, I would have been upset, but, again, it wouldn't have been that big a deal. This Balanced Scorecard, however, communicates my strategy so well that a competitor seeing this would be able to block the strategy and cause it to become ineffective.

When Balanced Scorecards exhibit this degree of transparency, they clearly have succeeded in translating a strategy into a linked set of performance measures.

LINKING THE BALANCED SCORECARD MEASURES TO STRATEGY

How can we build a Balanced Scorecard that translates a strategy into measurements? We introduced, in Chapter 2, three principles that enable an organization's Balanced Scorecard to be linked to its strategy:

1. Cause-and-effect relationships
2. Performance drivers
3. Linkage to financials

We discuss each of these principles in turn.

Cause-and-Effect Relationships

A strategy is a set of hypotheses about cause and effect. Cause-and-effect relationships can be expressed by a sequence of if-then statements. For example, a link between improved sales training of employees and higher profits can be established through the following sequence of hypotheses:

> If *we increase employee training about products,* then *they will become more knowledgeable about the full range of products they can sell;* if *employees are more knowledgeable about products,* then *their sales effectiveness will improve.* If *their sales effectiveness improves,* then *the average margins of the products they sell will increase.*

A properly constructed scorecard should tell the story of the business unit's strategy through such a sequence of cause-and-effect relationships. The measurement system should make the relationships (hypotheses) among objectives (and measures) in the various perspectives explicit so that they can be managed and validated. It should identify and make explicit the sequence of hypotheses about the cause-and-effect relationships between outcome measures and the performance drivers of those outcomes. *Every measure selected for a Balanced Scorecard should be an element of a chain of cause-and-effect relationships that communicates the meaning of the business unit's strategy to the organization.*

Outcomes and Performance Drivers

As discussed in the previous four chapters, all Balanced Scorecards use certain generic measures. These generic measures tend to be core outcome measures, which reflect the common goals of many strategies, as well as similar structures across industries and companies. These generic outcome measures tend to be lag indicators, such as profitability, market share, customer satisfaction, customer retention, and employee skills. The performance drivers, the lead indicators, are the ones that tend to be unique for a particular business unit. The performance drivers reflect the uniqueness of the business unit's strategy; for example, the financial drivers of profitability, the market segments in which the unit chooses to compete, and the particular internal processes and learning and growth objectives that will deliver the value propositions to targeted customers and market segments.

A good Balanced Scorecard should have a mix of outcome measures and performance drivers. Outcome measures without performance drivers do not communicate how the outcomes are to be achieved. They also do not provide an early indication about whether the strategy is being implemented successfully. Conversely, performance drivers—such as cycle times and part-per-million defect rates—without outcome measures may enable the business unit to achieve short-term operational improvements, but will fail to reveal whether the operational improvements have been translated into expanded business with existing and new customers, and, eventually, to enhanced financial performance. *A good Balanced Scorecard should have an appropriate mix of outcomes (lagging indicators) and performance drivers (leading indicators) that have been customized to the business unit's strategy.*

Linkage to Financials

With the proliferation of change programs under way in most organizations today, it is easy to become preoccupied with such goals as quality, customer satisfaction, innovation, and employee empowerment for their own sake. While these goals can lead to improved business-unit performance, they may not if these goals are taken as ends in themselves. The financial problems of some recent Baldrige Award winners give testimony to the need to link operational improvements to economic results.

A Balanced Scorecard must retain a strong emphasis on outcomes, especially financial ones like return-on-capital-employed or economic value-added. Many managers fail to link programs, such as total quality management, cycle time reduction, reengineering, and employee empowerment, to outcomes that directly influence customers and that deliver future financial performance. In such organizations, the improvement programs have incorrectly been taken as the ultimate objective. They have not been linked to specific targets for improving customer and, eventually, financial performance. The inevitable result is that such organizations eventually become disillusioned about the lack of tangible payoffs from their change programs. *Ultimately, causal paths from all the measures on a scorecard should be linked to financial objectives.*

We can illustrate the applications of these three principles in two case studies: Metro Bank and National Insurance.

METRO BANK

Metro Bank was confronted with two problems: (1) excessive reliance on a single product (deposits) and (2) a cost structure that made it unprofitable to service 80% of its customers at prevailing interest rates. Metro embarked upon a two-pronged strategy to deal with these two problems:

1. Revenue Growth. Reduce volatility of earnings by broadening the sources of revenue with additional products for current customers.

2. Productivity. Improve operating efficiency by shifting nonprofitable customers to more cost-effective channels of distribution (e.g., electronic banking).

The process of developing a Balanced Scorecard at Metro translated each of these strategies into objectives and measures in the four perspectives. Particular emphasis was placed on understanding and describing the cause-and-effect relationships on which the strategy was based. A simplified version of the results of this effort is shown in Figure 7-1. For the revenue growth strategy, the financial objectives were clear: broaden the mix of revenues. Strategically, this meant that Metro would focus on its current customer base, identify the customers who would be likely candidates for a broader range of services, and then sell an expanded set of financial products and services to these targeted customers. When customer objectives were analyzed, however, Metro's executives determined that its targeted customers did not view the bank, or their banker, as the logical source for a broader array of products such as mutual funds, credit cards, mortgages, and financial advice. The executives concluded that if the bank's new strategy were to be successful, they must shift customers' perception of the bank from that of a transactions processor of checks and deposits to a financial adviser.

Having identified the financial objective, *broaden revenue mix,* and the new customer value proposition, *increase customer confidence in our finan-*

Figure 7-1   The Metro Bank Strategy

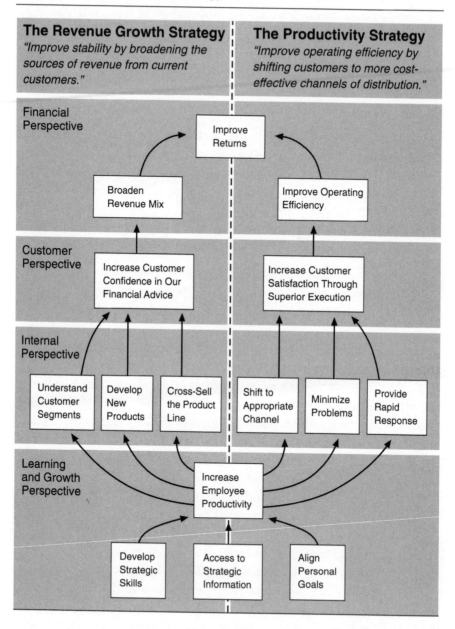

cial advice, dictated by the financial objective, the scorecard design process then focused on the internal activities that had to be mastered if the strategy were to succeed. Three cross-business processes were identified: (1) understand customers, (2) develop new products and services, and (3) cross-sell multiple products and services. Each business process would have to be redesigned to reflect the demands of the new strategy. The selling process, for example, had historically been dominated by institutional advertising of the bank's services. Good advertising plus good location brought the customers to the banks. The branch personnel were reactive, helping customers open accounts and providing ongoing service. The bank did not have a selling culture. In fact, one study indicated that only 10% of a salesperson's time was spent with customers. The bank launched a major reengineering program to redefine the sales process. The new sales process was designed to create a relationship-selling approach where the salesperson became more of a financial adviser. Two measures of this process were included on the Balanced Scorecard. The cross-sell ratio—the average number of products sold to a household—measured selling effectiveness. This "lag indicator" would tell whether or not the new process was working. The second measure, hours spent with customers, was included to send a signal to salespersons throughout the organization of the new culture required by the strategy. A relationship-based sales approach could not work unless face time with customers increased. Hours with customers therefore was a lead indicator for the success of this piece of the strategy.

The internal objectives led naturally to a final set of factors, on improving employee effectiveness, to implement the revenue growth strategy. The learning and growth component of the scorecard identified the need for (1) salespersons to acquire a broader set of skills (to become a financial counselor with broad knowledge of the product line), (2) improved access to information (integrated customer files), and (3) realignment of the incentive systems to encourage the new behavior. The lag indicators included a productivity measure, average sales per salesperson, as well as the attitudes of the work force as measured by an employee satisfaction survey. The lead indicators focused on the major changes that had to be orchestrated in the work force: (1) the upgrading of the skill base and qualified people—strategic job coverage ratio, (2) the access to information technology tools and data—strategic information availability ratio, and (3) the realignment of individual goals and incentives to reflect the new priorities—personal goal alignment.

These measures, in turn, provided the basis for introducing entirely new management processes. For example, consider the measure, strategic job coverage ratio. Every strategy for change, including Metro Bank's, ultimately requires a selected set of the work force to be reskilled and equipped to take on the new demands. The availability of these strategic competencies is either an asset (when you have them) or a liability (when you don't). Developing such intellectual assets is usually the longest-lead event for determining the ultimate success of the business unit's strategy. The most effective measure that we have found for strategic competencies, deceptive in its simplicity, is derived from the answers to three questions: (1) What are the required competencies?, (2) What currently exists?, and (3) What and how large is the gap? The strategic job coverage ratio measure defines the strategic liability (recall the gap displayed in Figure 6-4). While the measure is fundamental and simple, very few organizations are able to construct it because their human resource and planning systems are unable to answer the three questions posed above. The definition of this measure has caused several companies to redesign the basic structure of their staff development process. Figure 7-2 illustrates the relationship of the scorecard

Figure 7-2 Increasing Employee Productivity

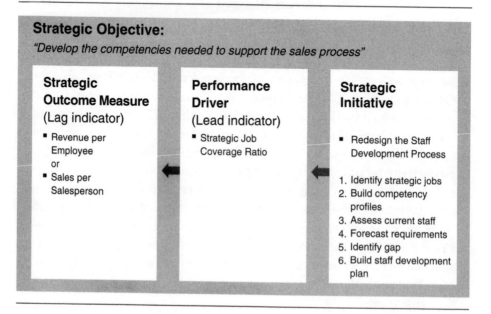

measures to the strategic initiative that was instituted to close the strategic job coverage gap. The logic of defining the strategic priorities and the measures that best describe it led to the redefinition of a basic management program required to execute the strategy. Had it not been for the construction of the Balanced Scorecard and the logical systems thinking that it fostered, these organizations would most likely not have addressed the staff deficiencies in such a focused way with such a sense of urgency.

Figure 7-3 summarizes the objectives and measures for Metro Bank's Balanced Scorecard, indicating the mixture of leading and lagging indicators. Not surprisingly, the financial and customer measures contain few

Figure 7-3   Metro Bank's Balanced Scorecard

Strategic Objectives	Strategic Measurements	
	(Lag Indicators)	(Lead Indicators)
Financial F1 - Improve Returns F2 - Broaden Revenue Mix F3 - Reduce Cost Structure	Return-on-Investment Revenue Growth Deposit Service Cost Change	Revenue Mix

Customer
C1- Increase Customer
   Satisfaction with Our Products
   and People
C2- Increase Satisfaction "After the Sale"
	Share of Segment
	
	Customer Retention
		Depth of Relationship
		
		Satisfaction Survey

Internal I1 - Understand Our Customers I2 - Create Innovative Products I3 - Cross-Sell Products I4 - Shift Customers to Cost-Effective Channels I5 - Minimize Operational Problems I6 - Responsive Service	New Product Revenue Cross-Sell Ratio Channel Mix Change Service Error Rate Request Fulfillment Time	Product Development Cycle Hours with Customers
Learning L1 - Develop Strategic Skills L2 - Provide Strategic Information L3 - Align Personal Goals	 Employee Satisfaction Revenue per Employee	Strategic Job Coverage Ratio Strategic Information Availability Ratio Personal Goals Alignment (%)

lead indicators; most of the leading or driving indicators occur for the internal-business-process and learning and growth measures. Figures 7-1 and 7-3 show how Metro's scorecard describes a system of cause-and-effect relationships, incorporating a mix of leading and lagging indicators, all of which eventually point to improving future financial performance.

National Insurance Company (long lag times)

The importance of linking outcome measures to performance drivers is perhaps most powerfully illustrated in the insurance industry. Insurance is an information- and measurement-intense industry characterized by long delays between the time that routine decisions are made and the corresponding outcomes occur. For example, the effectiveness of the central event of underwriting—evaluating a risk and pricing it—is not known until subsequent claims are made and resolved. The incidence of insured events and resolution through the claims process can take between two and five years, although in extreme cases, as in asbestos litigation, the exposure can go on for decades. In such a setting, having a mixture of leading and lagging measures is vital for motivating and measuring business unit performance.

National Insurance was a major property and casualty insurance firm that had been plagued by unsatisfactory results for the past decade. A new management team was brought in to turn the situation around. Its strategy was to move the company away from its generalist approach—providing a full range of services to the full market—to that of a specialist, a company that would focus on more narrowly defined niches. The new senior executive team identified several key success factors for its new specialist strategy:

- Become better at understanding and targeting desired market segments;
- Better select, educate, and motivate agents to pursue these segments;
- Improve the underwriting process as the focal point for executing this strategy; and
- Better integrate information about claims into the underwriting process to improve market selectivity.

National's executives selected the Balanced Scorecard as the primary tool for the new management team to use to lead the turnaround. They selected the scorecard because they believed it would help clarify the

meaning of the new strategy to the organization, and provide early feedback
that the ship was turning.

In the first step, the executives defined the strategic objectives for the
new specialist strategy, shown in the lefthand column of Figure 7-4. They
selected measures to make each objective operational by gaining agreement
on the answer to a simple question, "How would we know if National
Insurance achieved this objective?" The answers to this question yielded
the measures shown in the center column, "Core Outcomes," of Figure
7-4. The core outcome measures were also referred to as "strategic outcome
measures" because they described the outcomes that the executives wished
to achieve from each part of their new strategy.

Figure 7-4   The Balanced Scorecard at National Insurance

Strategic Objectives	Strategic Measurements	
	Core Outcomes (Lag)	Performance Drivers (Lead)
Financial		
F1 - Meet Shareholder Expectations	Return-on-Equity	
F2 - Improve Operating Performance	Combined Ratio	
F3 - Achieve Profitable Growth	Business Mix	
F4 - Reduce Shareholder Risk	Catastrophic Losses	
Customer		
C1 - Improve Agency Performance	Acquisition/Retention (vs. plan)	Agency Performance (vs. plan)
C2 - Satisfy Target Policyholders	Acquisition/Retention (by segment)	Policyholder Satisfaction Survey
Internal		
I1 - Develop Target Markets	Business Mix (by segment)	Business Development (vs. plan)
I2 - Underwrite Profitably	Loss Ratio	Underwriting Quality Audit
I3 - Align Claims with Business	Claims Frequency Claims Severity	Claims Quality Audit
I4 - Improve Productivity	Expense Ratio	Headcount Movement Managed Spending Movement
Learning		
L1 - Upgrade Staff Competencies	Staff Productivity	Staff Development (vs. plan)
L2 - Access to Strategic Information		Strategic I/T Availability (vs. plan)

As with many outcome measures, the measures shown in the center column were the obvious ones that any company in the property and casualty insurance industry would be using. The scorecard would not be meaningful if such industry-specific measures did not appear, but these measures, by themselves, would be inadequate to signal the factors that would lead to superior performance within the industry. Having only industry-generic measures at this point in the scorecard development process highlighted an additional problem. Every one of the outcome measures was a lagging indicator, the reported results for any of the measures reflected decisions and actions taken much earlier. For example, if new underwriting criteria were implemented, the results would not be reflected in the claims frequency for at least a year; the impact on the loss ratio would occur with an even longer delay.

The strategic outcome measures presented a "balanced" view of the strategy, reflecting customer, internal process, and learning and growth measures, in addition to the traditional financial ones. But a scorecard consisting only of lagging indicators would not satisfy management's goal of providing early indicators of success. Nor would it help to focus the entire organization on the drivers of future success: what people should be doing day-by-day to produce successful outcomes in the future. While the issue of balancing lagging outcome measures with leading performance driver measures occurs for all organizations, the extremely long lags between actions today and outcomes in the future was more pronounced in the property and casualty insurance company than in any other we have encountered.

National Insurance executives went through a second design iteration to determine the actions that people should be taking in the short term to achieve the desired long-term outcomes. For each strategic outcome measure, they identified a complementary performance driver—see righthand column of Figure 7-4. In most cases, the performance drivers described how a business process was intended to change. For example, the strategic outcome measures for the underwriting process were:

- Loss ratio
- Claims frequency
- Claims severity

Improving performance of these measures required a significant improvement in the quality of the underwriting process itself. The executives developed criteria for what they considered good underwriting. The criteria defined the actions desired in underwriting a new opportunity. The executives introduced a new business process, to audit, periodically, a cross-section of policies for each underwriter to assess whether the policies issued by the underwriter conformed to these criteria. The audit would produce a measure, the underwriting quality audit score, that would show the percentage of new policies written that met the standards of the redesigned underwriting process. The theory behind this approach is that the underwriting quality audit score would be the leading indicator, the performance driver, of the outcomes—loss ratio, claims frequency, and claims severity—that would be revealed much later. In addition to the underwriting quality audit, similar programs were developed for outcome objectives related to agency management, new business development, and claims management. New metrics, representing performance drivers for these outcomes were constructed to communicate and monitor near-term performance. These included:

Outcome Measure	Performance Driver Measures
Key agent acquisition/retention	Agency performance versus plan
Customer acquisition/retention	Policyholder satisfaction survey
Business mix (by segment)	Business development versus plan
Claims frequency and severity	Claims quality audit
Expense ratio	Headcount movement; indirect spending
Staff productivity	Staff development versus plan; IT availability

The righthand column of Figure 7-4 shows the new set of leading indicators, the performance drivers, selected by National Insurance.

Figure 7-5 presents the Balanced Scorecard graphically, illustrating two directional chains of cause and effect: from learning and growth and internal-business-process objectives to customer and financial objectives; and with each outcome measure in the customer, internal, and learning perspectives linked to a performance driver measure.

The National Insurance case again illustrates how the process of building a Balanced Scorecard creates change and produces results. Development of the metrics for the performance drivers forced executives to think through the way that work should be done in the future, and to introduce entirely

Figure 7-5 National Insurance—Cause-and-Effect Relationships

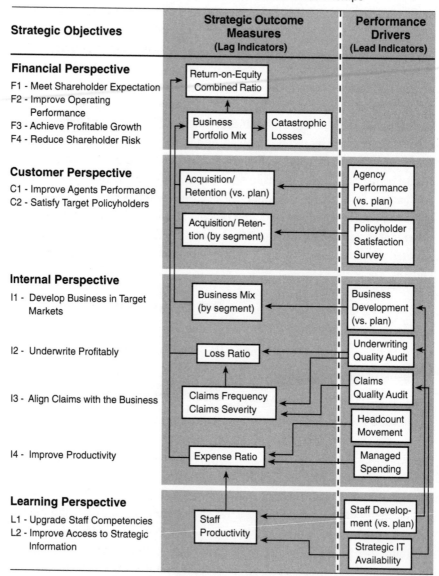

new business processes—the underwriting quality audit, the claims quality audit, and specific programs to enhance staff skills and expand information technology to employees. In addition to providing measures for the scorecard, the criteria developed by the executives for the underwriting quality and claims quality audits helped develop improved underwriting and claims processes that could be communicated to the work force. The underwriting and claims quality audit scores were not off-the-shelf measures. The executives developed customized measures to reflect the new underwriting and claims processes they wished to implement at National Insurance.

The detailed contents of the measures described National's strategy for success. The chain of cause-and-effect relationships diagrammed in Figure 7-5 represents the executives' hypotheses about the relationship of processes and decisions done today that were expected to favorably impact various core outcomes in the future. The underwriting and claims quality audit measures were not intended to be used punitively. The action after revelation of poor underwriting or claims-processing performance would be additional training, not dismissal. Therefore, the measures were intended to communicate the specifics of new work processes to the organization. The logical process of identifying the strategic priority, the strategic outcomes, and the performance drivers led to reengineered business processes. The process of measurement was indeed "the tail that wagged the dog" (of operations).

The ultimate success of this turnaround program at National Insurance will take some time to play out (we describe the evolution of the Balanced Scorecard at National Insurance in Chapter 12), and will, of course, be influenced by many factors beyond the measurement system. But executives readily concurred that the Balanced Scorecard has been a major part of their turnaround strategy and near-term success. The scorecard, by providing short-term indicators of long-term outcomes, has become National Insurance's guidance system to the future.

The Metro Bank and National Insurance cases illustrate the translation of an SBU business strategy into a measurement framework. In this macro-level design process, we have emphasized the importance of specifying the relationships among the measures as a basis for describing the strategy more than the construction of the individual measures themselves. Having established this overall strategic framework, however, the design and selection of specific measures or subsets of measures is where the execution of strategy begins. The Balanced Scorecard is not really a strategy formulation tool. We have implemented scorecards in organizations where the strategy has already been well articulated and accepted in the organization. But, more often we have found that even when the senior executive team thought it had prior agreement on the business unit's strategy, the translation of that strategy into operational measurements forced the clarification and redefinition of the strategy. In effect, the disciplined measurement framework enforced by the Balanced Scorecard stimulated a new round of dialogue about the specific meaning and implementation of the strategy. It is this debate that usually leads to elevating specific management processes into matters of strategic necessity.

Having a linked set of performance measures also enables organized learning at the executive level. By making explicit the cause-and-effect hypotheses of a strategy, managers can test their strategy and adapt as they learn more about the implementation and effectiveness of their strategy, a theme that we explicate in greater detail in Chapter 12. Without explicit cause-and-effect linkages, no strategic learning can occur.

STRATEGIC VERSUS DIAGNOSTIC MEASURES: HOW MANY MEASURES ON A BALANCED SCORECARD?

Considering that each of the four perspectives in the Balanced Scorecard can require between four and seven separate measures, businesses often have scorecards with up to 25 measures. Are 25 measures too many? Is it possible for any organization to focus on 25 separate things? The answer to both questions is NO! If a scorecard is viewed as 25 (or even 10) independent measures, it will be too complicated for an organization to absorb.

The Balanced Scorecard should be viewed as the instrumentation for a *single* strategy. When the scorecard is viewed as the manifestation of one strategy, the number of measures on the scorecard becomes irrelevant, for the multiple measures on the Balanced Scorecard are linked together in a cause-and-effect network that describes the business unit's strategy. While this is easier said than done, the examples of Metro Bank and National Insurance, as well as our experience with other companies, indicate that companies can indeed formulate and communicate their strategy with an integrated system of approximately two dozen measurements.

But today most organizations already have many more than 16 to 25 measures to keep themselves functioning. They are incredulous that a

Balanced Scorecard of no more than two dozen measures can be sufficient for measuring their operations. They are, of course, correct in a narrow sense, but they fail to distinguish between *diagnostic measures*[1]—those measures that monitor whether the business remains in control and can signal when unusual events are occurring that require immediate attention— and *strategic measures*—those that define a strategy designed for competitive excellence.

A simple example clarifies this point. Many aspects of our bodily functions must perform within fairly narrow operating parameters if we are to survive. If our body temperature departs from a normal 1–2° window (away from 98.6°F or 37°C), or our blood pressure drops too low or escalates too high, we have a serious problem. In such circumstances, all our energies (and those of skilled professionals) are mobilized to restore these parameters to their normal levels. But we don't devote enormous energy to optimizing our body temperature and blood pressure. Being able to control our body temperature to within 0.01 of the optimum will not be one of the strategic success factors that will determine whether we become a chief executive of a company, a senior partner in an international consulting firm, or a tenured full professor at a major university. Other factors are more decisive in determining whether we achieve our unique personal and professional objectives. Are body temperature and blood pressure important? Absolutely. Should these measurements fall outside certain control limits, we have a signal about a major problem that we must attend to and solve immediately. But while such measurements are necessary, they are not sufficient for the achievement of our long-run goals.

Similarly, corporations should have hundreds, perhaps thousands, of measures that they can monitor to ensure that they are functioning as expected, and to signal when corrective action must be taken. But these are not the drivers of competitive success. Such measures capture the necessary "hygiene factors" that enable the company to operate. These measures should be monitored diagnostically, with deviations from expectations noted rapidly; in effect, management by exception.

The outcome and performance driver measures on the Balanced Scorecard, in contrast, should be the subjects of intensive and extensive interactions among senior and mid-level managers as they evaluate strategies based on new information about competitors, customers, markets, technologies, and suppliers.[2] After he had implemented his first Balanced Scorecard one executive remarked: "Our division had always measured hundreds of operating variables. In building a Balanced Scorecard, we chose 12 measures as the key to implementing our strategy. Of these 12 measures, 7 were entirely new measurements for the division."[3]

The Balanced Scorecard is not a replacement for an organization's day-to-day measurement system. The scorecard measures are chosen to direct the attention of managers and employees to those factors expected to lead to competitive breakthroughs for an organization.

HOW BAD THINGS HAPPEN TO GOOD MEASURES: USING DIAGNOSTIC MEASURES TO BALANCE STRATEGIC MEASURES

Even the best objectives and measures can be achieved in bad ways. The Balanced Scorecard guards against some of the myopic suboptimization that occurs when only a single measure, especially a financial one, is used to motivate and evaluate business unit performance. But suboptimization is not unique to financial measures. For example, many companies use, in their customer perspective, the on-time delivery performance for targeted customers. On-time delivery has become an especially valued attribute by companies, especially manufacturers operating under a just-in-time discipline, where little inventory is held to buffer unreliable deliveries. Yet if too much pressure is placed on a single customer metric like OTD, managers could soon develop dysfunctional methods to achieve excellent OTD. For example, manufacturers can build a substantial inventory of all likely requested items so that almost any request could be filled by shipments from finished-goods inventory. For such companies, the OTD measure might be excellent but large amounts of capital would be tied up in inventory, storage, and handling facilities, and the company would run a high risk of obsolescence and spoilage. This is a very expensive way to achieve high OTD levels.

Alternatively, companies could achieve high OTD simply by quoting and committing to long lead times. For example, a customer might request delivery within 18 days. The company, because of backlogs, delays, and general confusion within its operations, may realize that it cannot deliver within 18 days, and offers the customer delivery only by day 30. The customer may not be happy with the extension, but in the short run may not have an alternative supplier for the good or service, and therefore accepts the 30-day delivery commitment. If the company does, in fact, deliver on day 30, it has satisfied its OTD objective, but it has not satisfied the customer that requested delivery on day 18.

Consider, as another example, an excellent performance measure for the innovation cycle of the internal-business-process perspective: the time-to-market measure for new products and services. Business units hope to improve their time-to-market by improving the management of their new-product introduction process, and by learning to produce the finished product with fewer design cycles, for example. But, lacking fundamental improvement in new-product introduction processes, and under the discipline of adhering to a demanding time-to-market performance measure, managers can release new products that are only incrementally different from existing products. They have achieved their performance target, but at the expense of fundamental innovation that has placed a competitive strength at risk.

A company's total measurement system should not encourage suboptimization along any single measure or perspective. Designers should attempt to anticipate the suboptimization that might occur for a given metric on the Balanced Scorecard, and provide supplemental metrics that discourage achieving the primary scorecard objective in undesirable ways. Rather than clutter up the scorecard with additional, nonstrategic measures, companies can use diagnostic measures to balance the strategic measures on the scorecard. As a specific example, Analog Devices, a prototype company for the Balanced Scorecard,[4] wanted to offset the temptation to achieve high OTD through long-lead-time quotes. Therefore, in addition to OTD, Analog measured the difference between the promised delivery date and the customer's requested delivery date. It also measured the percentage of time it could not commit to the customer's requested delivery date. It could also have used a diagnostic measure like inventory turns ratio to offset the temptation to achieve excellent OTD performance by carrying lots of inventory. The off-scorecard diagnostic measures like inventory turns and the difference between customer requested delivery dates and quoted delivery dates enable managers to detect when improved on-time delivery performance has been achieved by undesirable actions.

SUMMARY

Balanced Scorecards need to be more than a mixture of 15 to 25 financial and nonfinancial measures, grouped into four perspectives. The scorecard should tell the story of the business unit's strategy. This story is told by linking outcome and performance driver measures together via a series of cause-and-effect relationships. The outcome measures tend to be lagging indicators. They signal the ultimate objectives of the strategy and whether near-term efforts have led to desirable outcomes. The performance driver measures are leading indicators, which signal to all organizational partici-pants what they should be doing today to create value in the future. Outcome measures without performance drivers create ambiguity about how the outcomes are to be achieved, and may lead to suboptimal short-term actions. Performance driver measures that are not linked to outcomes will encourage local improvement programs that may deliver neither short- nor long-term value to the business unit. The best Balanced Scorecards will tell the story of the strategy so well that the strategy can be inferred by the collection of objectives and measures and the linkages among them.

NOTES

1. For a description of diagnostic measures, see Chap. 4 in Robert Simons, *Levers of Control: How Managers Use Innovative Control Systems to Drive Strategic Renewal* (Boston: Harvard Business School Press, 1995).
2. The important distinction between the measures monitored in an organization's diagnostic control systems and those that are part of the continual interactions among managers as they scan and debate key strategic uncertainties has been articulated by Simons, *Levers of Control*.
3. Experience reported in "Implementing the Balanced Scorecard at FMC Corpora-tion: An Interview with Larry D. Brady," *Harvard Business Review* (Septem-ber–October 1993): 143–147.
4. Robert S. Kaplan, "Analog Devices, Inc.: The Half-Life System," 9-190-061 (Boston: Harvard Business School, 1990) and A. Schneiderman, "Metrics for the Order Fulfillment Process: Parts I and II," *Journal of Cost Management* (Summer 1996, Fall 1996).

Chapter Eight

Structure and Strategy

THE BALANCED SCORECARD must reflect the structure of the organization for which the strategy has been formulated. The examples provided so far have illustrated Balanced Scorecards for autonomous business units. But Balanced Scorecards are useful for other organizational units as well. In this chapter we illustrate the development of scorecards for:

- Corporations that consist of a collection of strategic business units
- Joint ventures
- Support departments in corporations and business units
- Not-for-profit and governmental enterprises

BUSINESS UNIT VERSUS CORPORATE STRATEGY

Strategies are typically defined for an organizational unit, referred to as a strategic business unit. Metro Bank, for example, was just one operating unit in a major bank-holding company which also contained, among other SBUs, a credit card operation, a wholesale bank, a commercial bank, and an investment bank.

Some companies are focused in a single narrowly defined industry so that an SBU strategy coincides with the corporate strategy. Indeed, some of the early applications of the Balanced Scorecard were for companies in particular niches of the semiconductor industry, like Advanced Micro Devices and Analog Devices. These companies developed scorecards that also served as corporate scorecards (the term used at Analog Devices). Most SBUs, however, like Metro Bank, are members of a broader corporate or divisional portfolio. This raises the natural question about the relationship between a corporate-level scorecard and a divisional or SBU scorecard.

The theory of having a corporation consisting of several different SBUs is that synergies among the SBUs enable the corporate entity to be more valuable than the sum of its SBU parts. The theory of corporate-level strategy is an active research topic.[1] The theory attempts to identify how a corporate headquarters and a corporate strategy (as opposed to a business unit strategy) can create synergies among its operating units. At one extreme, a company like the FMC Corporation consists of more than two dozen independent operating companies, ranging from a company that mines gold, a defense contractor that builds armored personnel carriers, several industrial chemical companies, an airport equipment supplier, a lithium division, and divisions that build food and agricultural machinery. With such unrelated diversification, the corporate value-added role has typically consisted of corporate-level managers using the private information they can obtain from their operating units to assign capital and people among those units. Prior to introduction of the Balanced Scorecard at FMC, operating companies were held responsible for delivering consistent and superior financial performance, as measured by annual return-on-capital-employed. As long as targeted ROCE was achieved, corporate-level managers did not probe too deeply into how the financial results were produced.

The introduction of the Balanced Scorecard at FMC has provided a new corporate-level role, that of monitoring and evaluating the strategy of each operating company. The Balanced Scorecard allows a more intense dialogue not only about short-term financial results but also about whether the foundation for growth and future financial performance has been established. The corporate role for a diversified company, like FMC, however, probably remains best measured by the overall financial performance of the company. The strategies, objectives, and measures of the individual operating companies are likely so diverse that they cannot easily be aggregated into a corporate-level scorecard on perspectives other than the financial one.

At the other extreme, the various SBUs of a corporation may have strong interactions among them. They may share common customers. For example, Johnson & Johnson has more than 150 operating companies worldwide, but its companies are all in the health care field and share common customers, all of whom deliver health care products and services: hospitals, health-care delivery organizations, physicians, drug stores, supermarkets, and general retailers. Other company SBUs may share common technologies; for example, Hamel and Prahalad illustrated how Honda uses its superb capabilities in engine design and manufacture to produce superior products in different market segments: motorcycles, automobiles, power lawnmowers, and power generators.[2] NEC uses capabilities in microelectronics and miniaturization to be a leader in televisions, computers, and telecommunications. Other corporations may centralize certain key functions, such as purchasing, finance, or information technology, to achieve economies of scale that enable the centralized departments to deliver their services better than what could be achieved by independent departments operating within individual SBUs.

In each circumstance, a corporate scorecard should reflect the corporate-level strategy. It should articulate the theory of the corporation—the rationale for having several or many SBUs operating within the corporate structure, rather than having each SBU operating as an independent entity, with its own governance structure and independent source of financing. As with business unit strategy, the Balanced Scorecard does not define or originate the corporate-level strategy. Rather a corporate Balanced Scorecard should articulate, make operational, and help gain clarity and consensus as to what the corporate-level strategy is.

The development of corporate-level scorecards is still in its early development stages. To date, we have seen how a corporate scorecard can clarify two elements of a corporate-level strategy:

- Corporate Themes: values, beliefs, and themes that reflect the corporate identity and must be shared by all SBUs (e.g., safety at DuPont or innovation at 3M).

- Corporate Role: actions mandated at the corporate level that create synergies at the SBU level (e.g., cross-sell customers across SBUs, share common technologies, or centralize a shared service).

CORPORATE THEMES AND ROLES

We can illustrate the use of corporate themes and roles with Kenyon Stores. Kenyon consisted of 10 niche retailers, each with sales ranging from $500 million to $2 billion, and each with its own image and targeted customer markets. The CEO of Kenyon developed a strategic agenda of 10 items that would be the elements of the strategies for each retail division. The items were distributed across the four perspectives of the Balanced Scorecard, as shown below:

Financial

1. Aggressive growth
2. Maintain overall margins

Customer

3. Customer loyalty
4. Complete product-line offering

Internal Business Process

5. Build the brand
6. Fashion leader
7. Quality product
8. Superior shopping experience

Learning and Growth

9. Strategic skills
10. Personal growth

For each item on the corporate strategic agenda, the corporate executive team defined an associated guiding principle and a corporate-level measurement. For example, the aggressive growth item's guiding principle was stated as:

Each SBU should seek aggressive growth, measured relative to its market situation.

And the corporate-level measure was sales growth, measured on a year-to-year basis. The corporate strategic agenda item number 5, build the brand, the first objective for the internal-business-process perspective, was defined as:

Each SBU will create a dominant brand.

And this objective was measured on the corporate scorecard by percentage of SBUs that have achieved a dominant brand in their market segment.

The corporate scorecard served as a template for each SBU to define its own strategy and scorecards (see Figure 8-1). For example, consider the corporate financial objectives of aggressive revenue growth while maintaining overall margins. The corporate role was to allocate an overall growth target across its portfolio of retail businesses. This enabled the corporation to set more ambitious targets for those SBUs with considerable growth potential, and somewhat more modest targets for the SBUs in a mature and saturated market segment. Within the broad corporate objectives of growth and margins, individual SBUs could identify their own method for

Figure 8-1   The Corporate Scorecard Defines the Framework within Which Business Units Develop Their Scorecards

Corporate Strategic Agenda	Guiding Principles	Corporate Scorecard	SBU A (High-Growth)	SBU B (Mature)
Financial Perspective				
1 Aggressive Growth	Each SBU should seek aggressive growth, tailored to market situations	Sales Growth (vs. last year)	New Store Sales	Sales per Store Growth
2 Maintain Overall Margin	xxxx	xxxx	xxxx	xxxx
Customer Perspective				
1 Customer Loyalty	xxxx	xxxx	xxxx	xxxx
2 Complete Offering	xxxx	xxxx	xxxx	xxxx
Internal Perspective				
1 Build the Brand	Each SBU will create a dominant brand	% SBUs achieving dominant brands	% Revenue from Key Items	Market Share
2 Fashion Leader	xxxx	xxxx	xxxx	xxxx
3 Quality Product	xxxx	xxxx	xxxx	xxxx
4 Shopping Experience	xxxx	xxxx	xxxx	xxxx
Learning Perspective				
1 Strategic Skills	xxxx	xxxx	xxxx	xxxx
2 Personal Growth	xxxx	xxxx	xxxx	xxxx

achieving the corporate goal. For example, SBU A, a high-growth business, translated its growth objective into new store sales while mature SBU B looked for increases in sales per store. For the corporate theme focused on brand dominance, high-growth SBU A measured its performance by whether it achieved a high percentage of revenues from designated, key strategic merchandise items. Mature SBU B measured brand dominance by whether it maintained a leading market share in its retailing niche.

The Kenyon Stores example illustrates how one company, with SBUs that were organizationally independent but still operating within the same industry, could construct overall corporate objectives that provided the structure for the scorecards that each SBU would produce. The SBU Balanced Scorecards could be customized but all had a unity of purpose and focus derived from the corporate-level scorecard. In general, a corporate-level scorecard could articulate and communicate themes that all businesses within the corporation were expected to achieve.

As another example, top executives of Hoechst Celanese developed five core principles to guide employees' actions throughout the organization:

1. Customer-driven priorities, to be measured by customer satisfaction.

2. Continuous process improvement, to achieve processes that are effective, efficient, and flexible to meet customer needs, and incremental and breakthrough products.

3. Values-based leadership, so that everyone understands how they fit into the vision, mission, strategy, goals, objectives, and action plans; and where decisions and actions are based on values and long-term commitments.

4. Empowered people working together, in which decisions are made at the right level, accountability is accepted and welcomed, and there is commitment and ownership from everyone involved, leading to improved performance and productivity.

5. Excellent performance, as measured by customer satisfaction; preferred employer; environmental protection, safety, and health; and superior financial performance.

Such corporate-level themes could be translated into specific operational measures for each SBU in the corporation. The corporation would assign specific financial measures and targets for each SBU, but leave it up to the individual SBU to develop its own strategy to deliver the financial objective, consistent with the corporate themes. Each SBU was expected to measure customer satisfaction, employee empowerment and capabilities, and process capabilities, but the measures would be customized to their individual circumstances: market conditions, market strategy, and key innovation and operating processes.

JOINT VENTURES AND ALLIANCES

Achieving explicit synergies among related SBUs within a corporation has often been more rhetoric than reality. A specific example where such synergies are a fundamental component of the theory of the corporate form is the joint venture or strategic alliance between otherwise independent organizations. Joint ventures, while increasingly a part of the business landscape, have proven to be an operational challenge for many companies. Observers have noted that a prime obstacle is the difficulty of defining the goals that both parties have for the venture. The Balanced Scorecard has been used to define the shared agenda and measures of performance on which a joint venture would operate.

Consider the case of Oiltech, a joint venture of several companies in the oil-field services industry. The industry is highly fragmented, with many small players working at different points in the industry value chain (e.g., engineering, construction, logistics, and service companies all competing to support the same oil field). The Oiltech joint venture brought several of these companies together with the goal of improving productivity by eliminating the inefficiencies, duplications, and confusion that existed at the interfaces of their companies. The theory was that by combining efforts, Oiltech could provide a unified and integrated, even turnkey, perspective to customers (large, multinational oil and gas companies), and thereby provide benefits that could not be achieved by having each company operating independently.

The financial perspective for Oiltech included several traditional measures, such as return-on-capital, cash flow, and revenue growth. But it also included a new financial measure, revenue mix: the percentage of total business that involved multiple operating companies within Oiltech. This measure communicated an objective to obtain new business by providing integrated and turnkey services to customers.

The benefits to customers for working with multiple companies within the Oiltech joint venture was measured by one customer objective: reduce the cost per barrel at the wellhead. This was an excellent outcome measure because it described an objective desired by the customer and it clearly communicated the measure by which the joint venture's success could be evaluated. Oiltech's executives started by defining an industry cost curve (see Figure 8-2) that showed how each independent business (or function) contributed to the ultimate customer cost. The goal would be to obtain operating synergies that would lower the cost curve downward. The specific measure used for this objective was the $ per barrel life-cycle cost. The life-cycle per barrel cost was measured relative to that achievable by independent companies that worked without a joint-venture relationship among them.

With this clear customer-based objective for the joint venture, the executives derived performance drivers for internal processes that were expected to achieve this objective. They focused on the high-level behavior changes needed to execute the strategy; namely, working together in cross-business teams with the goal of achieving cost efficiencies. The measure—identified cost reductions resulting from cross-business initiatives—helped focus the

Figure 8-2   Strategic Objective: "Reduce the Life-Cycle Cost for the Customer by Integrating the Industry Value Chain"

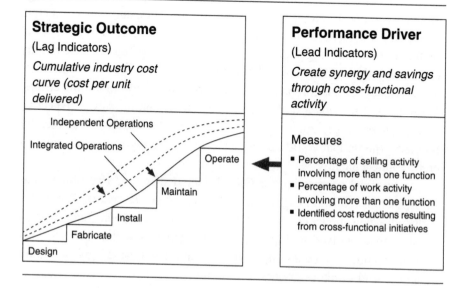

previously separate companies on their customer-driven goals for teamwork and cost reduction. Another internal measure, related to the create market objective, was the sales volume from contracts incorporating new service capabilities. The new service capabilities could include innovative financing mechanisms, project management techniques, and one-stop supply of integrated services for both operating expense businesses (OPEX) and capital expense businesses (CAPEX). The learning and growth perspective supported these initiatives by introducing measures that rewarded teaming relationships, enhancement of cross-functional skills, and alignment of incentives for performing systems integration work.

The development of the Balanced Scorecard at Oiltech facilitated the development of a new work model. The high-level strategic measures, and the linkage between a core outcome—reduction in life-cycle cost per barrel—and associated performance drivers triggered a set of strategic initiatives for reengineering the basic work processes that defined, at an operational level, how the joint venture participants would work as a team. The scorecard articulated the theory of how the previously separate companies in Oiltech could create unique and sustainable value for customers as a consequence of working better together.

FUNCTIONAL DEPARTMENTS: SHARED CORPORATE RESOURCES

We have discussed corporate strategies arising from establishing common themes that cut across operating companies, and explicit attempts to develop customer and operating synergies across different operating companies. Another source of corporate, or "parenting advantage" as it's called by Goold and colleagues, arises when operating companies can share a corporate-supplied resource.[3] A corporate resource provides a competitive advantage when it offers unique capabilities for the operating business units that they cannot acquire at comparable quality, price, and reliability from independent suppliers, including supplying it themselves through a self-contained resource unit. All too often, however, such corporate resources as maintenance, purchasing, human resources, information technology, or finance are not subjected to market tests and end up as a source of competitive disadvantage rather than an element of parenting advantage. Larry Brady, president of FMC Corporation, commented on how companies rarely apply discipline to their corporate staff groups:

Applying the scorecard to staff groups has been even more eye-opening than [with] our operating divisions. I doubt that many companies can respond crisply to the question, "How does staff provide competitive advantage?" Yet we ask that question every day about our line operations. We have just started to ask our staff departments to explain to us whether they are offering low-cost or differentiated services. If they are offering neither, we should probably outsource the function. This area is loaded with real potential for organizational development and improved strategic capability.[4]

This was the exact situation faced by Info Support (IS), the information and management systems unit of Telco, a major international telecommunications company. During the many decades when Telco operated as a regulated monopoly, business units were required to purchase all their information and technology services from Info Support, an internal corporate group. With outsourcing to external vendors precluded by corporate fiat, Info Support enjoyed rapid growth and high utilization, though with low levels of internal customer satisfaction. Entering the 1990s, Info Support was operating with mostly obsolete technology, a negative internal image, and a distinct lack of customer focus.

Most of Telco's business had been deregulated in the 1980s and its now highly competitive environment led to decentralization of its product and service delivery process into profit-center business units. The newly established business units needed higher services and technological capabilities from its information systems supplier. Telco, to encourage aggressive profit-seeking behavior from its operating units, empowered them to purchase services from their best supplier. Thus, Info Support either had to provide competitive services or watch its scale and scope of operations severely diminish.

The new CEO of Info Support turned to the Balanced Scorecard to transform an organization that had been a captive supplier of technology products and services into a customer-focused competitor. The CEO used the scorecard to:

- articulate a new customer-focused strategy,
- educate employees about the new approach, and
- change behavior to a strong customer focus.

Info Support knew that, because of decades of internal rather than external focus, the customer perspective would be most critical for its scorecard development. The project started by having team members interview customers in Telco's operating SBUs. The interviews revealed two different market segments among Telco's business units, each requiring quite different value propositions. One segment, analogous to Rockwater's Tier II customers, wanted basic information services, such as customer billing and payroll, provided at high levels of reliability and at minimum cost. The other segment, analogous to Rockwater's Tier I customers, wanted information technology that could provide them with competitive advantage in the marketplace. The Tier I business units wanted innovative technologies and long-term partnering relationships with its information systems supplier.

The Info Support project team developed specific measures for its two types of customers (see Figure 8-3). They developed customer satisfaction measures that reflected the value propositions for Tier I customers. They also included a measure, number of new customers, to emphasize the importance of developing technologies and services that could attract new customers. The BSC team introduced a measure of price versus market for supplying standardized services to Tier II customers, thus signaling the importance of delivering price-competitive services for these customers. The different measures provided clarity and focus for what Info Support had to excel at to retain its diverse internal customer base.

Figure 8-3 Objectives for Tier I and Tier II SBUs

Objective	Tier II (Price-Driven)		Tier I (Value-Added)			
	SBU A	SBU B	SBU C	SBU D	SBU E	SBU F
Low Price	√	√				
Value-Added			√	√	√	√
Quality/No Defects	√	√	√	√	√	√
Relationship			√	√	√	
Innovative Technologies			√	√	√	

The specific objectives developed for the customer perspective enabled Info Support to identify the critical internal processes if it were to succeed with its customers (see Figure 8-4). For Tier I customers, Info Support had to identify and develop new products and services. It measured this objective with percentage of revenues from products and services less than two years old and product-development cycle time. While neither of these measures would be startling to organizations like Hewlett-Packard, 3-M, and Analog

Figure 8-4   Translating Customer Objectives into Internal Priorities

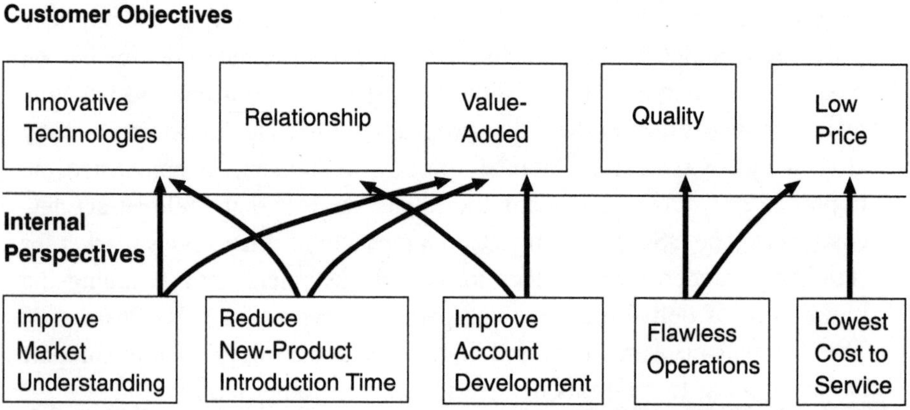

Customer Objectives

Objective	Measure
Market Understanding Improve our market understanding sufficiently to generate necessary future products, services, and customers that we don't have today	▪ Percent revenue from products and services less than 2 years old
Product Development Reduce product-introduction cycle time	▪ Product-development cycle time
Account Development Clarify the role of the account team as a focal point of value-added delivery	▪ Relationship audit
Flawless Operations Provide flawless implementation and operations at competitive cost	▪ Reliability (number faults/unit time) ▪ Serviceability (mean time to repair)
Low-cost Service Become the industry leader in cost per unit of service	▪ Competitive pricing index

Devices with deep and long-standing commitments to innovation, these measures represented a dramatic cultural change at Info Support since, as an internal captive supplier, it had never stressed the importance of product and service innovation. Its Tier I customers' desire for long-term partnering relationships would be measured by a score recorded on a relationship audit, which reflected both IS and customer employees' feedback on the quality of the supplier-customer relationship. The audit and reported score on the Balanced Scorecard communicated to all IS employees the importance of building excellent relationships with IS customers.

The scorecard process, particularly the development of the customer and internal-business-process objectives and measures, played a vital role in turning Info Support into a customer-focused organization. First, the process identified the two main customer segments and the value propositions for each segment so that a new strategy could be articulated for the different customer segments Info Support would attempt to serve. Second, the scorecard was communicated to all employees and embedded into Info Support's management processes so that critical internal processes could be continually directed to satisfying individual customer needs.

The Info Support's experience could likely be replicated by many organizational support and staff groups. Companies are now operating in an environment where partnering and strategic alliances are possible with a broad set of external suppliers of services—ranging across information technology, housekeeping, maintenance, and even product design and development. In this environment, corporate staff and support groups could benefit greatly from developing and communicating a strategy for delivering focused value propositions to internal customers, through excellent and aligned internal business processes. Corporate staff and support groups should be a source of competitive advantage. If they are not, their functions should either be assumed by the individual operating companies or else outsourced to more competitive and responsive external suppliers.

GOVERNMENT AND NOT-FOR-PROFIT ENTERPRISES

While the initial focus and application of the Balanced Scorecard has been in the for-profit (private) sector, the opportunity for the scorecard to improve the management of governmental and not-for-profit enterprises is, if anything, even greater. At least the financial perspective provides a clear long-run target for profit-seeking corporations. The financial perspective, however, provides a constraint, not an objective for government and not-for-profit organizations. These organizations must limit their spending to budgeted amounts. But the success of these organizations cannot be measured by how close they maintain spending to budgeted amounts, or even if they restrain spending so that actual expenses are well below budgeted amounts. For example, knowing that actual expenses for an agency came within 0.1% of budgeted amounts says nothing about whether the agency operated either effectively or efficiently during the period. Similarly, reducing expenses by 10% of budget is not a success story if the mission and constituencies of the agency have been severely compromised.

Success for government and not-for-profit organizations should be measured by how effectively and efficiently they meet the needs of their constituencies. Tangible objectives must be defined for customers and constituencies. Financial considerations can play an enabling or constraining role, but will rarely be the primary objective.

Recently, government agencies around the world are being held more accountable to taxpayers and constituents. Many governmental functions are being outsourced to the private sector or eliminated entirely. In the United States, an important early initiative of the Clinton administration that took office in January 1993 was to "reinvent government."[5] An initiative, under the leadership of Vice President Albert Gore, led to the publication of the *National Performance Review* (NPR).[6] This document emphasized the importance of a customer focus and performance measurement for governmental agencies. In a major section, "Empowering Employees to Get Results," this document has several recommendations for establishing performance measures for government agencies, including:

- All agencies will begin developing and using measurable objectives and reporting results.
- Clarify the objectives of federal programs.
- The president should develop written performance agreements with department and agency heads.

The report acknowledges that

Not everyone will welcome outcome measures. People will have trouble developing them. Public employees generally don't focus on the outcomes of their work. For one thing, they've been conditioned to think about process; for another, measures aren't always easy to develop. Consequently, they tend to measure their work volume, not their results.

If they are working hard, they believe they are doing all they can.
Public organizations will need several years . . . to develop useful
outcome measures and outcome reporting.[7]

One of the first applications of the NPR guidelines was carried out by
a performance measurement action team (PMAT), an interagency task force
created under the auspices of the federal Procurement Executive Association
(PEA) to evaluate the adequacy of the procurement systems in such agencies
as the Departments of Treasury, Transportation, Commerce, and Health
and Human Services, as well as the General Services Administration and
the U.S. Mint. The mission of the PMAT was to "assess the state of the
current [procurement] system, identify innovative approaches to measuring
performance, and develop strategies and recommendations for measuring
the health of agency acquisition systems."[8] The task force surveyed customers and employees, had senior procurement executives at each agency
perform a self-assessment, and collected available statistics about procurement performance. From this research, the task force developed a Balanced
Scorecard (see Figure 8-5). The scorecard retained the traditional four
perspectives of the corporate Balanced Scorecard, and added a fifth one,
employee empowerment, to emphasize the central role that federal employees must play in the new, more customer-focused approach for government
agencies.

The PMAT task force recommended the Balanced Scorecard because

It focuses on high impact measures. It is intended to be easy and
economical to use. It is balanced, and puts the emphasis on prevention
rather than detection. It is customer-oriented and cross-functional in
that it is not limited to areas of direct control. It empowers the procure-
ment organization to make improvements, rather than have headquar-
ters dictate the recommended changes to be made. It provides a method
to compare quality service with the goal of becoming best-in-class.

Moving from the federal government to municipal governments, the city
of Sunnyvale, California, has, for 20 years, produced an annual report that
discloses key objectives and actual performance against budgeted standards
for municipal services. In each policy area, the city defines sets of goals,
community condition indicators, objectives, and performance indicators. If
a program exceeds its objectives for quality and productivity, its manager
can receive a bonus of up to 10%. A 1990 comparison revealed that

Figure 8-5 The Balanced Scorecard for the Federal Procurement System

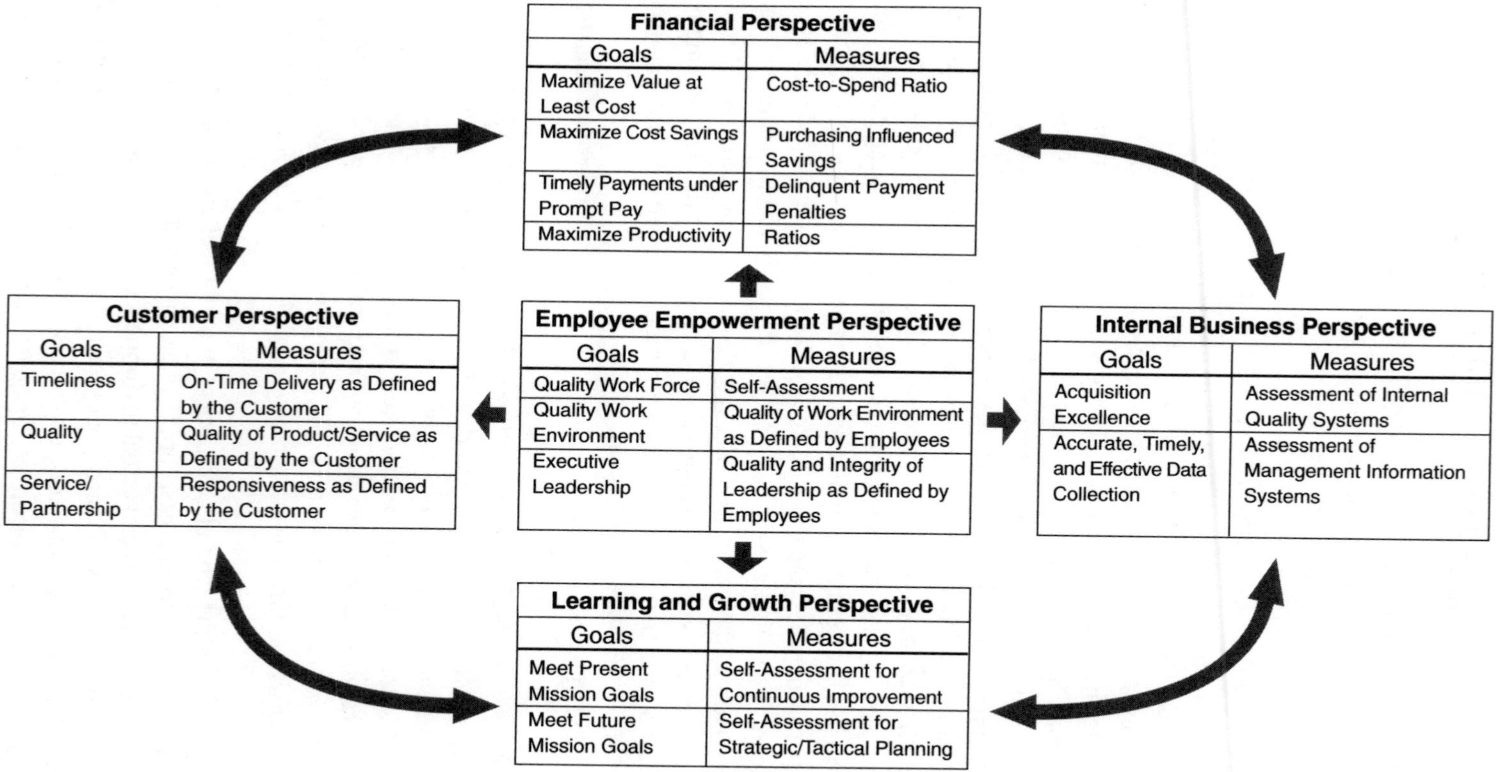

Financial Perspective

Goals	Measures
Maximize Value at Least Cost	Cost-to-Spend Ratio
Maximize Cost Savings	Purchasing Influenced Savings
Timely Payments under Prompt Pay	Delinquent Payment Penalties
Maximize Productivity	Ratios

Internal Business Perspective

Goals	Measures
Acquisition Excellence	Assessment of Internal Quality Systems
Accurate, Timely, and Effective Data Collection	Assessment of Management Information Systems

Employee Empowerment Perspective

Goals	Measures
Quality Work Force	Self-Assessment
Quality Work Environment	Quality of Work Environment as Defined by Employees
Executive Leadership	Quality and Integrity of Leadership as Defined by Employees

Customer Perspective

Goals	Measures
Timeliness	On-Time Delivery as Defined by the Customer
Quality	Quality of Product/Service as Defined by the Customer
Service/ Partnership	Responsiveness as Defined by the Customer

Learning and Growth Perspective

Goals	Measures
Meet Present Mission Goals	Self-Assessment for Continuous Improvement
Meet Future Mission Goals	Self-Assessment for Strategic/Tactical Planning

Source: Adapted from Robert S. Kaplan and David P. Norton, "The Balanced Scorecard—Measures That Drive Performance," *Harvard Business Review* (January–February 1992): 76. Reprinted with permission.

Sunnyvale uses 35–45% fewer people to deliver more services than other cities of similar size and type.[9]

More recently, the city of Charlotte, North Carolina, issued, in September 1995, a year-end objectives scorecard. The first part of the report reported on the city's major accomplishments during fiscal year 1995 in five focus areas:

- Community safety
- City within a city (targeted, local neighborhood initiatives)
- Restructuring government (to implement competition and asset management in city agencies)
- Economic development
- Transportation

The second part of the report summarized performance measured by major success indicators in four perspectives: financial, customer service, internal work efficiencies, and innovation and learning. Examples of the objectives and measures in these four scorecard perspectives included:

Customer Service: To Provide Excellent Customer Service to the Citizens of Charlotte

Status

- 89% of customer satisfaction on information about new procedures for garbage service
- Fire companies investigating and responding to local community needs
- Planning Department received 95.3% positive rating in its handling of more than 41,000 customer inquiries.
- Airport authority provided customer service training to shuttle bus drivers; survey of customers using the shuttle bus indicated very favorable responses.
- Transit authority had 25–35% more passenger pickups per hour of revenue service than comparable cities.
- Of 36,000 inquiries to the Transportation Department, only 26 (<0.01%) made a subsequent follow-up to the mayor's or City Council's office.

Financial Accountability: To Be Good Stewards of the City's Money

Status

- City's water/sewage rates were fourth lowest of 13 comparable cities. Annual rate increase was 25% below projected increase.

- Solid waste collection services was next to lowest among four largest national solid waste companies. Lost time from preventable accidents declined by 60% from previous year, saving about $130,000.

- Planning Department's per capita cost was lowest among six comparable cities.

- Worker's compensation medical treatment process was streamlined, saving $238,000 in employee time.

Internal Work Efficiencies: To Continue to Improve Cost Effectiveness of Services Within a No-Growth Budget, by Increasing Operating Efficiencies

Status

- Productivity of maintenance and utility meter reading substantially increased.

- Human Resources implemented an automated payroll system, reducing errors and redundant work. Provided better management reports on sick leave and other leaves.

- Improved efficiencies in Engineering and Property Management, Solid Waste, Transit, Transportation, Planning, and Aviation Departments by reduced staffing, reengineering several key processes, and outsourcing many functions (Note: details provided in actual report).

Innovation and Learning: To Explore New Products and Processes to Improve Our Performance in the Future

Status

- New Department of Transportation Information System introduced, containing information on street closings, project status, traffic counts, job openings, and business agendas.

- Initiated implementation of activity-based cost management for city departments.

- Exploring new initiatives for crime prevention.
- Developed a technology plan to increase productivity with a reduced work force.
- Employees undergoing training; post-test indicated a 51% skill improvement in targeted area.
- Employing two electric vehicles for fire and storm water field inspections
- Career development plan implemented for the Information Technology Division.

The city of Charlotte scorecard, while just a beginning and clearly a work-in-process, nevertheless provided a new focus and accountability for the municipal departments that previously were evaluated solely on whether or not their spending stayed within budgeted amounts. The city manager introduced the scorecard objectives and measures by stating: "I am especially pleased with our financial accountability and internal work efficiency achievements. . . . This report captures the 'success spirit' of our organization."

Not-for-profit organizations, especially those chartered to provide social service to the needy, have a particular requirement for communicating their mission and articulating the objectives and measures against which their performance should be measured. The entire rationale for such not-for-profit enterprises is to provide particular services to targeted constituents. As with government agencies, the financial perspective serves more as a constraint than as an objective for these organizations.

One of the first applications of the Balanced Scorecard to a not-for-profit social enterprise occurred for the Massachusetts Special Olympics.[10] The framework of the Special Olympics (SO) Balanced Scorecard was virtually identical to that used for companies and business units.

The financial perspective focused on the expectations of financial donors. Three principal objectives were selected:

- Public Recognition/Publicity: Position the Special Olympics as a favored charity through aggressive public relations and cause-related marketing.
- Community Involvement: Provide positive and fulfilling volunteer opportunities for corporate and individual volunteers.

- Athlete Outreach/Program Expansion: Expand programs and promote them to underserved areas to allow all potential athletes the
option to participate.

The measures selected for these objectives were:

- Number of new programs/athletes
- Volunteer retention/recruitment
- New donors
- Donor feedback
- Number of athletes in outreach programs

In addition, more traditional financial measures for a not-for-profit Balanced
Scorecard could include fund-raising targets, and administrative and fund-
raising expenses as a percentage of total funds raised.

The customer perspective focused on the athletes—the targeted audience
for the Special Olympics. Four objectives were selected:

- Training and Competition: Develop strong infrastructure for all
sports in order to provide convenient training times and locations.
- Controlled Cost: Minimize participation fees for athletes and families.
- Quality Programs: Focus on maintaining and improving quality of
training programs and competitive events.
- Community for Athletes: Foster opportunities for social interaction
among athletes.

The five measures for these objectives were:

- Number of athletes not able to find a team
- Cities with no registered athletes
- Fee increase
- Family feedback
- Number of social activities outside of competition

The internal operations perspective focused on the processes that would
enable the customer/athlete and financial donor objectives to be achieved:

- Organization and Administration: Communicate three-year plans to area management teams and coordinate within sections.
- Public Relations: Support outreach and fund-raising efforts through effective education of the public about the mission and operations of SO.
- Training: Continuously train and retrain athletic coaches.
- Outreach: Identify and target areas currently underserved by SO.

The measures included:

- Percentage of plans distributed
- Number of area management team meetings
- Funds raised
- Public awareness
- Number of training classes offered
- Number of first-time athletes

And the learning and growth perspective focused on the three key enablers typically identified for this perspective: people, systems, and organizational alignment:

- Knowledge of SO: Broaden understanding of the SO "big picture" among staff committee members, volunteers, and coaches.
- Management: Staff and develop strong area-management teams.
- Data Base Management: Maintain and effectively use data bases of donors, coaches, and volunteers.
- Recognition: Appropriately recognize volunteers, coaches, and staff.

The selected measures included:

- Number of volunteers trained in SO and sports
- Registration forms in on time
- Program guide distribution
- Volunteers in data base
- Coaches' training meetings

These examples—U.S. Government Procurement Executive Association, city of Charlotte, and Special Olympics—show how the Balanced Scorecard can translate a vision and strategy for government and not-for-profit organizations into tangible objectives and measures for the organizations' Balanced Scorecards. The scorecards for these organizations look remarkably similar to those developed at for-profit corporations, though they emphasize an even stronger role for customers and employees in specifying their objectives and performance drivers.

SUMMARY

In this chapter, we presented Balanced Scorecards for organizations that are structurally different from the strategic business units that have occupied our attention in prior chapters. A corporate scorecard requires an explicit corporate-level strategy that articulates the theory of how the corporation adds value to its collection of strategic business units. Such corporate value-added can arise from several sources, including common themes that pervade all business units, shared corporate services, and explicit interactions and transactions among business units that create unique competitive advantages in market segments. These themes and synergies should be explicitly identified, communicated with a corporate scorecard, and linked to business unit scorecards.

A Balanced Scorecard can also provide substantial focus, motivation, and accountability in government and not-for-profit organizations. In such organizations, the scorecard provides the rationale for their existence (serving customers and constituents, not simply containing spending to within budgetary constraints), and communicates to external constituents and internal employees the outcomes and performance drivers by which the organization will achieve its mission and strategic objectives.

NOTES

1. See D. J. Collis and C. A. Montgomery, "Competing on Resources: Strategy in the 1990s," *Harvard Business Review* (July–August 1995): 118–128; M. Goold, A. Campbell, and M. Alexander, *Corporate-Level Strategy: Creating Value in the Multibusiness Company* (New York: John Wiley & Sons, 1994); and G. Hamel and C. K. Prahalad, *Competing for the Future: Breakthrough Strategies for Seizing Control of Your Industry and Creating the Markets of Tomorrow* (Boston: Harvard Business School Press, 1994).

2. See C. K. Prahalad and G. Hamel, "The Core Competence of the Corporation," *Harvard Business Review* (May–June 1990): 79–91.

3. Goold, Campbell, and Alexander, *Corporate-Level Strategy.*

4. Experience reported in "Implementing the Balanced Scorecard at FMC Corporation: An Interview with Larry D. Brady," *Harvard Business Review* (September–October 1993): 146.

5. D. Osborne and T. Gaebler, *Reinventing Government: How the Entrepreneurial Spirit Is Transforming the Public Sector* (Reading, Mass.: Addison-Wesley, 1992).

6. *Creating a Government That Works Better and Costs Less: Report of the National Performance Review* (Washington, D.C.: U.S. Government Printing Office, 1993).

7. Ibid., 74–75.

8. Performance Measurement Action Team, "Performance Measurement Report," unpublished manuscript, Procurement Executive Association: Washington, D.C., December 1994.

9. *Creating a Government,* 76.

10. We are indebted to Laura Downing and Marissa Hendrickson of Renaissance Solutions, Inc. for the information on the Massachusetts Special Olympics study.

PART TWO

MANAGING BUSINESS STRATEGY

ONCE BUSINESSES HAVE BUILT their initial Balanced Scorecard, they should soon embed the scorecard in their ongoing management systems. In Part Two of the book, we illustrate how several companies are using the Balanced Scorecard as the cornerstone of a new strategic management system. Company managers have discovered that the scorecard enables them to bridge a major gap that formerly existed in their organizations: a fundamental disconnect between the *development and formulation* of strategy and its *implementation.*

The disconnect between strategy formulation and strategy implementation is caused by barriers erected by traditional management systems—the systems organizations use to:

- establish and communicate strategy and directions;
- allocate resources;
- define departmental, team, and individual goals and directions; and
- provide feedback.

In particular, we have identified four specific barriers (see Figure II-1) to effective strategy implementation:

Figure II-1 The Four Barriers to Strategic Implementation

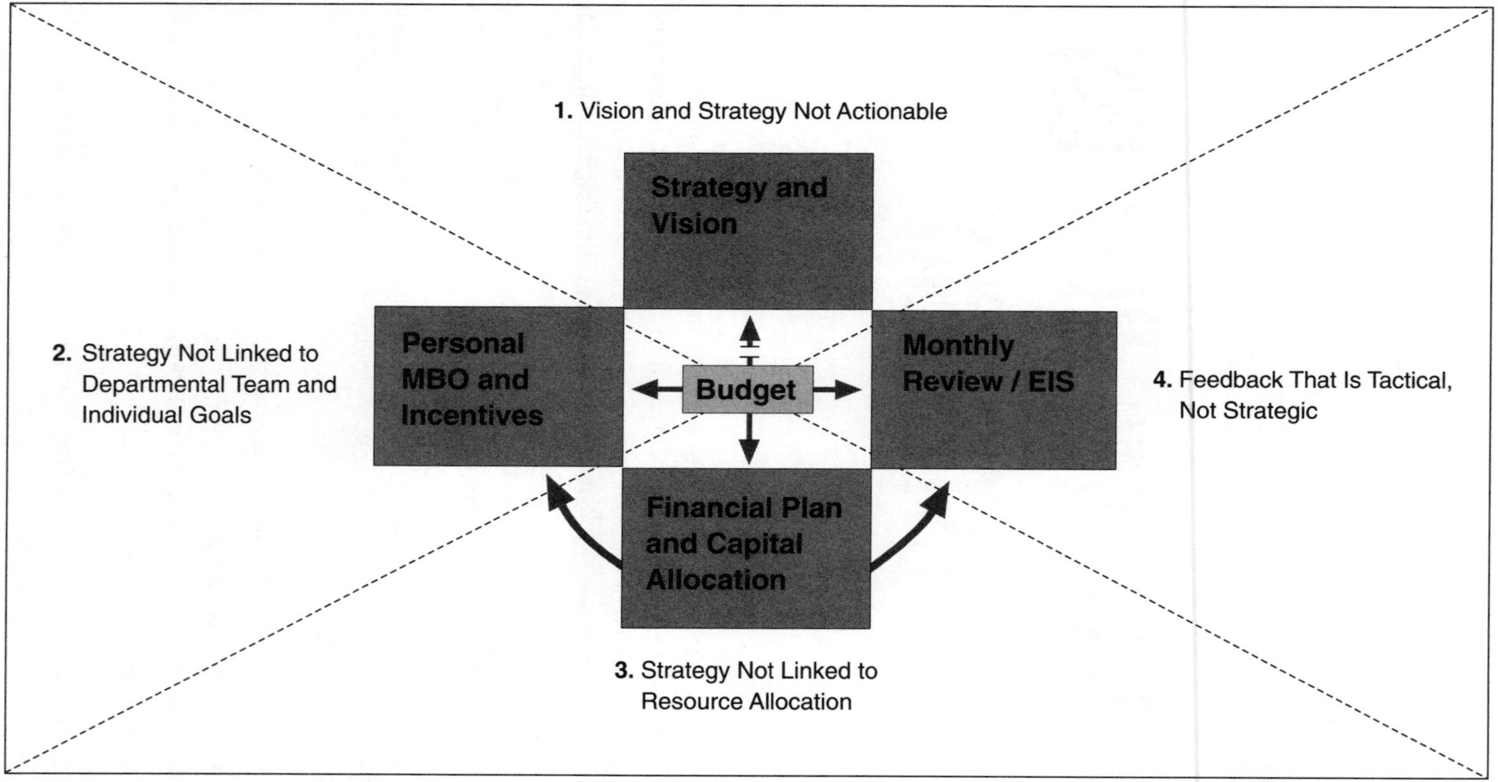

1. Visions and strategies that are not actionable
2. Strategies that are not linked to departmental, team, and individual goals
3. Strategies that are not linked to long- and short-term resource allocation
4. Feedback that is tactical, not strategic

Each barrier can be overcome by integrating the Balanced Scorecard into a new strategic management system. Let us pause here and be more specific about the defects of current management systems, driven mainly by a traditional, historical-cost financial model, that lead to a disconnect between strategy formulation and strategy implementation.

We recently conducted, with Business Intelligence, a conference organizer in the United Kingdom, a survey of management practices related to performance measurement and performance management systems. The survey was designed to learn how companies were currently managing the four components of a strategic management system: translating vision into shared understanding and commonality of purpose, communicating strategy and linking strategy to performance measurement, planning and target setting, and feedback and review of performance relative to strategy. We received responses from more than one hundred managers. The findings provided quantitative evidence on the phenomena we had observed in the individual companies that were implementing the Balanced Scorecard as a strategic management system.

BARRIER #1: VISION AND STRATEGY NOT ACTIONABLE

The first barrier to strategic implementation occurs when the organization cannot translate its vision and strategy into terms that can be understood and acted upon. Where fundamental disagreement exists about how to translate the lofty vision and mission statements into actions, the consequence is fragmentation and suboptimization of efforts. The CEO and the senior executive team have failed to gain consensus among themselves about what their vision and strategy really mean. Lacking consensus and clarity, different groups pursue different agendas—quality, continuous improvement, reengineering, empowerment—according to their own interpretations of vision and strategy. Their efforts are neither integrated nor cumulative since they are not linked coherently to an overall strategy. While our survey revealed that 59% of senior management teams feel they have a clear understanding of how to implement the vision, only 7% of middle managers and front-line employees do. This finding corroborates Senge's observation that even a leader with a clear vision lacks mechanisms for sharing this vision with all organizational employees in terms that make the vision actionable.

We have found that the process of building a Balanced Scorecard (as described in Chapters 3–8) clarifies the strategic objectives and identifies the critical few drivers for strategic success. The process creates consensus and teamwork among all senior executives, regardless of their previous employment history, job experience, or functional expertise. The scorecard translates a vision into key strategic themes that can then be communicated and acted upon throughout the organization.

BARRIER #2: STRATEGY NOT LINKED TO DEPARTMENTAL, TEAM, AND INDIVIDUAL GOALS

The second barrier arises when the long-term requirements of the business unit's strategy are not translated into goals for departments, teams, and individuals. Instead, departmental performance remains focused on meeting the financial budgets established as part of the traditional management control process. And teams and individuals within departments have their goals linked to achieving departmental short-term and tactical goals, to the exclusion of building capabilities that will enable longer-term strategic goals to be achieved. This barrier can perhaps be attributed to the failure of human resource managers to facilitate the alignment of individual and team goals to overall organizational objectives.

In our survey, respondents indicated that 74% of their senior executives had their compensation linked to the organization's annual goals. Fewer than one-third, however, reported that incentive compensation was linked in any way to achieving long-term strategic objectives. At lower levels, the disconnect was even more dramatic. Fewer than 10% of middle managers and front-line employees had incentive compensation linked to long-term strategy. Given this disconnect, it is not surprising that organizations have difficulty focusing their employees on implementing strategies, no matter how well-conceived and -formulated the strategies are. The incentive system, linked to short-term financial measures, simply reinforces the old ways of doing business.

In Chapter 9, we describe how organizations are using the Balanced Scorecard to communicate their new strategies to all employees, and then aligning departmental, team, and individual goals to successful implementation of the strategy. While senior managers disagree about the benefits of rapidly and explicitly linking compensation to scorecard measures, they do agree that the communication and goal-setting process has dramatically improved the alignment of all organizational participants to the strategy.

BARRIER #3: STRATEGY NOT LINKED TO RESOURCE ALLOCATION

The third barrier to implementing strategy is the failure to link action programs and resource allocation to long-term strategic priorities. Currently, many organizations have separate processes for long-term strategic planning and for short-term (annual) budgeting. The consequence is that discretionary funding and capital allocations are often unrelated to strategic priorities. Major initiatives—like reengineering—are undertaken with little sense of priority or strategic impact, and monthly and quarterly reviews focus on explaining deviations between actual and budgeted operations, not on whether progress is being made on strategic objectives. The failure here can be jointly attributed to the vice presidents of strategic planning and finance for not seeing how their efforts need to be integrated, not pursued as separate, functional agendas.

In Chapter 10, we present a comprehensive process, built around the Balanced Scorecard, for integrating an organization's planning, resource allocation, and budgeting processes. In particular, we describe the critical elements of a program that translates strategy into action:

- Establish long-term, quantifiable, and stretch targets for scorecard measures that managers and employees believe are achievable

- Identify the initiatives (investments and action programs) and resources for these initiatives that will enable the long-term targets for the strategic measures on the scorecard to be achieved

- Coordinate the plans and initiatives across related organizational units

- Establish short-term milestones that link the long-term scorecard targets to short-term budgeted measures.

BARRIER #4: FEEDBACK THAT IS TACTICAL, NOT STRATEGIC

The final barrier to implementing strategy is the lack of feedback on how the strategy is being implemented and whether it is working. Most management systems today provide feedback only about short-term, operational performance, and the bulk of this feedback is on financial measures, usually comparing actual results to monthly and quarterly budgets. Little or no time is spent examining indicators of strategy implementation and success. Our survey revealed that 45% of companies spent no time in periodic performance review meetings either reviewing strategy or making decisions about strategy. The gap here may be attributed to inadequate information, under the responsibility of the vice president of information systems, as well as to the tactical review processes, organized and run by the authority of the vice president of finance. The consequence is that organizations have no way of getting feedback on their strategy. And without feedback they have no way to test and learn about their strategy.

The ultimate payoff of using the Balanced Scorecard as a strategic management system occurs when organizations conduct regular strategic reviews, not just operational reviews. A strategic feedback and learning process based on the Balanced Scorecard has three essential ingredients:

1. A shared strategic framework that communicates the strategy and allows participants to see how their individual activities contribute to achieving the overall strategy;

2. A feedback process that collects performance data about the strategy and allows the hypotheses about interrelationships among strategic objectives and initiatives to be tested; and

3. A team problem-solving process that analyzes and learns from the performance data and adapts the strategy to emerging conditions and issues.

Chapter 11 illustrates how organizations can use the Balanced Scorecard to develop such a strategic feedback and learning process. At present, this process is the most undeveloped of the four major management processes we describe in Part Two. To our knowledge, only a few companies have moved far enough along to have implemented a strategic review process, but the ones that have recognize what a powerful new management tool

Figure II-2 A Different Management System for Strategic Implementation

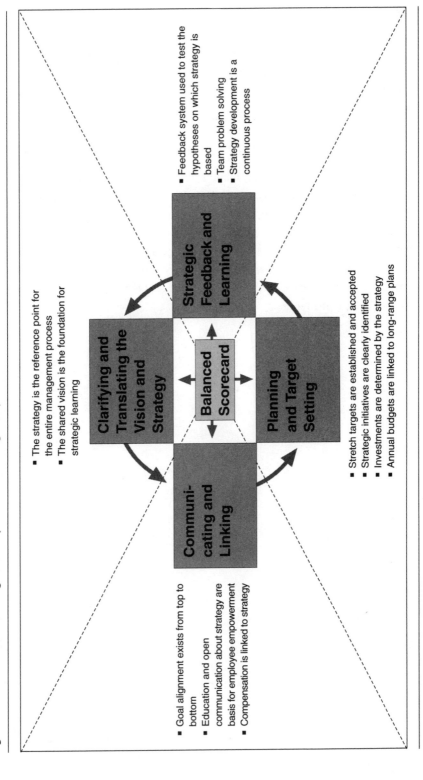

- The strategy is the reference point for the entire management process
- The shared vision is the foundation for strategic learning

Clarifying and Translating the Vision and Strategy

Strategic Feedback and Learning

Balanced Scorecard

Communi-cating and Linking

Planning and Target Setting

- Feedback system used to test the hypotheses on which strategy is based
- Team problem solving
- Strategy development is a continuous process

- Goal alignment exists from top to bottom
- Education and open communication about strategy are basis for employee empowerment
- Compensation is linked to strategy

- Stretch targets are established and accepted
- Strategic initiatives are clearly identified
- Investments are determined by the strategy
- Annual budgets are linked to long-range plans

it is. The updating of the strategy cycles the organization back to the first management process—clarifying and gaining consensus on vision and strategy—allowing the strategy to evolve as competitive, market, and technological conditions change.

BUILDING THE INTEGRATED MANAGEMENT SYSTEM

The final chapter of the book, Chapter 12, describes the evolutionary path followed by two organizations, National Insurance and Kenyon Stores, to build, over a 24-month period, a new strategic management system (see Figure II-2). The chapter identifies pitfalls that some organizations have encountered in developing a Balanced Scorecard and deploying it as the central framework for a new management system. It concludes with recommendations for organizing the development and the implementation phases of a scorecard project.

Achieving Strategic Alignment: From Top to Bottom

IMPLEMENTING A STRATEGY begins by educating and involving the people who must execute it. Some organizations hold their strategy secret, shared only among the senior executive group. The group implements the strategy through central command and control. While this approach was widely used by senior executives for much of the twentieth century, most executives of today's technology- and customer-driven organizations realize that they cannot determine and communicate all the local actions required to implement a successful strategy. Organizations that wish to have every employee contribute to the implementation of the strategy will share their long-term vision and strategy—embodied in the business unit's Balanced Scorecard—with their employees, and will actively encourage them to suggest ways by which the vision and strategy can be achieved. Such feedback and advice engages employees in the future of the organization, and encourages them to be part of the formulation and implementation of its strategy.

In an ideal world, every person in the organization, from the board room to the back room, would understand the strategy and how his or her individual actions support the "big picture." The Balanced Scorecard permits such a top-to-bottom alignment. The development of the scorecard should begin with the executive team (see the Appendix). Executive team building and commitment are an essential part of gaining benefits from the scorecard. But, they are only the first step. To gain maximum benefit, the executive team should share its vision and strategy with the whole organization, and with key outside constituents. By communicating the strategy and by linking it to personal goals, the scorecard creates a shared understanding and commitment among all organizational participants. When everyone understands the business unit's long-term goals, as well as the strategy for achieving these goals, all organizational efforts and initiatives can become aligned to the needed transformation processes. Individuals can see how their particular actions contribute to achieving business unit objectives (see Figure 9-1).

The alignment of an organization to a shared vision and common direction is an extended and complex process. Some organizations, in our experience, have eventually involved 5,000 or more of their employees in the alignment process. No single program or event can align this many people. Instead, these large organizations use several interrelated mechanisms to translate the strategy and the Balanced Scorecard into local objectives and measures that will influence personal and team priorities. Typically, three distinct mechanisms are used.

1. Communication and Education Programs. A prerequisite for implementing strategy is that all employees, senior corporate executives, and the board of directors understand the strategy and the required behavior to achieve the strategic objectives. A consistent and continuing program to educate the organization on the components of the strategy, as well as reinforcing this education with feedback on actual performance, is the foundation of organizational alignment.

2. Goal-Setting Programs. Once a base level of understanding exists, individuals and teams throughout the business unit must translate the higher-level strategic objectives into personal and team objectives. The traditional management-by-objectives (MBO) programs used by most organizations should be linked to the objectives and measures articulated in the Balanced Scorecard.

3. Reward System Linkage. Alignment of the organization toward the strategy must ultimately be motivated through the incentive and reward systems. While this linkage should be approached carefully, and only after the education and communication programs are in place, many organizations are already benefiting from linking incentive compensation systems to their Balanced Scorecards.

Figure 9-1 A Different Management System—Communicating and Linking

- Goal alignment exists from top to bottom
- Education and open communication about strategy are basis for employee empowerment
- Compensation is linked to strategy

Clarifying and Translating the Vision and Strategy

Communicating and Linking

Balanced Scorecard

Strategic Feedback and Learning

Planning and Target Setting

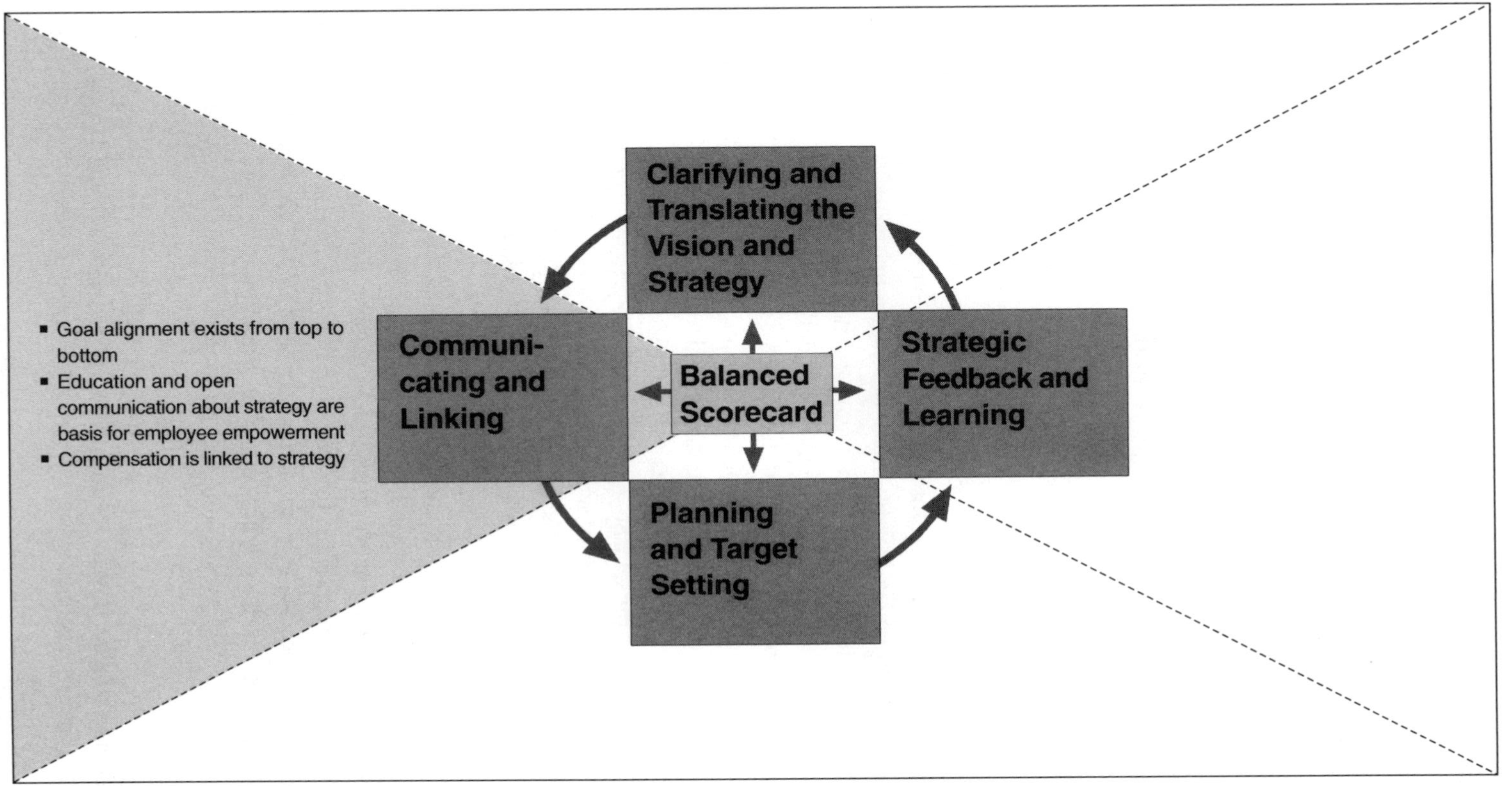

This chapter will explore the experiences of several organizations that have used these three mechanisms, in orchestrated campaigns, to align their people with strategic objectives. Strategic alignment of a business unit must take place in multiple directions. The obvious need is to achieve downward alignment to the employee base. This process, frequently referred to as "cascading," is the most complex because of the sheer numbers and logistics involved. Frequently overlooked is the need for upward alignment, to corporate boards and shareholders. Both types of alignment are discussed here.

COMMUNICATION AND EDUCATION PROGRAMS

Communication to employees about an organization's vision and strategy should be viewed as an internal marketing campaign. The goals of such a campaign are identical to those of traditional marketing campaigns: to create awareness and to affect behavior. The communication of the Balanced Scorecard should increase each individual's understanding of the organization's strategy and enhance motivation for acting to achieve strategic objectives. One executive described her organization's education program as a "campaign to win the hearts and minds of our people." She recognized that an essential part of successfully implementing the strategy was a shared vision among those who must execute it: "If they don't understand the vision, they can't share or act upon it."

A business unit implementing a Balanced Scorecard can have as many as 10,000 to 15,000 employees. A communication program to this many people requires a sustained, comprehensive plan. Some organizations, however, treat the Balanced Scorecard as a one-time event. Having just spent several months developing the scorecard and a shared consensus among the senior management group, they rush to share their new insight with all their employees. But they never follow up the initial publicity splash, and the employees treat the announcement as just another program-of-the-month that can be safely shelved and eventually ignored.

The organizational communication and education program should not only be comprehensive but also periodic. Multiple communication devices can be used to launch the Balanced Scorecard program: executive announcements, videos, town meetings, brochures, and newsletters. These initial announcements should then be followed up continually, by reporting scorecard measures and outcomes on bulletin boards, newsletters, groupware, and electronic networks.

Several companies have prepared brochures to communicate their strategy to the workforce. For example, see Figure 9-2 for the brochure used by a major European airline. The brochure identifies seven major corporate themes and communicates both the outcomes the airline wishes to achieve, as well as the drivers that will enable those outcomes to be achieved. Instead of a statement of broad, general themes, the brochure describes the specific measures the executives use to monitor the success of their strategy. The airline updates the brochure periodically to report trends and current performance along each of the seven goals, and to describe the initiatives the airline is using to accomplish its goals. In general, we encourage companies to communicate the objectives, measures, and targets embodied in the unit's Balanced Scorecard by distributing such brochures throughout the organization.

Many organizations use the company newsletter to embed the Balanced Scorecard in their ongoing communication programs with employees. Pioneer Petroleum devotes a section of each monthly newsletter to scorecard information. In the beginning of the program, this section was used to educate employees. Each issue reviewed one scorecard perspective, explaining its importance, articulating the reasoning behind the specific objectives that had been selected, and describing the measures that would be used to motivate and monitor performance for that perspective. After communicating the purpose and content of the scorecard in the first few issues, the section shifted from education to feedback. Each issue reported recent results on the measures for one perspective. Raw numbers and trends were supplemented with stories on how a department or an individual was contributing to the reported performance. The vignettes communicated to the workforce how individuals and teams were taking local initiatives to help the organization implement its strategy. The stories created role models of individual employees contributing to strategy implementation through their day-to-day activities.

Some organizations, however, deliberately choose not to communicate the Balanced Scorecard, as such, to their employees. These organizations feel that their employees have been bombarded, during the past 5 to 10 years, with all manner of vision and change programs, and that the employees have become cynical and inured to high-level pronouncements about the latest management fad that is sure to imminently transform the organization to breakthrough performance. In order to overcome individual resistance to named programs, the senior executives use their newsletters to disseminate the broad themes of the scorecard without specifically labeling or naming

Figure 9-2   A Strategy Brochure Based on the Balanced Scorecard

Our Mission

**What Does It
Mean to Our:**

Shareholders

Customers

**Internal
Processes**

Employees

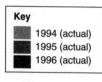

Key
- 1994 (actual)
- 1995 (actual)
- 1996 (actual)

Corporate Goals

Safe and Secure
To be a safe and secure airline

Financially Strong
To deliver strong and consistent financial
performance

Global Leader
To secure a leading share of air travel business
worldwide, with a significant presence in all major
markets

Service and Value
To provide overall superior service and good value
for money in every market segment in which we
compete

Customer Driven
To excel in anticipating and quickly responding to
customer needs and competitor activity

Good Employer
To sustain a working environment that attracts,
retains, and develops committed employees who
share in the success of the company

Good Neighbor
To be a good neighbor, concerned for the
community and the environment

Figure 9-2   Continued

Targets

Public perception as a safe airline

Cash flow as % of revenue

Presence in world markets

Standards achieved

Recommend to a friend

Employee satisfaction

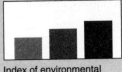

Index of environmental performance

Initiatives

- Undertook safety audits across all operational areas
- Continual improvement of established safety trends
- Continued to improve the security awareness of staff throughout the company

- Continued to reduce departmental unit costs with gap closure
- Optimized traffic mix, yields, and third-party revenues
- Improved the performance of the airline's capital assets

- Arrangements made for access to North American and Asia/Pacific markets
- Further presence negotiated in Europe
- Loyalty schemes developed in major markets

- Executive Club expanded to identify core customers and track their travel
- Sustained improvement in punctuality of the operation

- Executive Club members recognized by Service Delivery
- Mechanisms to encourage the innovations of staff and respond to customers

- Half the airline's staff attended Winning for Customers
- Assessed training requirements and developed quality program
- Developed improved performance and career management methods

- Key targets set from internal environmental audit program
- Increased communication/dialogue with local communities
- Increased involvement in educational, community, and conservation initiatives

this new corporate initiative. That is, the executives talk about the customer focus of the organization, and identify the targeted customer segments and the image, quality, time, product, and service attributes that the organization wishes to deliver to key customers, but do not label them as the "value propositions for targeted customers." Having stressed the importance of satisfying specific preferences of key customer segments, the communication program then emphasizes the internal business processes that are most important for the organization to excel at if customer satisfaction, acquisition, and retention are to be achieved.

For example, when we visited the corporate headquarters of Metro Bank, we asked whether the scorecard had been communicated to personnel in the street-level branch at the corporate office. An executive responded that the branch employees would not yet have heard of the Balanced Scorecard, but they *would* know about the new, targeted customer focus of the bank, and how they must strive to avoid operational defects, like billing errors and downtime at the ATMs.

Electronic networks and groupware, like Lotus Notes, provide additional opportunities for organizations to communicate and gain commitment to Balanced Scorecard objectives. We envision companies in the near future posting the complete set of scorecard objectives and measures on their electronic bulletin boards. The textual presentation can be enhanced with video clips of customers, internal processes, and employees, and audio recordings of the chief executive explaining why a particular objective has been chosen, and the rationale for the measures selected for each objective. Actual results and trends of past performance on each scorecard measure can be updated and displayed monthly on the groupware and internal electronic network. To encourage dialogue and debate, bulletin boards would be established for each scorecard measure, allowing managers and all other employees to comment about the root causes for exceeding or falling short on any particular measure.

Brochures, newsletters, and electronic bulletin boards are the tools of a communication/education program. To be effective, however, these tools must be woven together into a comprehensive communication effort that is directed at achieving strategic alignment over the long term. The design of such a program should begin by answering several fundamental questions.

- What are the objectives of the communication strategy?
- Who are the target audiences?

- What is the key message for each audience?
- What are the appropriate media for each audience?
- What is the time frame for each stage of the communication strategy?
- How will we know that the communication has been received?

Figure 9-3 is an example of the comprehensive communication program used at Kenyon Stores.

The corporate communications director, in partnership with the director of strategic planning, developed a program tailored to the needs of each constituent. The communications director was responsible for the communication process itself, while the strategic planning director supplied the content for the messages to the various constituents. The two directors then

Figure 9-3 A Comprehensive Communications Program—Kenyon Stores

Target Audiences	Communication Vehicles					
	Strategic Dialogue	Detailed Monthly Reports	Review Meeting	Kickoff/ Leadership Roadshow	Video	Periodic Update Brochure/ Newsletter
Corporate	√		Semiannually		√	Quarterly
SBU Leadership Team	Semiannually	√	Monthly Meeting Year End	Kickoff	√	Monthly
Directors	Semiannually	√	Monthly Meeting	Kickoff for Directors	√	Monthly
Stores		As Needed	As Needed	Kickoff for Group Leaders Road Show by Group Leaders	√	Monthly
Distribution Center		As Needed	As Needed	√	√	Monthly
Support Groups ■ Real Estate ■ Store Planning ■ Key Suppliers	As Needed	√ √		√	√	As Needed

monitored the effectiveness of the program with a quarterly employee survey, which solicited feedback about how well and how pervasively the education process was working.

While open communications about strategic priorities are a prerequisite for implementation at the local level, such programs must also deal with the legitimate needs for secrecy and confidentiality. As we described in Chapter 7, a good strategy should be explicit and not generic; it should identify particular customer and market segments that have been targeted for aggressive building of market share, and the particular mechanisms that will be deployed to take market share away from competitors. Were such a strategy to be clearly disclosed to thousands of employees throughout an organization, it could soon be known by rival companies—through terminated or disgruntled employees, by managers and employees hired by other organizations, or even by casual discussion by employees unaccustomed to having access to highly sensitive information (as the wartime expression goes, "Loose Lips Sink Ships"). Premature disclosure of the new strategy could enable competitors to blunt its impact.

Each business unit must assess the relative benefits of extensive communication, commitment, and buy-in from all organizational employees versus the potential costs of disclosure and the possible loss of competitive advantage. One approach is to communicate the generic outcome measures (market share, customer satisfaction, retention, and acquisition) and generic performance drivers (quality, response time, and cost performance) to which the organization is striving. But the executives would restrict, on a need-to-know basis, the particular customer segments and competitors that the organization is targeting. Indices can also be used instead of actual numbers.

COMMUNICATING WITH THE BOARD OF DIRECTORS AND EXTERNAL SHAREHOLDERS

The Balanced Scorecard, as the embodiment of business unit strategy, should be communicated upward in an organization to corporate headquarters, and the corporate board of directors. Conventional rhetoric declares that a principal responsibility of the board is to provide oversight of corporate and business unit strategy. In practice, however, corporate boards spend more time reviewing and analyzing quarterly financial results than engaging in detailed strategic reviews and analysis. When the primary communication between senior corporate executives and its outside board of directors consists of short-term financial measures, it is not surprising that meetings focus more on short-term operational results than long-term strategic vision.

Jay Lorsch, among others, has argued that boards of directors must play a more active role in monitoring corporate strategy and corporate performance.

> . . . outside directors [must] have the capability and independence to monitor the performance of top management and the company; to influence management to change the strategic direction of the company if its performance does not meet the board's expectations; and, in the most extreme cases, to change corporate leadership. . . . If boards are to be effective in evaluating the CEO and approving corporate strategy, they need to develop knowledge not only about the company's financial results, which are an indication of past performance, but also about the company's progress in accomplishing its strategy. That means understanding progress in developing new technology and new products and services, and in entering new markets. It means under-standing changing customer requirements and what competitors are doing. Similarly, directors need the data to build knowledge about the organizational health of the company. In essence, they need their own version of the "balanced scorecard."[1]

The Balanced Scorecard can and should be the mechanism by which senior corporate executives present their corporate and business unit strategies to the board of directors. This communication not only informs the board in specific terms that long-term strategies designed for competitive success are in place. It also provides the basis for feedback and accountability to the board.

Ultimately, the question is whether the Balanced Scorecard should be communicated beyond the boardroom to external shareholders. Historically, companies have been reluctant to disclose information beyond the minimum required by regulatory authorities. This reluctance stems from several sources. First, executives are properly concerned that anything beyond minimal disclosure could benefit competitors more than existing shareholders. Especially if the Balanced Scorecard is a clear articulation of business unit and corporate strategy, its public revelation could enable competitors to sabotage a well-formulated and executed strategy. A second concern is with liability, particularly in today's litigious environment. By voluntarily communicating the scorecard, managers fear that failure to achieve or improve on these "supplemental" measures could become the basis for shareholder suits. Class-action securities lawsuits are often triggered by even a mild deviation from projected goals. A third reason comes from the apathy of much of the investment community about nonfinancial information, especially when that information explicitly communicates long-term goals (for many analysts, anything beyond next quarter's earnings is a long-term goal). One company president whose organization was an early implementor of the Balanced Scorecard described an experience with financial analysts:

> I was giving a presentation to a group of analysts of a major mutual fund organization that, collectively among all its funds, owned up to 40% of our shares. As long as I was describing plans and forecasts for next period's earnings, the analysts were on the edge of their seats, hanging on every word I said. When I started to talk about our program to improve quality and customer response times, 90% of the analysts got up to make phone calls.

If financial analysts remain indifferent to measures of a company's long-term strategy, we are not optimistic that Balanced Scorecard reporting will become part of an organization's communication program to outside shareholders.

We believe, however, that the best financial reporting policies will eventually be derived from the best internal reporting policies. At present, most companies are still experimenting internally with developing, communicating, and evaluating performance using the Balanced Scorecard. As senior executives become more experienced and confident about the ability of scorecard measures to monitor strategic performance and predict future financial performance, we believe they will find ways to communicate these measures to outside investors, without disclosing competitively sensitive information.

Skandia: How One Company Communicates Its Balanced Scorecard to Shareholders

As a precursor for how key performance drivers can be communicated to external investors, take Skandia, a Swedish insurance and financial services company. Skandia issues a supplement, called the *Business Navigator*, to its annual report. The supplement describes the company's strategy, the strategic measures it uses to communicate, motivate, and evaluate the strategy, and performance along these measures during the past year. The introduction in Skandia's 1994 annual report supplement, entitled "Visualizing Intellectual Capital at Skandia," declares:

> *Commercial enterprises have always been valued according to their financial assets and sales, their real estate holdings, or other tangible assets. These views of the industrial age dominate our perception of businesses to this day—even though the underlying reality began changing decades ago. Today it is the service sector that stands for dynamism and innovative capacity. . . . The service sector has few visible assets, however. What price does one assign to creativity, service standards or unique computer systems? Auditors, analysts, and accounting people have long lacked instruments and generally accepted norms for accurately valuing service companies and their "intellectual capital."*

The supplement presents a *Business Navigator* for eight major lines of business.[2] The navigator for one line of business is shown in Figure 9-4.

Skandia is clearly taking a "lead-steer" position in voluntarily disclosing its business-unit scorecard objectives and measures to the financial community. It is doing so as part of its reporting and disclosure strategy, hoping to attract shareholders that are willing to invest for long-term results. These relationship investors take a significant long-term position in a company and, therefore, have a more intense interest in how the company is being managed for long-term economic results. Early indications are promising since investment analysis of Skandia now includes discussion of its products, technology, customers, and employee capabilities, not just financial forecasts.

LINKING THE BALANCED SCORECARD TO TEAM AND PERSONAL GOALS

Communication of the Balanced Scorecard's objectives and measures is a first step in gaining individual commitment to the business unit's strategy. But awareness is usually not sufficient by itself to change behavior. Somehow, the organization's high-level strategic objectives and measures need to be translated into actions that each individual can take to contribute to the organization's goals. For example, an on-time delivery objective for the business unit's customer perspective can be translated into an objective to reduce setup times at a bottleneck machine, or for rapid transfer of orders from one process to the next. In this way, local improvement efforts become aligned with overall organizational success factors.

Many organizations, however, have found it difficult to decompose high-level strategic measures, especially nonfinancial ones, into local, operational measures. In the past, when managers relied exclusively on top-down financial controls, they could exploit an elegant decomposition of an aggregate measure, like return-on-investment or economic value-added, into local measures, like inventory turns, days sales in accounts receivable, operating expenses, and gross margins. Unfortunately, nonfinancial measures, such as customer satisfaction and information systems availability, are more difficult to decompose into more disaggregate elements. The Balanced

Figure 9-4 Skandia's Business Navigator

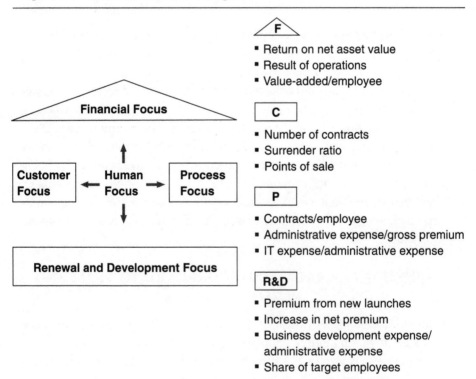

Scorecard can make a unique contribution here since it is based on a "performance model" that identifies the drivers of strategy at the highest level. The scorecard's framework of linked cause-and-effect relationships can be used to guide the selection of lower-level objectives and measures that will be consistent with high-level strategy. As illustrated in Figure 9-5, the high-level performance model reflected in the scorecard becomes the starting point for a decomposition process that cascades high-level measures down to lower organizational levels. The central concept is that an integrated performance model that defines that drivers of strategic performance at different organizational levels should be used as the central organizing framework for setting goals and objectives at all organizational levels. Thus, the Balanced Scorecard at the SBU level can be translated into a linked scorecard for lower-level departments, teams, and individuals. Several examples illustrate different approaches for implementing this concept.

In one company concerned with gaining buy-in from middle management, the senior executive group defined its strategy for only the financial and customer perspectives—including the customer segments in which it wanted to compete and the value proposition it should be delivering to customers in those segments. The next two levels of middle managers were then brought in to participate in the process to develop the internal-business-process and learning and growth objectives that could enable the company's financial and customer objectives to be achieved.

The real estate division of a large retailer set out to cascade its SBU scorecard to the next level of departments and teams. As illustrated in Figure 9-6, each team used the SBU scorecard as its point of reference. The team then identified the objectives and measures on the SBU scorecard that it could influence. The managers developed a team scorecard that translated the higher-level strategic objectives and measures into local team initiatives and measures that they could influence. These two examples illustrate an approach that engaged middle managers and enabled them to use their local and specific knowledge to make operational the key elements of their business unit's strategy. Also, the managers themselves became more committed to implementing the strategy and achieving the overall organizational goals. On reviewing the scorecards from his various teams, the CEO of the real estate division observed, "I sleep more easily at night knowing that my goal of growth with profitability has been translated into such operational details as 'type of paint and wall covering.' This is what alignment is all about."

Figure 9-5   Cascading the Scorecard

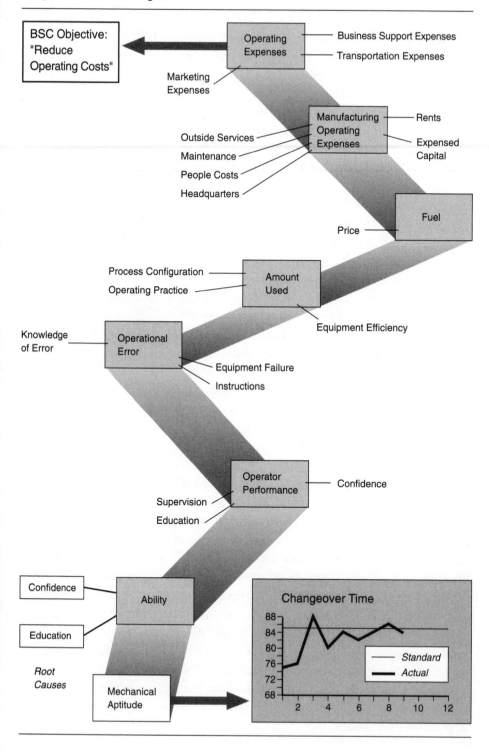

Figure 9-6   Cascading Division Objectives into Specific Team Objectives

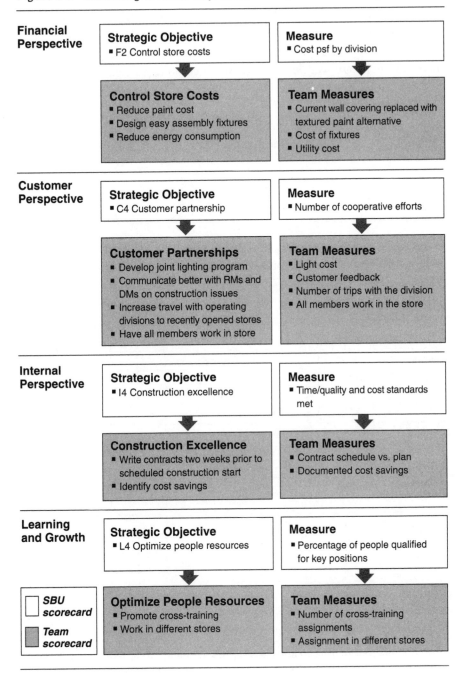

Financial Perspective

Strategic Objective
- F2 Control store costs

Measure
- Cost psf by division

Control Store Costs
- Reduce paint cost
- Design easy assembly fixtures
- Reduce energy consumption

Team Measures
- Current wall covering replaced with textured paint alternative
- Cost of fixtures
- Utility cost

Customer Perspective

Strategic Objective
- C4 Customer partnership

Measure
- Number of cooperative efforts

Customer Partnerships
- Develop joint lighting program
- Communicate better with RMs and DMs on construction issues
- Increase travel with operating divisions to recently opened stores
- Have all members work in store

Team Measures
- Light cost
- Customer feedback
- Number of trips with the division
- All members work in the store

Internal Perspective

Strategic Objective
- I4 Construction excellence

Measure
- Time/quality and cost standards met

Construction Excellence
- Write contracts two weeks prior to scheduled construction start
- Identify cost savings

Team Measures
- Contract schedule vs. plan
- Documented cost savings

Learning and Growth

Strategic Objective
- L4 Optimize people resources

Measure
- Percentage of people qualified for key positions

☐ SBU scorecard
▨ Team scorecard

Optimize People Resources
- Promote cross-training
- Work in different stores

Team Measures
- Number of cross-training assignments
- Assignment in different stores

As a third example, the exploration group of a large oil company developed an innovative approach to foster individual goal setting consistent with overall group goals. The group created a small, fold-up personal scorecard (see Figure 9-7) for each individual in the organization. The personal scorecard was designed so that it could be carried in a shirt pocket or purse at all times. The scorecard contained three levels of information. The first level, preprinted on the left side of the scorecard, described the corporate objectives and measures. The second level, printed in the middle, provided space for the business unit to translate the corporate goals into

Figure 9-7 The Personal Scorecard

Corporate Objectives
- Double our corporate value in seven years
- Increase our earnings by an average of 20% per year
- Achieve an internal rate-of-return 2% above the cost of capital
- Increase both production and reserves by 20% in the next decade

	Corporate Targets*			Scorecard Measures	Business Unit Targets			Team/Individual Objectives and Initiatives
	1997	1998	1999		1997	1998	1999	
Financial	160	180	250	Earnings (in millions of dollars)				1.
	200	210	225	Net cash flow				
	80	75	70	Overhead and operating expenses				2.
Operating	73	70	64	Production costs per barrel				
	93	90	82	Development costs per barrel				
	108	108	110	Total annual production				3.

Team/Individual Measures	**Targets**			
1.				
2.				4.
3.				
4.				
5.				5.
Name:				
Location:				

* 1995 level = 100

Source: Adapted from Robert S. Kaplan and David P. Norton, "Using the Balanced Scorecard as a Strategic Management System," *Harvard Business Review* (January–February 1996): 81. Reprinted with permission.

its specific goals. The third, and most important, level enabled individuals and teams to define their personal performance objectives and the near-term action steps they would take to achieve the objectives. Individuals also defined up to five personal performance measures for the personal objectives, as well as targets for these objectives that would be consistent with achieving the higher-level business unit and corporate objectives. This mechanism enabled the business and corporate-level objectives to be communicated down and translated into objectives that were internalized by all employees and teams. The device of the personal scorecard kept the three levels of objectives, measures, and actions readily accessible, on a daily basis, to all employees.

While such programs to establish goals linked to high-level strategy are typically triggered by the creation of a Balanced Scorecard at the SBU level, many organizations already have a normal, ongoing process, generally referred to as management-by-objectives, for setting individual, team, and local organizational goals. Obviously, a company should have only one process for setting goals for departments, teams, and individuals. Most MBO programs are quite consistent with the scorecard framework, so that the business unit need only link its existing MBO process to establishing team and personal scorecards that are consistent with and will drive the achievement of scorecard strategic objectives and measures.

REWARD SYSTEMS LINKAGE

The big question faced by all companies is whether and how to link their formal compensation system to the scorecard measures. Currently, companies are following different strategies in how soon they link their compensation system to the measures. Ultimately, for the scorecard to create the cultural change, incentive compensation must be connected to achievement of scorecard objectives. The issue is not whether, but when and how the connection should be made.

Because financial compensation is such a powerful lever, some companies want to tie their compensation policy for senior managers to the scorecard measures as soon as possible. One organization shifted its bonus calculation for senior executives away from annual return-on-capital-employed targets; bonuses are now based 50% on achieving economic value-added targets over a three-year period, with the remaining 50% based on the formulation and achievement of scorecard measures in the three nonfinancial perspectives. This policy has the obvious advantages of aligning the financial interests of the senior managers with achieving their business unit's strategic objectives.

As another example, Pioneer Petroleum moved quickly to use its Balanced Scorecard as the sole basis for computing senior executive incentive compensation. As shown in Figure 9-8, it tied 60% of the executive bonus to financial performance. Pioneer, rather than relying on a single number for this component, developed a weighted average among five financial indicators: operating margin and return-on-capital, both measured against competitive benchmarks; cost reduction versus plan; and growth in both existing and new markets. It based the remaining 40% of the bonus on indicators drawn from the customer, internal process, and learning and growth perspectives, including a key indicator on community and environmental responsibility. The CEO expressed his pleasure with the results from this plan: "Our organization is aligned with its strategy. I know of no competitor that has this degree of alignment. It is producing results for us."

Obviously, tying incentive compensation to scorecard measures is attractive, but it has some risks. Are the right measures on the scorecard? Are the data for the selected measures reliable? Could there be unintended or

Figure 9-8   Incentive Compensation Based on the Balanced Scorecard

Category	Measure	Weighting
Financial (60%)	Margin vs. Competition	18.0%
	ROCE vs. Competition	18.0%
	Cost Reduction vs. Plan	18.0%
	New Market Growth	3.0%
	Existing Market Growth	3.0%
Customers (10%)	Market Share	2.5%
	Customer Satisfaction Survey	2.5%
	Dealer Satisfaction Survey	2.5%
	Dealer Profitability	2.5%
Internal (10%)	Community/Environmental Index	10.0%
Learning and Growth (20%)	Employee Climate Survey	10.0%
	Strategic Skill Rating	7.0%
	Strategic Information Availability	3.0%

unexpected consequences in how the targets for the measures are achieved? The disadvantages occur when the initial scorecard measures are not perfect surrogates for the strategic objectives, and when the actions that improve the short-term measured results may be inconsistent with achieving the long-term objectives.

Some companies, concerned about these questions and recognizing that compensation is such a powerful lever, don't want it to operate when the Balanced Scorecard is first being implemented. For them, the initial score-card represents a tentative statement of the unit's strategy. The scorecard expresses hypotheses about the cause-and-effect relationships among the measures for creating superior, long-run financial performance. Executives, as they translate strategy into measures and formulate hypotheses about the linkages among the measures, may not be confident at first that they have chosen the right measures. They may be reluctant to expose the initial measures to the efforts by highly motivated (and compensated) executives to achieve maximal scores on the selected measures. For this reason, many companies are cautious about switching their formula-based compensation system over to scorecard measures. Of course, if compensation is not tied explicitly to the scorecard measures, traditional formula-based incentive systems using short-term financial results, will likely have to be turned off. Otherwise, senior business unit managers will be asked to pay attention to achieving a balanced set of strategic objectives, while being rewarded for achieving short-term financial performance.

A second concern arises from the traditional mechanism for handling multiple objectives in a compensation function. This mechanism, as illus-trated in the Pioneer Petroleum example, assigns weights to the individual objectives, with incentive compensation calculated by the percentage of achievement on each objective. This permits substantial incentive compen-sation to be paid even when performance is unbalanced; that is, the business unit overachieves on a few objectives, while falling far short on some others.

The Balanced Scorecard offers an alternative approach for determining when incentive compensation is paid. Corporate executives can establish minimum threshold levels across all, or a critical subset, of the strategic measures for the upcoming periods. Managers earn no incentive compensa-tion if actual performance in a period falls short of the threshold on any of the designated measures. This constraint should motivate balanced per-formance across financial, customer, internal-business-process, and learning and growth objectives. The threshold constraint should also balance short-term outcome measures and the performance drivers of future economic value. If the minimum thresholds are achieved on all measures, incentive compensation can be linked to outstanding performance across a smaller subset of measures. The subset used to determine the amount of incentive compensation will be the measures from the four perspectives felt to be most valuable for the organization to excel at in the upcoming period.

Some companies allow business unit managers to set their own targets for scorecard measures. But then the senior executive team makes a judgment about the degree of difficulty of the targets, and this degree of difficulty, analogous to how diving competitions are scored, influences the size of the bonus paid when targets are achieved. The senior executives use a combination of external benchmarking and subjective judgments to assess the stretch or slack in the unit managers' targets.

Such use of subjective judgments reflects a belief that results-based compensation may not always be the ideal scheme for rewarding managers. Many factors not under the control or influence of managers also affect reported performance. Further, many managerial actions create (or destroy) economic value but may not be measured. Ideally, managers should be compensated for their abilities, their efforts, and the quality of their decisions and actions. Ability, effort, and decision quality are typically not used in formal compensation plans because of the difficulty of observing and measuring them. Pay-for-performance is a second-best approach, but one that is widely used because the other factors are so difficult to observe in practice.

Interestingly, the active use of the Balanced Scorecard provides much greater visibility about managerial abilities, efforts, and decision quality than traditional summary financial measures. The companies that, at least for the short run, abandon formula-based incentive systems often find that the dialogue among executives and managers about the scorecard—both the formulation of the objectives, measures, and targets, and the explanation of actual versus targeted results—provides many opportunities to observe managers' performance and abilities. Consequently, even subjectively determined incentive rewards become easier and more defensible to administer. The subjective evaluations are also less susceptible to the game playing associated with explicit, formula-based rules.

A further consideration arises from the recognition that incentive compensation is an example of extrinsic motivation, in which individuals act because they either have been told what to do, or because they will be rewarded for achieving certain clearly defined targets. Extrinsic motivation is important. Rewards and recognition should be associated with achieving business unit and corporate goals. But extrinsic motivation alone may be inadequate to encourage creative problem solving and innovative decision making. Several studies have found that intrinsic motivation, employees acting because of their personal preferences and beliefs, leads to more creative problem solving and innovation. In the context of the Balanced Scorecard, intrinsic motivation exists when employees' personal goals and actions are consistent with achieving business unit objectives and measures. Intrinsically motivated individuals have internalized the organizational goals and strive to achieve those goals even when they are not explicitly tied to compensation incentives. In fact, explicit rewards may actually reduce or crowd out intrinsic motivation.

In several organizations, the clear articulation in a Balanced Scorecard of business unit strategic objectives, with links to associated performance drivers, has enabled many individuals to see, often for the first time, the links between what they do and the organization's long-term objectives. Rather than behaving as automata, with bonuses tied to achieving or exceeding targets in the performance of their local tasks, individuals can now identify the tasks they should be doing exceptionally well to help achieve the organization's objectives. This articulation of how individual tasks align with overall business unit objectives has created intrinsic motivation among large numbers of organizational employees. Their innovation and problem-solving energies have become unleashed, even without explicit ties to compensation incentives. Of course, since extrinsic motivation remains important, should the organization begin to achieve breakthrough performance by meeting or exceeding the stretch targets for its strategic measures, the employees who made such performance happen should be recognized and rewarded. Pioneer Petroleum, for example, has now implemented a variable compensation approach for all its nonunion employees, with rewards linked to achievement of business unit and company performance targets. Pioneer believes that tying compensation for the great majority of its employees to business unit scorecard measures has built deep organizational commitment to its strategic objectives.

In expressing caution about using Balanced Scorecard measures in formal compensation schemes, we do not advocate that such linkage not be used. The role of the scorecard in determining explicit rewards is still in its embryonic stages. Clearly, attempting to gain organizational commitment to balanced performance across a broad set of leading and lagging indicators will be difficult if existing bonus and reward systems remain anchored to short-term financial results. At the very least, such short-term focus must be de-emphasized.

Several approaches may be attractive to pursue. In the short term, tying incentive compensation of all senior managers to a balanced set of business unit scorecard measures will foster commitment to overall organizational goals, rather than suboptimization within functional departments. The dialogue that leads to formulation of the goals and the actions that help to achieve them will often reveal much about managerial ability and effort, enabling subjective judgments to be combined with quantitative outcome measures in calculating incentive compensation. Further experimentation and experience will provide additional evidence on the appropriate balance between explicit, objective formulas and subjective evaluation for linking incentive compensation to achievement of scorecard objectives.

SUMMARY

Formulating a Balanced Scorecard that links a business unit's mission and strategy to explicit objectives and measures is only the start of using the scorecard as a management system. The Balanced Scorecard must be communicated to a variety of organizational constituents, especially employees, corporate-level managers, and boards of directors. The goal of the communication process is to align all employees within the organization, as well as individuals to whom the business unit is accountable (corporate executives and the board), to the strategy. The knowledge and alignment among these constituents will facilitate local goal setting, feedback, and accountability to the SBU's strategic path.

Alignment and accountability will clearly be enhanced when individual contributions to achieving scorecard objectives are linked to recognition, promotion, and compensation programs. Whether such linkages should be explicit, based on predetermined formulas, or applied judgmentally, using the heightened visibility and observability gained from formulation, dialogue, and review about scorecard objectives and measures, will likely vary from company to company. More knowledge about the benefits and costs of explicit linkages will undoubtedly continue to be accumulated in the years ahead.

NOTES

1. Jay W. Lorsch, "Empowering the Board," *Harvard Business Review* (January–February 1995): 107, 115–116.
2. Skandia calls its system of describing human, structural, and customer capital the *Skandia Navigator,* because it is used as "an instrument to help us navigate into the future and thereby stimulate renewal and development."

Targets, Resource Allocation, Initiatives, and Budgets

MANAGERS SHOULD USE their Balanced Scorecard to implement an integrated strategy and budgeting process. The organizational, team, and individual employee processes, described in Chapter 9, align human resources to the business unit's strategy. But this is not sufficient. The business must also align its financial and physical resources to the strategy. Long-run capital budgets, strategic initiatives, and annual discretionary expenses must all be directed to achieving ambitious targets for the objectives and measures on the business' scorecard.

We have found that four steps are needed to use the scorecard in an integrated long-range strategic planning and operational budgeting process (see Figure 10-1):

1. Set stretch targets. Managers should set ambitious targets for measures that all employees can accept and buy into. The cause-and-effect interrelationships in the scorecard help identify the critical drivers that will allow breakthrough performance on important outcome measures, particularly financial and customer ones.

2. Identify and rationalize strategic initiatives. The gaps between the ambitious targets set for scorecard measures and the current performance on those measures enable managers to set priorities for capital investments and action programs intended to close the gaps.

Figure 10-1 A Different Management System—Planning and Target Setting

Clarifying and Translating the Vision and Strategy

Communi-cating and Linking

Balanced Scorecard

Planning and Target Setting

Strategic Feedback and Learning

- Stretch targets are established and accepted
- Strategic initiatives are clearly identified
- Investments are determined by the strategy
- Annual budgets are linked to long-range plans

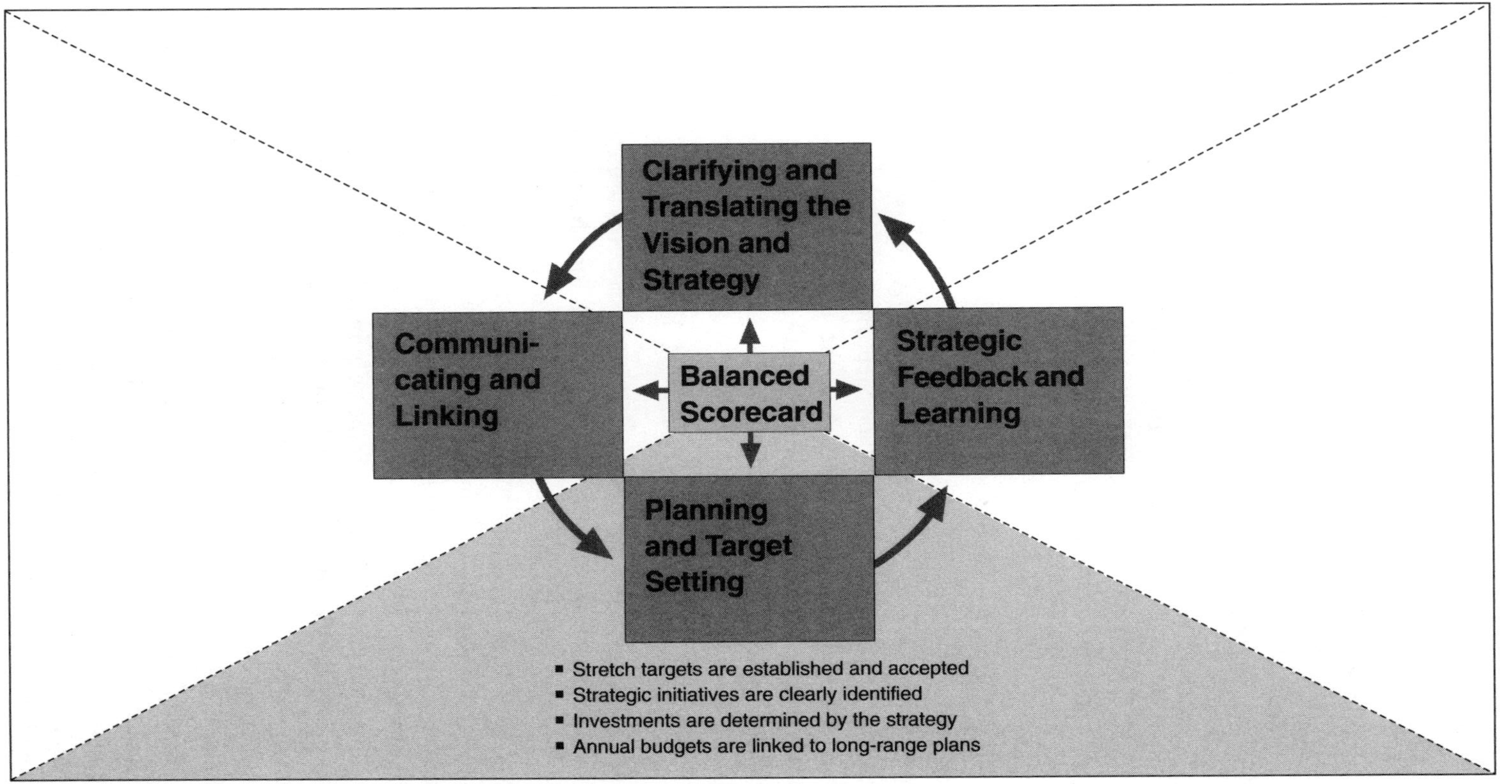

Managers eliminate or de-emphasize initiatives that will not have a major impact on one or more scorecard objectives.

3. Identify critical cross-business initiatives. Managers identify the initiatives that will deliver benefits (synergies) to the strategic objectives of other business units or the corporate parent.

4. Link to annual resource allocation and budgets. Managers link the three- to five-year strategic plan to discretionary expenses and budgeted performance (milestones) for the upcoming year. These milestones enable them to track the business unit's trajectory along its strategic journey.

This four-step process identifies the long-term outcomes the organization wishes to achieve. The outcomes include not only the measures that the organization wishes to improve but also explicit and ambitious targets for these measures. The process then identifies the mechanism by how these outcomes are to be achieved. And the unified planning and budgeting process concludes by establishing short-term milestones for the financial and nonfinancial measures on the scorecard.

SET STRETCH TARGETS

The Balanced Scorecard is most effective when it is used to drive organizational change. To communicate the need for change, managers should establish targets for the measures, three to five years out, that, if achieved, will transform the company. The targets should represent a discontinuity in business unit performance. For example, if the business unit were a public company, target achievement should lead to a doubling or more of the stock price. Typical financial targets have included doubling the return on invested capital, or a 150% increase in sales during the next five years. An electronics company set a financial target to increase sales at a rate nearly double the expected growth rate of its existing customers.

While most executives are not shy about setting stretch financial targets, the credibility of the targets is frequently questioned by those who must achieve them. Steve Kerr, described as the "chief learning officer" at General Electric, explains why many companies have difficulties with stretch targets: "It's popular today for companies to ask their people to double sales or increase speed-to-market threefold. But then they don't provide their people with the knowledge, tools, and means to meet such ambitious goals."[1]

The problem with most stretch-targeting exercises is that they are fragmented approaches that attempt to establish ambitious objectives for isolated issues or measures. Best-in-class benchmarking typifies this approach: make a concerted effort to study the performance of other organizations along a particular dimension, define those organizations' level of performance as a target, and develop a program to achieve that performance. While conceptually appealing, even if the organization achieves its ambitious objectives for isolated business processes, benchmarking may not lead to the desired breakthrough in future financial performance.

The Balanced Scorecard has proven to be a powerful tool to gain acceptance for aggressive targets because it stresses the linkages for achieving outstanding performance in related measures, not just improving performance in isolated measures. Consider the target-setting process used by the executive team of a high-tech engineering firm just after completing its first Balanced Scorecard. The CEO asked his team to develop an aggressive set of targets that, if achieved, "would make us proud and make our sister divisions envious." At an off-site workshop, the team split into four subgroups, one for each perspective of the scorecard. The customer/business development group, led by the vice president of marketing, proposed aggressive targets for new customer acquisition, average size of sale, and customer retention. The group concurred on the targets because of their newly formulated strategy for building customer partnerships. The service delivery group, headed by the vice president of operations, developed stretch targets for on-time, on-spec performance, reductions in rework, and higher quality and safety. The targets assumed the implementation of a dramatically improved project management process. The learning and growth group, led by the vice president of human resources, developed aggressive targets, based on employee-driven innovations, for cost reduction and customer-partnering initiatives. The staff innovations were expected to flow from greatly expanded employee empowerment that, in turn, would be driven by improved skill development and more open communications. The financial group, however, led by the chief financial officer, was not as aggressive. This group felt that profitability could be increased, but only by about 20%. The CFO resisted higher targets, because he did not want to commit his peers to stretch performance that they would have to deliver on. He felt that it was better to set low targets and hit them than to set high expectations and miss them.

After all the subgroup presentations at a plenary session, the CEO declared that the modest targets proposed by the financial group were unacceptable. The members of the other groups concurred with the CEO. Their opinions were well expressed by the vice president of operations: "If we are able to achieve the targets that we set for marketing, for innovation, and for customer service, the profitability will follow—and the increase will be enormous. We are committed to making these things happen. I will personally commit to doubling our profits." The executive team, in concert, agreed to a stretch target on profitability that would make the firm the industry leader. If the target had been set in isolation, no such consensus would have occurred. But every member of the executive team could now see that the drivers for future financial performance were in place and had the commitment of the entire executive team. The team unanimously concluded that breakthrough financial performance would result from these efforts.

The inclusion of performance drivers and lead indicators on the scorecard enables managers to identify the operational factors, such as strategic investments, market research, innovative products and services, reskilled employees, and enhanced information systems, that must be created if the ambitious financial targets are to be achieved. In our experience, operating executives often agree on stretch targets even beyond those requested by senior management, if they can be sure of having the investment, resources, and time to execute a long-term plan.

CEOs can motivate stretch targets for Balanced Scorecard measures by creating a performance gap in critical high-level financial objectives. For example, Figure 10-2 shows how one division of Kenyon Stores used the logic of the scorecard to become comfortable with what initially seemed an "impossible" target: double revenues during the next five years. Current plans were considerably short of this goal, creating a revenue gap of $1 billion. At first, the operating managers of the retail chain thought that closing this gap could not be done. But the CEO led the management team through scenario planning, based on the underlying cause-and-effect performance model (see Chapter 7) embedded in the Balanced Scorecard. This scenario-planning approach enabled the team to propose and test the feasibility of different strategies before agreeing to a final set of targets. The team systematically decomposed the revenue growth target into the increase required in:

- number of new stores,
- number of new customers attracted into each store,

Figure 10-2 Setting Stretch Targets Based on Cause and Effect at Kenyon Stores

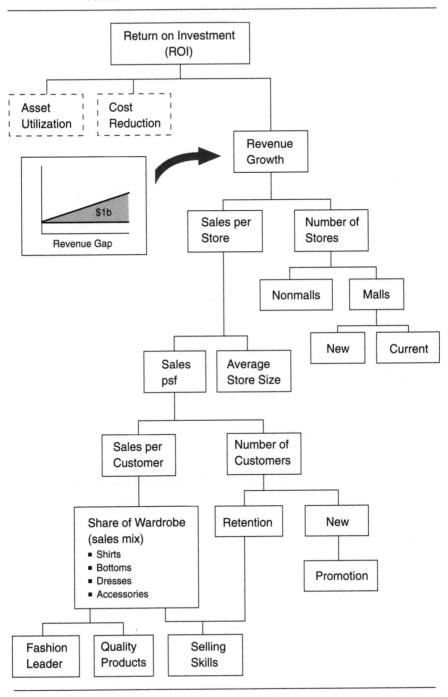

- percentage of shoppers in each store converted into actual purchasers,

- retention of existing customers, and

- average sales per customer.

Several scenarios were evaluated. One scenario assumed the division would keep the same mall-based real estate strategy. Under this scenario, the revenue growth target could only be achieved by having sales-per-square-foot more than 50% greater than anyone in the industry had ever achieved. No one was willing to commit to such an increase in this measure. In an alternative scenario, the team considered creating a new type of store that could be positioned in nontraditional locations. Upon further reflection and evaluation, the executive team felt this scenario was feasible and it became the foundation for a revised strategy that, at the end of the exercise, enabled the executive team to commit to the revenue growth target of a doubling, or more, of sales.

The scenario-planning process enabled a seemingly impossible objective to be decomposed into a series of smaller objectives that, taken together, would enable the revenue growth target to be achieved. By defining the key drivers for the revenue growth objective, and by committing to targets and initiatives for each driver, the managers agreed that they could reach the stretch target for revenue growth. Further, the scorecard provided a tool to monitor how well the strategy was being implemented.

IDENTIFY STRATEGIC INITIATIVES

Once targets for financial, customer, internal process, and learning and growth measures have been established, managers can assess whether current initiatives will help achieve these ambitious targets, or whether new initiatives are required. Currently, many organizations have a myriad of initiatives under way—for example, total quality management, time-based competition, employee empowerment, and reengineering.

Unfortunately, these initiatives are frequently not linked to achieving targeted improvement for strategic objectives. Thus, the efforts are managed independently, sponsored by different champions, and compete with each other for scarce resources, including the scarcest resource of all, senior management time and attention. When the Balanced Scorecard is used as the cornerstone of a company's management system, the various initiatives can be focused on achieving the organizational objectives, measures, and targets.

While the formulation and mobilization of initiatives to achieve stretch performance targets is largely a creative process, there are three ways in which a planning process, based on the Balanced Scorecard, can improve and channel this creativity:

1. The "missing measurement" program

2. Continuous improvement programs linked to rate-of-change metrics

3. Strategic initiatives, such as reengineering and transformation programs, linked to radical improvement in key performance drivers

The "Missing Measurement" Program

The first set of opportunities for performance improvement occurs immediately after the design of a Balanced Scorecard. We invariably discover that data are not available for at least 20% of the measures on the scorecard. Recall the discussion in Chapter 6 on the paucity of measures for employee development and reskilling. Here too, missing measurements are generally not a data problem. They reveal a management problem: "If you can't measure it, you can't manage it." If data do not exist to support a measure, the management process for a key strategic objective is likely to be inadequate or nonexistent.

As specific examples, the missing measures at National Insurance included such items as regulatory compliance, claims effectiveness, policyholder satisfaction, and competency levels. The missing measures at Metro Bank included deposit service cost, share of target market segment, service error rate, and competency levels. The missing measures at Pioneer Petroleum included customer retention, dealer quality, service quality, and technical competency. For each of these organizations, the missing measures indicated that managers were not currently able to manage several critical processes, now considered essential for strategic success.

For example, Metro's inability to measure deposit service cost meant that marketing managers could not determine if a customer relationship was profitable. The development of this measure led to extending its activity-based costing model from just measuring only product costs to measuring customer profitability. This initiative ultimately enabled Metro to restructure its prices and service offerings to more targeted market segments. National

Insurance's inability to measure claims effectiveness meant that it could not tailor its claims management process for the specialist niches in which it intended to operate. The lack of a customized claims management process was a barrier to National's entire strategy. To correct this gap, the company developed a new claims management approach that could be tailored to individual niches. Pioneer's inability to measure customer retention meant that its marketing managers could not effectively manage the market segmentation program. In developing the program to obtain this measure, Pioneer's managers also obtained mechanisms for collecting information about and monitoring targeted consumers' preferences.

In each of these cases, the missing measure was just the tip of the iceberg. Instituting a process to collect data for the measure led the organization to develop strategic initiatives that would not only gather relevant information but also facilitate better management of a critical internal process. Both factors are essential to superior performance.

Continuous Improvement Programs Linked to Rate-of-Change Metrics

Managers must determine whether their stretch targets can be achieved by continuous improvement, such as a total quality management approach to business processes, or whether they require discontinuous improvement, such as a reengineering or transformation program. The TQM approach works within existing processes and applies systematic problem solving to reduce and eventually eliminate defects in the processes (such as late deliveries, non-value-added time within the process cycle, defective products, process errors, and unskilled employees). A discontinuous or reengineering approach develops an entirely new method for accomplishing a process. It assumes that the existing process is flawed in a fundamental way, and requires an entire redesign to fix it.

If a continuous improvement approach is adopted, a rate-of-improvement metric should be used to track whether near-term efforts are on the right trajectory to achieve the ambitious long-term target. One example is the half-life metric developed at Analog Devices (see Chapter 6). The half-life measures how many months are required to reduce process defects by 50%. The metric assumes that when TQM teams are successfully applying formal quality improvement processes, they should be able to reduce defects at a constant rate (each 50% reduction in defects takes about the same number of months). By establishing the rate at which they expect defects to be eliminated from the system, managers can validate whether they are on a continuous improvement trajectory that will yield the desired performance over the specified time period.

One company, a producer of industrial commodities, used the half-life concept to develop an innovative measure. The continuous improvement index was based on eight, strategically important business process measures, including such items as:

- Customer complaint frequency
- Problem resolution period
- Safety incident rate
- Waste levels
- Not right first time percentage

For each factor, the company established a targeted rate-of-improvement, using the half-life philosophy, as well as action initiatives to achieve these improvements. The continuous improvement index measured the percentage of the eight strategic measures that were meeting or exceeding their targets for rates-of-improvement.

Strategic Initiatives Directed to Radical Improvement of Performance Drivers

Frequently, managers conclude that local problem solving to continuously improve critical processes will not enable the three- to five-year stretch targets to be achieved. This gap signals the need to develop and deploy entirely new ways of accomplishing these processes. Thus, the scorecard approach provides the front-end justification and focus for organizational reengineering and transformation. Rather than just apply fundamental process redesign to any local process, where gains might be easily obtained, managers develop or reengineer processes that will be critical for the organization's strategic success. And unlike conventional reengineering programs, where the objective is massive cost cutting (the slash and burn rationale), the objective for a reengineering or transformation program need not be measured by dollars saved. The targets for the strategic initiative can be dramatic time reductions in order fulfillment cycles, shorter time-to-market in product development processes, and enhanced employee capabilities. These nonfinancial targets can be used to justify and monitor strategic initiatives since the Balanced Scorecard has established the linkage of these measures to dramatic improvements in future financial performance.

Most important, when the power of the scorecard is used to drive reengineering and transformation programs, the organization can focus on the issues that create growth, not just those that reduce costs and increase efficiency. Again, the key ingredient for setting priorities for reengineering programs is the cause-and-effect relationships embedded in the Balanced Scorecard. Recall the example of National Insurance (described in Chapter 7), which developed a scorecard to clarify its new vision of becoming a specialist insurer. The Balanced Scorecard became the point of departure for reengineering the underwriting, claims management, and agency-management business processes.

Figure 10-3 illustrates how high-level scorecard measures led to developing a more detailed performance model for the underwriting process. The Underwriting Performance Model identified the factors in the underwriting process that contributed most heavily to the results desired on the Balanced Scorecard. For example, the scorecard outcome measure, loss ratio, was driven by three factors: account selection, accurate pricing, and reduced claims. These factors, in turn, were driven by whether the organization had the capabilities to learn about specific hazards and exposures. As illustrated in Figure 10-4, the Underwriting Performance Model generated the foundation of a Desktop System designed to support the underwriter in the field. Each outcome identified in the performance model generated specifications for the design of an information and work support system. The design specifications identified the more detailed knowledge and experience sharing that was fundamental to the new process design. The performance model, linked to the Balanced Scorecard, allowed the development of an information technology platform that was focused on the strategic objective—improve the underwriting process. The scorecard objective enabled National's executive team to invest in the long-term drivers, including significant investments in data acquisition and information technology, that would ultimately create financial success for the organization.

Conversely, companies should also review all their current initiatives to determine whether they are contributing to achievement of one or more scorecard objectives. For instance, shortly after the merger that created it,

Figure 10-3 National Insurance's Performance Measures Reflect Complex
Underlying Business Processes

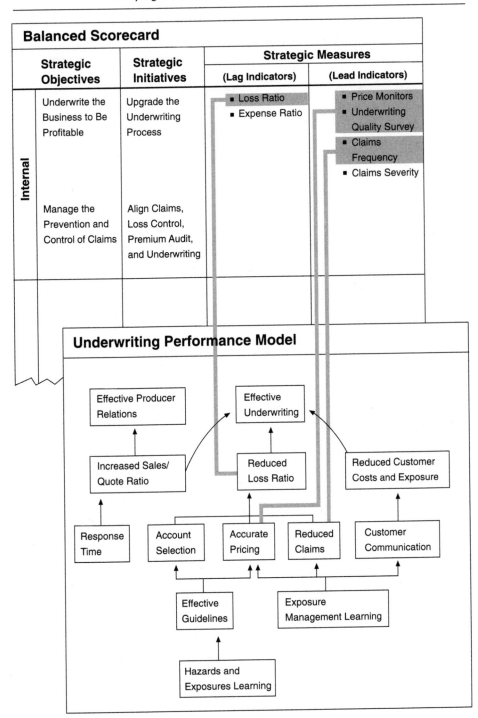

Figure 10-4 National Insurance's Business Transformation through a Structured Design Process

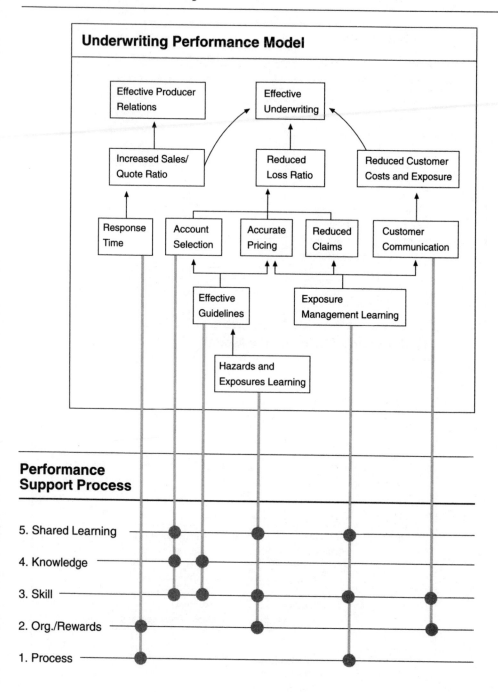

Figure 10-4 Continued

Balanced Scorecard

	Strategic Objectives	Strategic Initiatives	Strategic Measures	
			(Lag Indicators)	(Lead Indicators)
Internal	Underwrite the Business to Be Profitable	Upgrade the Underwriting Process	▪ Loss Ratio ▪ Expense Ratio	▪ Price Monitors ▪ Underwriting Quality Survey ▪ Claims Frequency ▪ Claims Severity
	Manage the Prevention and Control of Claims	Align Claims, Loss Control, Premium Audit, and Underwriting		

Desktop System Design

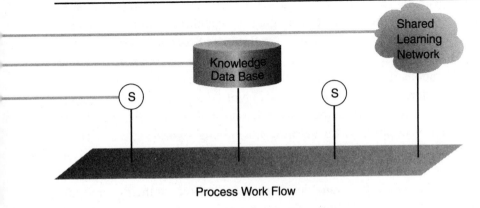

Process Work Flow

Metro Bank had launched more than 70 different action programs. Each was intended to produce a more competitive and successful institution, but none was integrated into an overall strategy. When building its Balanced Scorecard, Metro executives dropped or consolidated many of these action programs. For example, a marketing effort directed at very high net worth individuals was dropped as was a sales force operational improvement program aimed at enhancing existing low-level selling skills. Managers replaced the latter with a major reskilling program more aligned with the strategic objective to transform salespersons into trusted financial advisers, capable of cross-selling a broad range of newly introduced products.

Obviously, organizations should also link their investment decisions to their strategic plans. While this goal seems obvious and is part of the rhetoric of most strategic planning exercises, many organizations do not, in practice, link their investments to long-term strategic priorities.[2] The justification for most capital investments remains tied to narrow financial measures, such as payback and discounted cash flow and these financial metrics are not necessarily linked to developing strategic capabilities, or even tactical improvements in nonfinancial variables, such as quality, customer satisfaction, and organizational and employee skills.[3]

Senior executives deny that they rely exclusively on financial metrics for capital investment decisions. They contend that formal discounted cash flow analysis is only part of a more complex resource-allocation process. They claim to recognize that the impact of an investment on competitors, the organization, and the capital markets may exceed the importance of DCF calculations.[4] Yet most organizations continue to allocate resources using incremental, tactical capital-budgeting mechanisms that stress easily quantified financial measures of near-term cash flows. They do not formally incorporate the development of long-term capabilities into their resource allocation processes and decisions. The Balanced Scorecard overcomes this gap by providing executives with a mechanism to incorporate strategic considerations into the resource allocation process.

For example, one organization (see Figure 10-5) now uses its scorecard measures to assess the impact of each potential investment. A relative weighting is established for the measures, giving significant emphasis to financial measures, such as return-on-capital and profitability, but also to the drivers of future financial performance, such as quality, service, and customer retention. Individual investments are ranked on their overall impact on the scorecard formula. The top-ranked investments that fit within the available capital budget are selected.

Chem-Pro, a manufacturer of polymer-based industrial products, used a variation of this approach to rationalize its strategic investments. Chem-Pro's senior executives believed that investment opportunities should not be a series of independent, stand-alone projects that must be evaluated and justified one by one, using traditional financial criteria. Rather, they recognized that to achieve strategic objectives, several linked programs must be initiated, each focused on a different but related factor. Chem-Pro's Balanced Scorecard identified five strategic initiatives necessary to execute its strategy (see Figure 10-6). For each initiative, the drivers of performance were made explicit. As shown in Figure 10-7, one strategic initiative—increase sales and marketing effectiveness—consisted of nine action programs, each one targeted at a particular driver to increase sales and marketing efficiency. A traditional capital budgeting approach would evaluate each program independently. Many might be considered discretionary expense programs that would require funding from current year operating budgets, not from a budget dedicated to achieving long-term strategic objectives. Managers, operating under a traditional evaluation process, would be unlikely to see the cumulative impact from investing in the entire package of linked initiatives, and, indeed, many of the individual programs would fail in the operating and capital budgeting review process.

Figure 10-5 The Capital Budgeting Process Using Balanced Scorecard Criteria

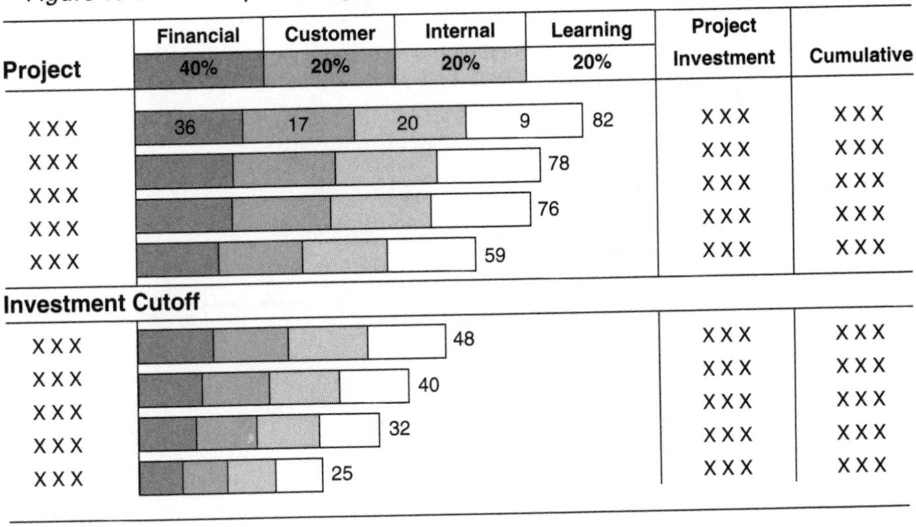

Project	Financial 40%	Customer 20%	Internal 20%	Learning 20%		Project Investment	Cumulative
XXX	36	17	20	9	82	XXX	XXX
XXX					78	XXX	XXX
XXX					76	XXX	XXX
XXX						XXX	XXX
XXX					59	XXX	XXX
Investment Cutoff							
XXX					48	XXX	XXX
XXX					40	XXX	XXX
XXX					32	XXX	XXX
XXX						XXX	XXX
XXX					25	XXX	XXX

Figure 10-6 Chem-Pro's Scorecard and Strategic Initiatives

The Mission

"We will help our customers be the best by providing world-class services and we will use our expertise to help us win in the marketplace."

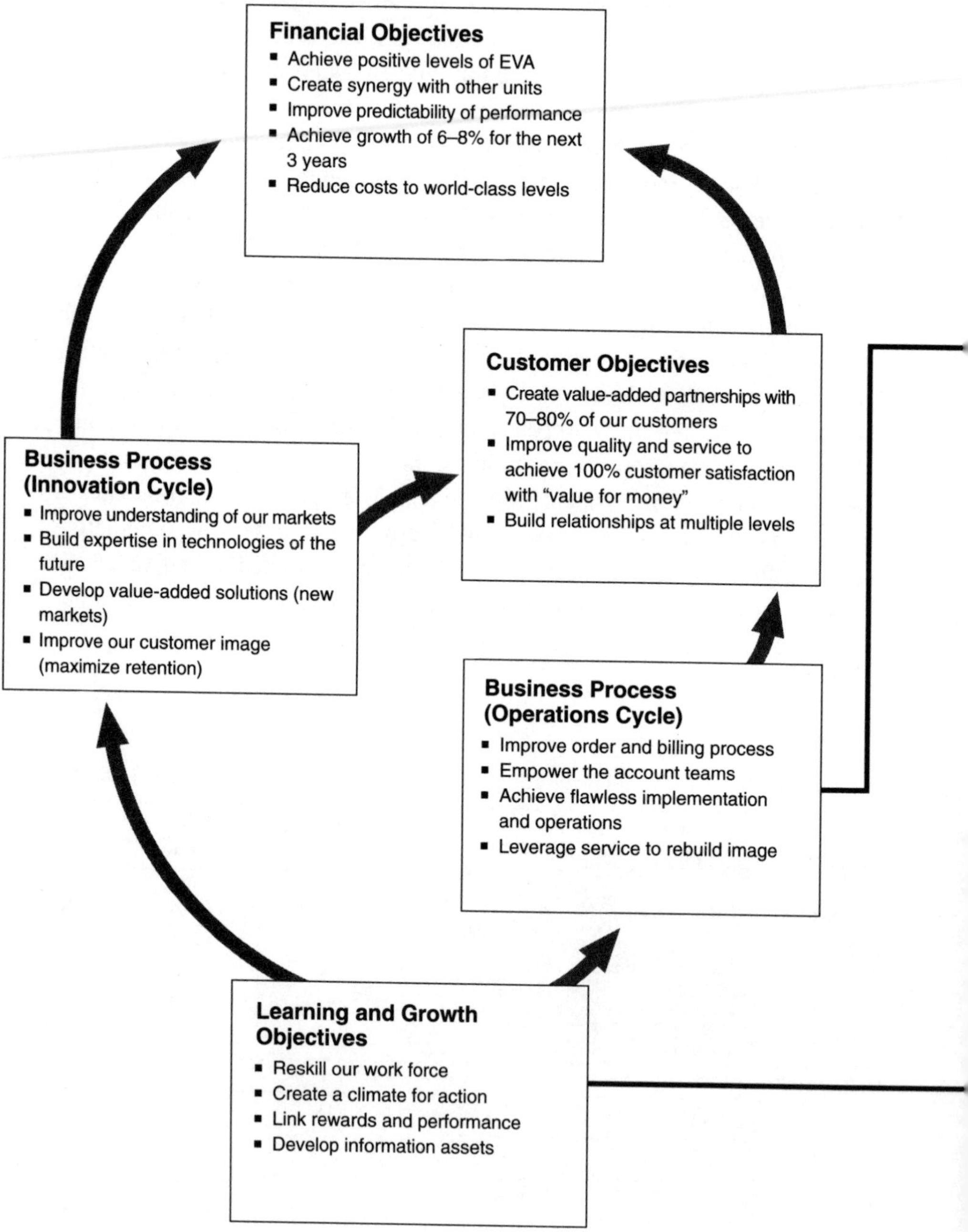

Financial Objectives
- Achieve positive levels of EVA
- Create synergy with other units
- Improve predictability of performance
- Achieve growth of 6–8% for the next 3 years
- Reduce costs to world-class levels

Customer Objectives
- Create value-added partnerships with 70–80% of our customers
- Improve quality and service to achieve 100% customer satisfaction with "value for money"
- Build relationships at multiple levels

Business Process (Innovation Cycle)
- Improve understanding of our markets
- Build expertise in technologies of the future
- Develop value-added solutions (new markets)
- Improve our customer image (maximize retention)

Business Process (Operations Cycle)
- Improve order and billing process
- Empower the account teams
- Achieve flawless implementation and operations
- Leverage service to rebuild image

Learning and Growth Objectives
- Reskill our work force
- Create a climate for action
- Link rewards and performance
- Develop information assets

Figure 10-6 Continued

Strategic Initiatives

1. Development Cycle

Improve the business development cycle in order to achieve 75% of our revenues from value-added partnerships and drive annual revenue growth of 15% by 1998.

2. Account Management/Selling

Dramatically improve the sales and marketing process in order to achieve sales growth that exceeds market growth by 2% and adds 5 points of margin by 1998.

3. Order and Billing Management

Develop a reliable order tracking and billing process that will reduce lost revenue to 1%, reduce the error rate to 1%, reduce the cost per order by 50%, and dramatically improve customer satisfaction.

4. Staff Skills

Develop the skills of our staff such that 100% of 1998 strategic requirements are in place.

5. Information Assets

Develop the customer and performance databases necessary to support the strategy.

The strategic initiative approach used by Chem-Pro ensured that the full complement of programs required to achieve dramatic improvements in future performance would be in place. As the first part of the planning process, all capital budgeting and discretionary expense programs were identified. Only those that supported a strategic initiative were approved. Chem-Pro managers had initially proposed many spending programs that were unrelated to achieving strategic objectives. This first screen eliminated more than 40% of these proposals. A second pass, evaluating the impact of the survivors on the strategic targets, eliminated another 10% of the spending programs. The process also revealed gaps, where no investment programs had been proposed to achieve the ambitious targets for some of

Figure 10-7   Chem-Pro's Account Management/Selling Strategic Initiative

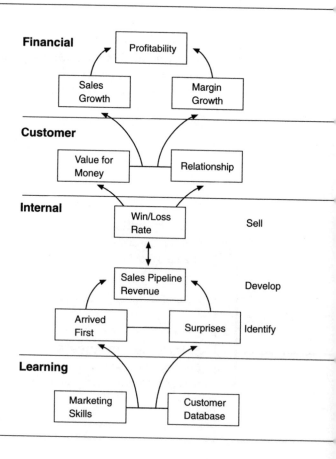

Strategic Initiative:
Dramatically improve the sales and marketing process in order to achieve sales growth that exceeds market growth by 2% and adds 5 points of margin by 1998

the Balanced Scorecard objectives. Identifying these gaps led to several new initiatives being funded. Chem-Pro used its scorecard as the focal point for all of its discretionary expense and capital investment decisions. After seeing this process function for the first time, one member of the executive committee said: "In the past, we had unfocused activities occurring everywhere. It was like 'a thousand points of light.' The activities made us a little better off but a lot of effort was counterproductive and much of it was not cumulative. The Balanced Scorecard is like a prism through which all of our investments are focused. Instead of a thousand points of light, we now have a laser. All of our energies are directed at a critical few targets."

Figure 10-7 Continued

Objective	Measurement	Target	Action Program
Exceed market growth Profitable growth	Sales growth Margin growth	Market growth + 2% +5 points in 3 years	
Perceived value for money Relationships at multiple levels	Customer survey # contacts with targeted sponsors	Rated #1 by 75% 100%	Focus Group Program Account Penetration Program
Maximize retention Develop regional markets Identify profitable new markets	Win/loss rate Potential revenue in sales pipeline # potential customers arrived first # surprises	Exceed 60% in targeted segments Increase by 30% Double current # in 2 years Reduce by 50% in 2 years	Critical Opportunity Sales Support Reference Sell Program Pull Marketing and Image Program Target Marketing Program
Develop marketing skills Develop customer database	Percent of strategic skills available Percent of customers with key attributes known	100% in 2 years 80% in 2 years	Selling Skills Program Customer Database Sales Learning System

Once the Balanced Scorecard has articulated the strategy and identified the drivers for accomplishing the strategy, companies can:

- identify new strategic initiatives;
- focus a multitude of strategic initiatives—continuous improvement, reengineering, and transformation programs; and
- align investment and discretionary spending programs

to close the gap between ambitious three- to five-year targets for critical scorecard measures and current performance levels. It is this process that most clearly mobilizes the scorecard to translate strategy into action.

Identify Critical Cross-Business and Corporate Initiatives

An important element in the planning process is to identify the linkages of the strategic business unit to other SBUs in the corporation and to functional activities done at the corporate level. The linkage to other SBUs provides opportunities for mutually reinforcing action and sharing of best practices. These opportunities include developing and sharing knowledge about critical technologies and core competencies, coordinating marketing efforts to common customers, and sharing production and distribution resources where significant economies of scale or scope exist. One of the important corporate-level functions is to provide mechanisms whereby such opportunities for synergy across decentralized SBUs can be identified and exploited. The Balanced Scorecard provides such a mechanism.

For example, Figure 10-8 shows how Kenyon Stores used the scorecard to coordinate strategic planning and action for its individual operating companies. The corporate scorecard defined the common strategic priorities for all the operating companies. Each SBU then developed its own strategy and Balanced Scorecard, in which the corporate agenda was tailored to its specific circumstances. Kenyon's centralized support functions could then build on the scorecards of the individual operating companies to develop their own strategic plans and initiatives that would service the objectives of individual SBUs and also achieve the economy-of-scale operations that justified a centralized resource. For example, the operating company SBUs all leased real estate in malls around the country. Since real estate was not a differentiator for each operating company, the corporation established a central real estate department that developed expertise in identifying outstanding locations and in contracting with real estate developers and shopping-mall management groups. The real estate department deployed its considerable experience to the benefit and individual needs of each SBU.

The coordination process, facilitated by the information exchange via corporate, SBU, and support department Balanced Scorecards, enabled the real estate department to identify where leases could be transferred across operating company SBUs; for example, when one SBU was

Figure 10-8 Using the Balanced Scorecard to Manage Cross-Business Synergies

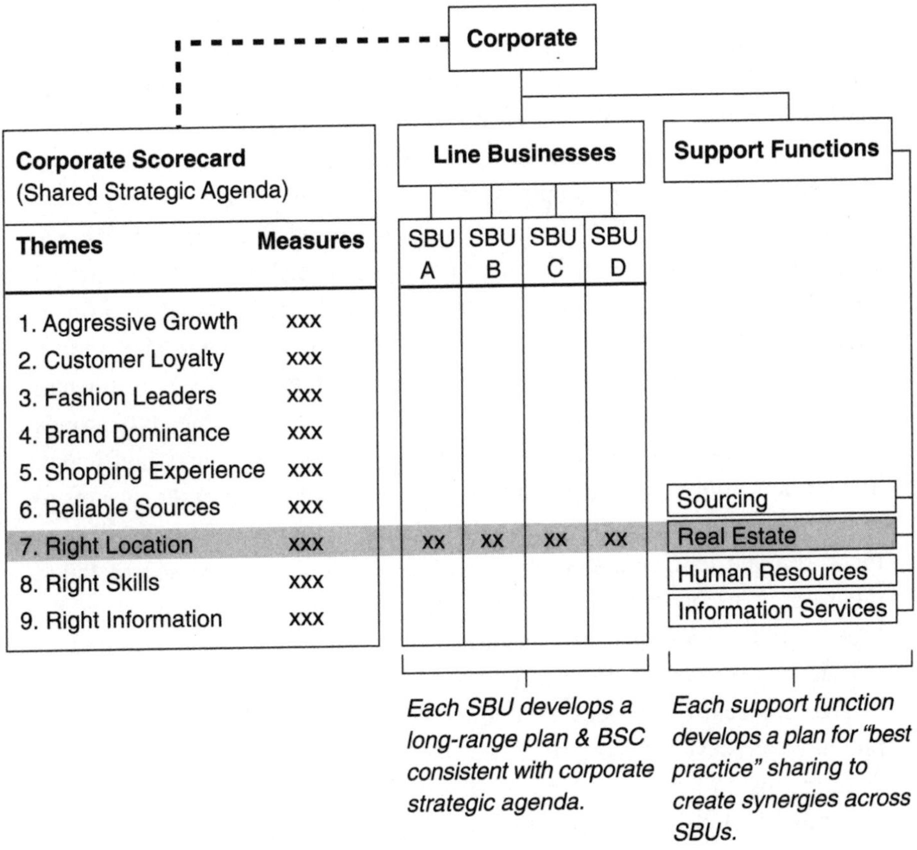

Corporate Scorecard (Shared Strategic Agenda)		Line Businesses				Support Functions
Themes	**Measures**	SBU A	SBU B	SBU C	SBU D	
1. Aggressive Growth	xxx					
2. Customer Loyalty	xxx					
3. Fashion Leaders	xxx					
4. Brand Dominance	xxx					
5. Shopping Experience	xxx					
6. Reliable Sources	xxx					Sourcing
7. Right Location	xxx	xx	xx	xx	xx	Real Estate
8. Right Skills	xxx					Human Resources
9. Right Information	xxx					Information Services

Each SBU develops a long-range plan & BSC consistent with corporate strategic agenda.

Each support function develops a plan for "best practice" sharing to create synergies across SBUs.

contracting stores in an area, another SBU was growing in the same area. While such coordination could, theoretically, have been done in the past, in practice, information sharing about the individual SBU strategies was not sufficiently detailed to accomplish such cross-SBU coordination. The explicit articulation of multiyear objectives and initiatives through the Balanced Scorecards enabled corporate support departments to deliver dramatically better service to the operating company SBUs.

Other companies are also using their balanced scorecards to force their corporate-level functions to become more efficient and more customer focused. As discussed in Chapter 8, Larry Brady of FMC Corporation has queried his staff departments about their strategy. Are they being retained because they are lower cost than external suppliers of the service or relative to smaller groups that could be located within each operating company? Or are the groups retained at the corporate level because they offer unique or superior services that could not be obtained from outside suppliers, or from decentralized groups in the operating companies? If the centrally supplied service is not offering lower cost, unique products, or superior service, the theory for having a corporate-level group supplying this service evaporates.

Similarly, Pioneer Petroleum used a structured approach to achieve cross-functional integration. Pioneer knew that it had to break a historical culture of staff unit domination of the business. It realized that significant economies of scale resulted from the shared management and supply of certain issues like franchise development, advertising, environmental performance, and safety programs. The problem was that the staff groups had lost touch with the market and had become costly and inefficient. To reorient the business, Pioneer required each corporate group to develop a "service agreement" that defined the relationship between the group and its customers, the operating SBUs. The agreement detailed the service to be provided to the SBU, as well as its cost, response time, and level of quality. The service agreement was incorporated in a Balanced Scorecard for the corporate-level staff group.

The scorecard provides a common framework for organizing the planning process of corporate support departments. It enables these departments to understand the strategies of the entire corporation and the individual SBUs so that the support departments can develop and deliver better services that help the operating units and corporation achieve their strategic objectives.

Link to Annual Resource Allocation and Budgets

Currently, most organizations have separate processes and separate organizational units for strategic planning and for operational budgeting. The strategic planning process—such as the process that defines long-range plans, targets, and strategic initiatives discussed so far in this chapter—operates on an annual cycle. In the middle of each fiscal year, senior executives go off-site, for several days, to engage in active discussion, facilitated by senior planning and development managers, and, occasionally, external consultants. The outcome from this exercise is a strategic plan for where the company expects (or hopes, or prays) to be in three, five, and ten years. Typically, these expectations are codified into documents that sit on executive bookshelves for the next 12 months.

Ongoing throughout the year is a separate budgeting process, run by the finance staff, to set financial targets for revenues, expenses, profits, and investments for the next fiscal year. This process culminates in month 10 or 11 of the year with an approved budget for the upcoming year. The budget consists almost entirely of financial numbers, typically bearing little relationship to the five-year targets in the now-hibernating strategic plan.

Which document gets discussed during the next year when business unit and corporate managers meet monthly and quarterly? Usually only the budget, as the periodic reviews focus on comparison of actual with budgeted results, line item by line item, with explanations demanded for large variances. When is the strategic plan discussed? Probably during the next off-site annual strategic planning meeting, when new three-, five-, and ten-year plans are formulated.

Strategic planning and operational budgeting processes are too important to be treated as independent processes. Strategic planning must be linked to operational budgeting if action is to be tied to vision. The targeting process described earlier in this chapter sets aspirations for what the business unit must achieve for breakthrough performance in the strategic measures in the four scorecard perspectives. Resources and initiatives are deployed to start the journey, to close the gap between current performance and the stretch targets to be achieved during the next three to five years. But managers cannot wait for three to five years to determine whether their strategy, their theory of the business, is valid. They need to continually test both the theory underlying the strategy and how the strategy is being implemented. A necessary condition for such testing is the formulation of specific short-term targets for the scorecard measures. These short-term targets, or milestones, are the tangible expression of managers' beliefs about the speed and impact of current programs and initiatives on strategic measures.

In effect, this process expands the traditional budgeting process to incorporate strategic as well as operational targets. Traditionally, the annual budgeting process establishes detailed short-term targets for financial measures, such as sales, operating expenses, gross margin, general and administrative expenses, operating margin, net profit, cash flow, and return on investment. It also establishes and authorizes spending levels for capital investments, research and development, and for marketing and promotional activities. Such detailed, short-term financial planning remains important, but the budgeting process should encompass, as well, expected short-term performance on the strategic objectives and measures of the other three scorecard perspectives. That is, as part of the integrated planning and budgeting process, executives should establish short-term targets for where they expect to be, monthly or quarterly, on the outcome and performance driver measures for customers and consumers, innovation, operational processes, as well as employees, systems, and organizational alignment. These milestones, for the upcoming year, establish the expectations for the short-term achievements along the long-term strategic path the organization has chosen.

If the target-setting process of the long-range plan is conducted appropriately, the short-term budgeting process simply involves translating the first year of a five-year plan into operational budgets for strategic objectives and measures in the four scorecard perspectives.

SUMMARY

The processes described in this chapter—planning, targeting, aligning resource allocation and strategic initiatives, and budgeting—are critical if lofty and ambitious strategic objectives are to be translated into actions and reality. For many companies, the scorecard process emphasizes the early stage of the new management process: translating vision and strategy into objectives and measures that can be communicated to participants internal and external to the organization. Unless, however, real resources are directed toward achieving these objectives, the objectives will remain distant goals, not tangible targets to which the organization is committed. By establishing long-term targets for the strategic measures, by directing strategic initiatives and significant resources toward achieving them, and by specifying short-term milestones along the strategic path, managers become committed to and accountable for achieving the organizational vision.

NOTES

1. S. Sherman, "Stretch Goals: The Dark Side of Asking for Miracles," *Fortune* (November 13, 1995), 231–232.
2. C. Y. Baldwin and K. B. Clark, "Capital-Budgeting Systems and Capabilities Investments in U.S. Companies after the Second World War," *Business History Review* (Spring 1994): 73–109.
3. Ibid.; and R. S. Kaplan, "Must CIM Be Justified by Faith Alone," *Harvard Business Review* (March–April 1986): 87–97; R. L. Hayes and D. A. Garvin, "Managing as If Tomorrow Mattered," *Harvard Business Review* (May–June 1982): 71–79.
4. G. Donaldson, *Managing Corporate Wealth: The Operation of a Comprehensive Financial Goals System* (New York: Basic Books, 1984).

Chapter Eleven

Feedback and the Strategic Learning Process

IN PREVIOUS CHAPTERS, we described:

- how a business strategy can be articulated as a set of hypotheses about cause-and-effect relationships among scorecard measures (Chapter 7),

- how execution of the strategy is enhanced when human resources are committed to and aligned with the strategy (Chapter 9), and

- how the organization's strategic initiatives and financial and physical resources should all be linked to the strategy (Chapter 10).

These actions are consistent with a clear formulation of a strategy and its translation into action. One final element, however, must be added to have a complete strategic management system: a process of feedback, analysis, and reflection that tests and adapts the strategy to emerging conditions.

FROM COMMAND AND CONTROL TO STRATEGIC LEARNING

Many companies still retain the hierarchical planning and control systems designed for industrial age competition. Strategy is determined at the top as senior executives establish long-term objectives, policies, and resource deployment.[1] They then order lower-level managers and employees to act according to these plans. The executives and managers use a management control system to monitor the acquisition and use of resources in accordance with the strategic plan. And further down the organization, operational control systems monitor the short-term performance of specific operational processes and front-line employees.

This hierarchical approach to strategy formulation and implementation works fine when senior executives have a clear vision of organizational destination and the actions that must be taken to reach that destination. It is a single-loop feedback process in which the objective has already been determined and will not change. Departures from planned results do not cause people to question whether the planned results are still the desirable outcomes. Nor do they question whether the methods used to accomplish the planned objectives are still appropriate. Departures from the planned trajectory are treated as defects, with remedial actions launched to bring the organization back to the intended path.

The strategies for today's information-age organizations, however, cannot be this linear or stable. Senior managers need feedback about more complicated strategies and more turbulent competitive environments. The planned strategy, though initiated with the best of intentions and with the best available information, may no longer be appropriate or valid for contemporary conditions.

Organizations need the capacity for double-loop learning, the learning that occurs when managers question their assumptions and reflect on whether the theory under which they were operating is still consistent with current evidence, observations, and experience.[2] They need, on occasion, to be able to devise new strategies to capitalize on new opportunities, or to counter new threats that were not anticipated when the initial strategic plan was articulated. Frequently, ideas for seizing new opportunities come from managers further down in the organization. Mintzberg and Simons identify key aspects of this newer or emergent view of strategy:[3]

- Strategies are incremental and emerge over time
- Intended strategies can be superseded
- Strategy formulation and implementation are intertwined
- Strategic ideas can arise throughout the organization
- A strategy is a process

In practice, of course, both the hierarchical and emergent views of strategy formulation and implementation co-exist. Day by day organizational participants implement previously formulated plans. But they should be alert for opportunities to capitalize on changes among customers, markets, technology, and competitors. Management processes built around the strategy articulated in the Balanced Scorecard must provide regular opportunities for double-loop learning—by collecting data about the strategy, testing the strategy, reflecting on whether the strategy is still appropriate in light of recent developments, and soliciting ideas throughout the organization about new strategic opportunities and directions.

TOWARD A STRATEGIC LEARNING PROCESS

Many organizations today are reengineering several of their critical business processes. Their efforts tend to focus on improving operational processes, such as product development, customer service, and product delivery. They are also applying learning at the operational level, for individuals and teams.[4] Improving existing operations to achieve prespecified strategic goals is a good example of single-loop learning. But companies are starting to use the Balanced Scorecard to extend their operational and management review processes into a strategic learning process, which extends single-loop operational learning to double-loop strategic learning at the management team and SBU level (see Figure 11-1).

An effective strategic learning process has three essential ingredients:

1. a shared strategic framework that communicates the strategy and allows each participant to see how his or her activities contribute to achievement of the overall strategy;

2. a feedback process that collects performance data about the strategy and allows the hypotheses about interrelationships among strategic objectives and initiatives to be tested; and

3. a team problem-solving process that analyzes and learns from the performance data and then adapts the strategy to emerging conditions and issues.

SHARED STRATEGIC FRAMEWORK

The Balanced Scorecard is, as we have discussed throughout this book, a representation of the organization's shared vision. The scorecard's objectives and measures clarify and communicate this vision to mobilize and

Figure 11-1   A Different Management System—Strategic Feedback and Learning

Clarifying and Translating the Vision and Strategy

Communi-cating and Linking

Balanced Scorecard

Planning and Target Setting

Strategic Feedback and Learning

- Feedback system used to test the hypotheses on which strategy is based
- Team problem solving
- Strategy development is a continuous process

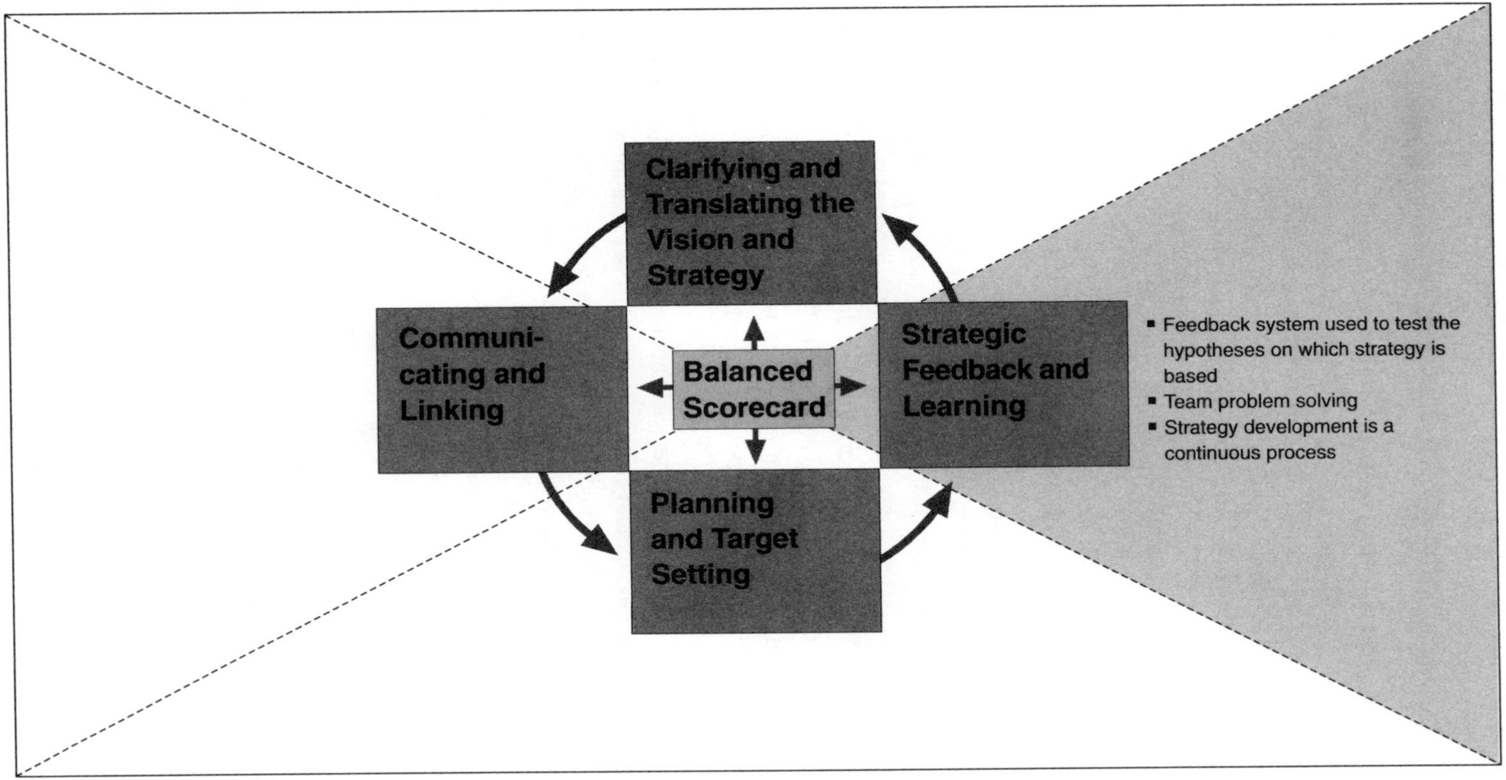

focus the organization. Having a shared vision is an essential starting point for the strategic learning process because it defines, in clear and operational terms, the results that the whole organization is attempting to achieve. Beyond a shared vision, the balanced scorecard establishes a common model of performance, and communicates a holistic approach to linking individual efforts and accomplishments to business unit objectives. The shared vision and shared performance model, structured around the Balanced Scorecard, provides the first element for a strategic learning process.

STRATEGIC FEEDBACK

A strategic feedback system should be designed to test, validate, and modify the hypotheses embedded in a business unit strategy. The cause-and-effect relationships embodied in a Balanced Scorecard enable executives to establish short-term targets that reflect their best forecast about the lags and impacts between changes in performance drivers and the associated changes in one or more outcome measures. For example, how much time will it take until improvements in employee training and information system availability enable employees to cross-sell multiple financial products to an expanded customer base? What is the impact of a 10% improvement in on-time delivery on customer satisfaction? How long is the delay between quality improvements and increases in customer retention?

Obviously, specifying such relationships is easier said than done. Initially, these impacts must be assessed subjectively and qualitatively. But just getting managers to think systematically about their strategy will be an improvement over the exclusive focus in most management review systems on operational-level processes. The following approaches have been used to promote strategic learning.

Correlation Analysis

Instead of simply reporting information on each scorecard measure, on an independent, stand-alone basis, managers can help validate hypothesized cause-and-effect relationships by measuring the correlation between two or more measures. Correlations among these variables provide powerful confirmation of the business unit's strategy. If hypothesized correlations are not found over time, the organization has evidence that the theory underlying its strategy is not working.

Consider the experience of Echo Engineering, as illustrated in Figure 11-2. Many organizations measure employee morale, but often only to be politically correct, as a "warm, fuzzy" measure, to demonstrate that even large corporations value their employees. But for investments in employee capabilities, skills, and individual goal alignment to be sustained for ex-

Figure 11-2   Echo Engineering—Linking Measures from the Four Perspectives

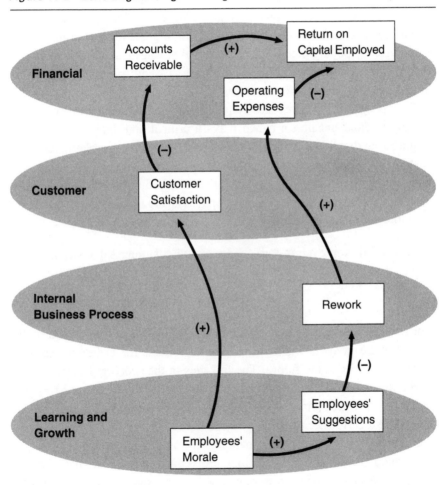

Source: Robert S. Kaplan and David P. Norton, "Using the Balanced Scorecard as a Strategic Management System," *Harvard Business Review* (January–February 1996): 83. Reprinted with permission.

tended periods of time, employee-based measures must be something more than warm fuzzies. More tangible benefits should be forthcoming. Indeed, through a correlation analysis, Echo Engineering discovered that its most satisfied customers were the ones served by the employees who scored highest in morale. Thus, employee morale was not something that had to be justified for its own sake; it was a necessary ingredient for Echo's strategy to be successful.

But, cynics contend, correlating employee morale with customer satisfaction just correlates an internal warm fuzzy and an external one. Real corporations, they argue, need profits and return-on-capital, not just happy employees and satisfied customers. After all, organizations can have loyal employees by paying them higher-than-market wages, and they can delight their customers by offering rock-bottom prices and many valued but un-priced delivery and support services.

That is where the scorecard requirement that all measures eventually link up to financial performance plays a critical and decisive role. Echo Engineering discovered a further correlation, an inverse correlation between customer satisfaction and the length of the accounts receivable cycle. The most satisfied customers paid their bills within 15 days, while dissatisfied customers often took up to 120 days to pay. The organization had discovered an entire sequence of linkages (as illustrated in Figure 11-2):

Improved employee morale → Increased customer satisfaction

→ Lower accounts receivable

→ Higher return-on-capital-employed.

Thus, employee morale did not have to be justified as a noble and paternalistic corporate goal. It was a necessary ingredient for achieving superior financial returns in the future. The linkages in the scorecard demonstrated a "hard" benefit (higher return-on-capital-employed) from improvements in "soft" measures (employee morale and customer satisfaction). Analyses like these clearly focus thinking on the necessary performance drivers for the strategy to deliver higher financial returns.

As another example of correlations across the four scorecard perspectives, the service profit chain[5] was developed after extensive research on the factors that drive highly successful service organizations, such as Progressive Corporation (insurance), Southwest Airlines, MCI, and Taco Bell. As shown in Figure 11-3, the service profit chain can be viewed as a generic Balanced Scorecard. It shows the explicit linkages between employee-based

Figure 11-3 The Service Profit Chain

Operating Strategy and Service Delivery System

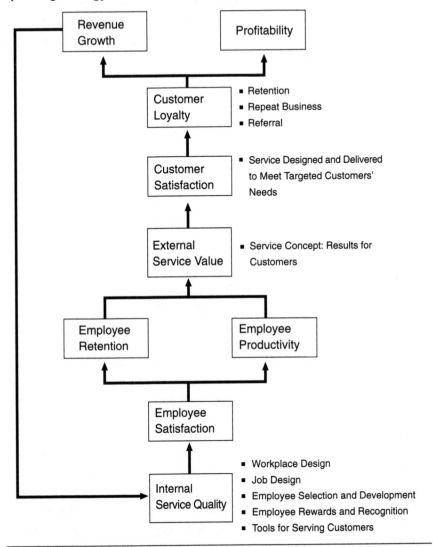

Source: James L. Heskett, Thomas O. Jones, Gary W. Loveman, W. Earl Sasser, and Leonard A. Schlesinger, "Putting the Service-Profit Chain to Work," *Harvard Business Review* (March–April 1994): 166. Reprinted with permission.

measures and internal and external service quality, with both employee and service quality (internal business process) measures driving improvements in customer satisfaction and customer loyalty. Satisfied and loyal customers, in turn, drive improved financial performance (revenue growth and profitability), which provides a feedback loop to further investments in employees and systems. Research on high-performing service companies has identified strong, often statistically significant, correlations between the elements in the service profit chain:

Employee satisfaction and capabilities $\leftrightarrow$ Excellent internal processes

$\leftrightarrow$ Satisfied and loyal customers

$\rightarrow$ Higher financial performance.

Management Gaming/Scenario Analysis

Senior managers at one organization used their hypothesized scorecard linkages as an innovative way to advance organizational strategic learning. On the first anniversary of the scorecard's implementation, but prior to updating the model for the subsequent year, management scheduled a two-day off-site meeting. Analysts had developed a management game based on the linkage model in the Balanced Scorecard. Statistical data from the previous year were compiled, stressing the correlations between critical variables. The management team was first asked to evaluate the previous year's strategy and identify any fatal flaws in it. If results were not being achieved on scorecard measures, the managers had to determine the likely causes. For example, was the external environment different from that anticipated when the strategy was formulated? Had important drivers been omitted from the model? Based on this analysis, the team was asked to construct an improved strategy for moving forward. The Balanced Scorecard was the basis for a management game simulation that quantified the new strategic scenarios. After the exercise, the managers agreed that the simulation analysis had renewed and stimulated their thinking about the drivers of strategic success.

Anecdotal Reporting

Often, and especially for large organizations, much time must elapse before sufficient data and evidence accumulate to obtain statistically significant conclusions about correlation and causation among the scorecard measures. To achieve statistical significance, performance may have to be embedded deeply into the core of the organization, perhaps for an extended period of time. While statistical significance and validity are important goals, a strategic learning system should provide early indications as to whether the strategy is working. Such early indicators may be found in small, perhaps isolated, examples.

For example, as Rockwater attempted to shift its marketing strategy toward Tier 1 customer partnerships, rather than Tier 2 price-driven business, managers constantly supplemented their quantitative performance reports with stories about strategic relationships with new customers—how they had been established and what lessons could be learned from the relationships. As Metro Bank shifted its marketing strategy toward cross-selling new financial products to targeted customer segments, the company newsletter cited examples, each month, about how a salesperson had succeeded in building a new customer relationship, emphasizing techniques used and benefits achieved. National Insurance constantly supplemented performance reports with stories of its agents becoming successful specialists. By telling the stories behind the numbers, these companies were getting informal feedback that the strategy was working, as well as helping educate the organization on the intention and specific details of the strategy. In this way, the organizations were able to use past experiences to influence future performance.

Initiative Review

In Chapter 10, we discussed the importance of identifying and funding the strategic initiatives that will enable an organization to achieve stretch targets for its scorecard measures. These initiatives should be reviewed during the strategic learning process. Such a periodic and comprehensive review will signal all managers that progress on the initiatives is continually being assessed. This knowledge should help keep the organization focused on implementing the initiatives and assessing whether they are still expected to lead to achievement of the ambitious targets.

For example, Figure 11-4 illustrates a group of typical strategic initiatives and the measures that they were intended to improve. In general, a one-to-one correspondence between initiative and measure will not exist. Rather, a set of programs may be required to achieve a set of outcomes. In this

Figure 11-4 Stretch Targets, Initiatives, and Accountability

Strategic Objective	Measure	Target	Initiatives	Accountable
Image Building Expand our image from successful private label to mature brand that is clearly defined by the customer	New Accounts Opened	97 – 100 98 – 115 99 – 150	Media Promotion Program Credit Card Expansion	RMN DPK
	Ever Active (%)	97 – 100 98 – 105 99 – 115	Card Usage Program	MSF

example, a combination of media advertising, acquisition of new credit-card customers, and expansion of credit card use were needed to affect the outcome measures, new accounts opened and percentage of active accounts. When the initiatives were chosen, managers selected those expected to have the greatest impact and dropped those with perceived lesser potential. Similar judgmental decisions must be made when assessing the impact of the initiatives. Typically, anecdotes provide the first evidence that the investments are bearing fruit. By continually evaluating the impact of the initiatives on the measures, managers further enhance their understanding of the cause-and-effect relationships of their business strategy.

Peer Review

Another effective mechanism for learning is to gain perspective from independent outsiders. HI-Tek, a manufacturer of electronic components, was using its scorecard program to improve organizational alignment. After a year, most of the bugs had been worked out of the program and the monthly scorecard review had become part of the normal management process. HI-Tek's CEO, however, was concerned that the monthly meetings were losing their strategic perspective. To counter the drift toward routine reviews of operational objectives, he adapted a peer review process, originally introduced in the company as part of its Baldrige Award application. Each six months, a team of three to five executives from another division would review HI-Tek's Balanced Scorecard. The peer review team revisited the strategy, the objectives and measures, and the strategic initiatives. The team also talked to employees at random locations in the organization to determine the program's awareness level and penetration. Then, the team delivered an independent and objective evaluation of the scorecard structure and process.

The peer review process enabled HI-Tek's executives to remove themselves from the daily and monthly routine so that they could reflect on the strategic issues of their business. The stimulus of the peer review added a sense of professionalism and formality to the process. The review also helped transfer best practice ideas from one division to another. While this approach would not work for every organization, HI-Tek's prior experience with independent peer reviews and feedback provided a foundation for introducing a Balanced Scorecard peer review process with great success.

All these mechanisms—correlation analysis, management gaming and scenario analysis, anecdotal reporting, strategic initiative reviews, and peer reviews—enable an organization to review and think about its strategic directions on a regular basis. Periodic management reviews shift from explaining the past to learning about the future. Deviations from planned performance are not used to point fingers or to establish blame and responsibility. Rather, the deviations are treated as opportunities for learning. The discrepancy between actual and planned performance encourages key executives to debate whether, given the evidence to date, their hypotheses about the strategy are valid. Are the value propositions being delivered to targeted customers leading to improved customer and financial outcomes? Is the organization progressing fast enough in performing activities and developing new products and services that are valued by targeted customers? The Balanced Scorecard, unlike ad hoc performance measurement systems, articulates the "theory of the business."[6] By having an explicit set of linkages among the scorecard measures, managers can test informally, if not statistically, the business theory's hypothesized causal chain of strategic initiatives, performance drivers, and outcomes.

TEAM PROBLEM SOLVING

The third element for strategic learning is an effective team problem-solving process.[7] The emphasis here is on "team." The values of team building were stressed when we described how organizations gain clarity and consensus on their strategy and then use the consensus to design Balanced Scorecards.

The same team orientation should be maintained as the strategy is implemented and evaluated.

Cross-Functional Teams

Maintaining a cross-functional perspective is an important component of the learning process. Companies should avoid the natural tendency to revert to functional specialization. For example, it may seem convenient to assign the vice president of finance responsibility for the objectives and measures in the financial perspective, for the vice presidents of marketing and of sales to take responsibility for the customer perspective, for the vice presidents of operations, R&D, and logistics to take on the internal-business-process perspective, and for the vice presidents of human resources and of information systems to manage the objectives and measures for the learning and growth perspective. Such functional compartmentalization is not consistent with team accountability and team problem solving. Responsibility for achieving the measures and mobilizing the initiatives should be shared across the entire management group.

Echo Engineering used the internal-business-process value chain to create five cross-functional teams to manage different facets of its strategy (see Figure 11-5). The team assigned to identify customer needs, typically a marketing function, had members from operations, engineering, and quality. Each team member brought a different view to understanding customer requirements. The synthesis of what previously had been dispersed knowledge greatly enhanced the effectiveness of the process.

Strategic Review Meeting

A formal, periodic strategic review meeting plays a critical role in the executive team strategic-learning process. Unfortunately, most management meetings focus on operational, not strategic issues. For example, the senior executive team of Kenyon Stores met monthly to review the performance of the previous month. The meetings were scheduled as close to the monthly closing as possible and generally took place on a Saturday morning to eliminate interruptions.

The agenda was organized by responsibility center. The controller handed out monthly reports at the meetings so no advance preparation was possible. The controller began the meeting with a review of financial performance, which was followed by presentations from the three merchandise managers and the director of the retail stores' division. Each manager reviewed the performance of his or her department. Sixty-five percent of the meeting time was spent in this one-way communication. The remaining 35% of the meeting was spent in group discussion, which all managers felt was clearly the most valuable part of the meeting. Of this interactive time, however, the greatest focus was on some short-range issues raised by the operational reports (e.g., how to ensure "freshness" in store layouts, or how buyers have to deliver better merchandise on a more timely basis). Only 10% of the meeting time focused on issues related to longer-term, strategic implications, such as creating a stronger organizational commitment to quality. Because the meeting was designed as a broad, balanced performance review, no nonfinancial item received more than five minutes of group discussion. The participants concluded the meeting by developing a list of seven follow-up items related to improving short-term performance.

Clearly this meeting was about operational or, at best, management, control issues. Its goal was to monitor performance relative to plan and to initiate short-term actions that would bring the organization back into

Figure 11-5   The Use of Cross-Functional Teams to Facilitate Executive Problem Solving

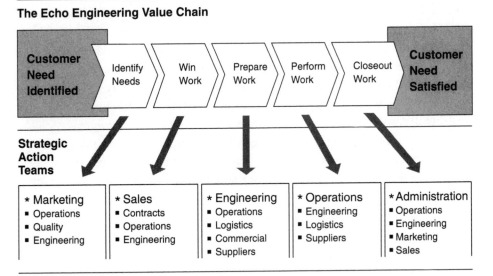

The Echo Engineering Value Chain

| Customer Need Identified | Identify Needs | Win Work | Prepare Work | Perform Work | Closeout Work | Customer Need Satisfied |

Strategic Action Teams

* Marketing	* Sales	* Engineering	* Operations	*Administration
▪ Operations	▪ Contracts	▪ Operations	▪ Engineering	▪ Operations
▪ Quality	▪ Operations	▪ Logistics	▪ Logistics	▪ Engineering
▪ Engineering	▪ Engineering	▪ Commercial	▪ Suppliers	▪ Marketing
		▪ Suppliers		▪ Sales

*Identifies Team Leader

compliance with the plan. By such criteria, the meeting could be considered a success. It fostered a team problem-solving atmosphere among the executive group. Much cross-functional education took place as managers from different parts of the organization and different functional expertise and responsibilities reviewed each other's plans and outcomes. In addition, two-thirds of the meeting was devoted to nonfinancial topics. On the negative side, most of the meeting was listening; there was little team problem solving. The agenda was structured around functional departmental responsibilities, not around strategic issues that required a solution from more than one department.

Arguably, this monthly management meeting worked well for operational and management control. But because it was the *only* meeting that Kenyon executives used to review performance, its limitations were ones of omission, not commission. Missing was a process to learn whether the organizational strategy was working and being implemented effectively.

Most companies continue to operate like Kenyon Stores. Prior to adoption of the Balanced Scorecard as a management system, the quarterly meetings at the FMC Corporation between corporate executives and individual operating company management focused on analyzing the most recent period's financial results. Dozens of managers from the operating company attended the meeting, most sitting around the perimeter of the room, in case they were needed to explain a variance in any of the 100+ line items on the quarterly financial statements. The discussion focused on past performance and on explanations for why financial objectives were not achieved.

To generalize, most organizations' periodic reviews assess whether recent performance is consistent with the short-term operating plan specified in the annual budget. The meetings review monthly or quarterly financial and operating statistics, discussing short-term, tactical results and processes. Virtually no time is devoted to reflecting on whether the organization's strategy is proceeding as expected; whether the competitive, market, and technological environment is still consistent with the strategic plan; and whether adequate resources are continuing to be committed to achieving the strategic plan. In our experience, the opportunity for strategic learning is missing in most organizations.

In contrast, by using the Balanced Scorecard as the cornerstone of its management system, FMC now has an entirely new process for its quarterly reviews. The change in focus is dramatic. Company presidents inform corporate executives, in advance, of any major deviation from the financial plan. Typically, that issue is resolved before the meeting. The face-to-face meetings have only three people from corporate and three or four top people from the operating company. And the discussion at every meeting focuses on strategy—whether the company is achieving its near-term objectives, whether its long-term objectives are going to be realized, and whether any modification to the strategy seems warranted.

For strategic review meetings to be effective, they should be separated in both time and place from operational review meetings. Also, while monthly meetings are appropriate for operational reviews, strategic reviews seem better suited to a quarterly cycle. Strategic factors like market share, customer satisfaction, new product introduction, and employee capabilities may not change meaningfully from month to month. A quarterly review also allows for more reflection on trends, on the drivers of strategy, and the correlation with results. The quarterly strategic review meeting should focus on issues, not performance of functional departments, with a goal of refining the strategy and its implementation.

The identification of strategic issues that require further exploration and clarification closes the loop on the strategic learning process. Quarterly reviews become opportunities to learn about the validity of the strategy and how well it is being executed. For example, a strategy review meeting at Metro Bank revealed a significant increase in customer complaints about quality. Internal quality statistics, however, did not confirm this increase. A small cross-functional team was formed to analyze the problem and recommend a solution. In this way, the strategy was partially validated and partially refined. Typically, in the quarterly strategic review, executives modify the current strategy; they don't introduce revolutionary new approaches.

The effectiveness of the learning process can be further enhanced by linking operational and strategic review meetings. As illustrated in Figure 11-6, the operational review process, while short-term in its focus, frequently identifies issues with longer-term impact. An operational performance review at Kenyon Stores found that three merchandise managers were experiencing similar problems with unreliable vendor performance on quality and reliability. The issue of the company's linkages with key vendors was much broader than could be effectively dealt with in the monthly review meeting. Instead, the issue was placed on the agenda of the quarterly strategic review. Similarly, issues can arise during the strategic review that require better execution at the operational level. These issues can then be

Figure 11-6   Operational and Strategic Management Processes Are Separated but Related

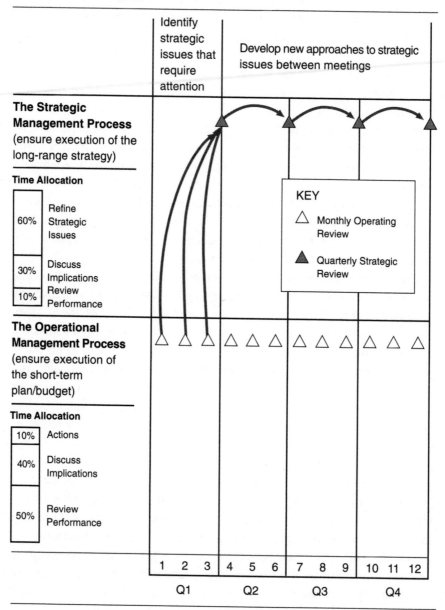

placed on the monthly agenda of the operational meetings to ensure that the company is responding rapidly. The linkages between operational and strategic reviews allow many such issues to be identified and acted upon as they emerge so that both strategy and operations can evolve accordingly.

Continual Double-Loop Learning about Strategy

Face-to-face contact at the strategy review meetings is clearly an important element of the team-building and problem-solving processes required for strategic learning. But approximately half the time of a typical meeting is still spent by someone reviewing and explaining the numbers. New technology can enhance the strategic learning process, by moving from event-driven learning (at the quarterly strategy review meetings) to a continual learning process. Groupware technologies like Lotus Notes permit a defined group of individuals to work continually on topics of shared interest and responsibility. Some executive groups have begun to embrace this technology-based approach to management. The Balanced Scorecard provides a perfect opportunity for the application of this technology as illustrated in Figure 11-7.

In the continual learning approach, the one-way reporting of the numbers can be eliminated from the team meeting. Reports are put on the network to be reviewed at any individual's convenience. The network permits ongoing dialogue about the numbers and their implications so that the shared time of the executive team can focus more heavily on issues and interpretation.

We can even envision a more formal process for using the evidence considered in the quarterly strategic review meeting to test, learn about, and update strategy. For example, suppose that at Metro Bank, executives at a quarterly meeting observe that growth in customer purchases of new banking products and services—a key measure in the customer perspective—is below expectations. With the cause-and-effect relationships specified in the Balanced Scorecard, managers would initially look back to see whether the enablers, the performance drivers, for this outcome measure had achieved their targets. Are the anticipated new products and services available to customers? Have employees been trained to market and sell these new products and services? Are information systems in place to enable employees to identify promising customer candidates for these new products and services and to provide information about the customers' existing relations with the bank as well as their anticipated demand for the new financial products? If one or more of the performance drivers have not achieved their targets, the failure to achieve targeted performance on an outcome measure (customer purchase of new products and services) can be attributed to poor implementation performance. Plans to correct these defects can be made in the upcoming period. This is a good example of single-loop learning. The managers observe deviations from the intended plan and initiate actions to bring the organization back to the planned strategic trajectory.

Figure 11-7 The Strategic Review Process of the Future

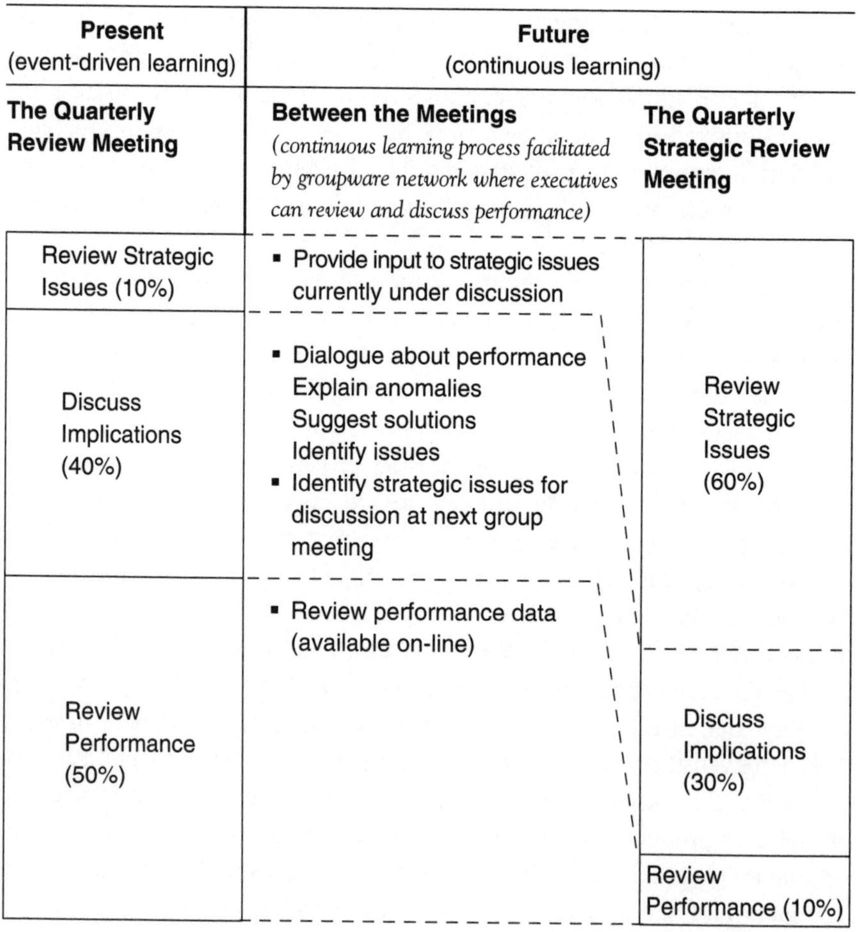

Present (event-driven learning)	Future (continuous learning)	
The Quarterly Review Meeting	**Between the Meetings** *(continuous learning process facilitated by groupware network where executives can review and discuss performance)*	**The Quarterly Strategic Review Meeting**
Review Strategic Issues (10%)	▪ Provide input to strategic issues currently under discussion	Review Strategic Issues (60%)

Discuss Implications (40%)	▪ Dialogue about performance
	  Explain anomalies
	  Suggest solutions
	  Identify issues
	▪ Identify strategic issues for discussion at next group meeting
		Review Strategic Issues (60%)

Review Performance (50%)	▪ Review performance data (available on-line)	Discuss Implications (30%)
		Review Performance (10%)

But suppose the data reveal that the organization's employees and managers have delivered on the performance drivers—employees have been re-skilled, information systems are available, and new financial products and services have been developed and introduced on schedule. Now, the failure to have achieved the expected outcomes—higher sales of multiple products—is an important signal: the theory embodied in Metro Bank's targeted customer strategy may not be valid. Managers should take such disconfirming evidence seriously by initiating a double-loop learning process. They should have an intense dialogue to review their shared assumptions about market conditions, value propositions for targeted customers, competitor behavior, and internal capabilities. Such a dialogue may lead to a reaffirmation of the current strategy, but also a need to adjust the milestones, which represent the quantitative interrelationships among the strategic measures on the Balanced Scorecard. In this case, managers maintain their belief in the extant theory of the business, but establish a different set of dynamic relationships. Alternatively, and potentially far more significant, the intensive strategic reviews may reveal that the business unit's strategy is not valid, that it needs to be modified in light of the new knowledge about market conditions, customer preferences, and internal capabilities. In our experience, this process of data gathering, hypothesis testing, reflection, strategic learning, and adaptation is fundamental to the successful implementation of business strategy. This capacity for enabling strategic learning at the executive level makes the Balanced Scorecard the cornerstone of a strategic management system.

Whether the managers reaffirm the existing strategy, but adjust their judgments about the speed and magnitude of the cause-and-effect relationship, or they adopt a modified or entirely new strategy, the scorecard will have successfully stimulated a strategic (double-loop) learning process among key executives about the viability and validity of their strategy. The executives can use this learning to cycle back to the initial scorecard implementation process, updating their vision and strategy, and translating the updated strategy into a modified set of objectives and measures for the upcoming year.

SUMMARY

The capacity for organizational learning at the executive level—what we refer to as strategic learning—is perhaps the most innovative aspect of the

Balanced Scorecard. Strategic learning makes the journey worthwhile for those who learn how to use the scorecard as a strategic management system. The process begins with the clarification of the shared vision which the entire organization is attempting to achieve. The use of measurement as a language helps translate complex and frequently nebulous concepts into more precise ideas that align and mobilize all individuals into actions directed at attaining organizational objectives. The emphasis on constructing cause-and-effect relationships in the scorecard introduces dynamic systems thinking. It enables individuals in various parts of the organization to understand how the pieces fit together, how their role influences that of others. It facilitates the definition of performance drivers and related initiatives that not only measure change but also foster it. Finally, the approach facilitates team learning. The scorecard should be developed by a management team and used by that same team to monitor the performance of the business. Because the scorecard defines the theory of the business on which the strategy is based, performance monitoring can take the form of hypothesis testing and double-loop learning. We feel that this process of strategic learning and adaptation is fundamental to the successful implementation of business strategy.

NOTES

1. See, for example, R. N. Anthony, *Planning and Control Systems: A Framework for Analysis* (Boston: Harvard Business School, 1965).

2. For extensive discussion of single- and double-loop learning in management processes, see C. Argyris, *Reasoning, Learning, and Action* (San Francisco: Jossey-Bass, 1982); *Strategy, Change and Defensive Routines* (New York: Harper & Row, 1985); and "Teaching Smart People How to Learn," *Harvard Business Review* (May–June 1991): 99–109.

3. See H. Mintzberg, "Crafting Strategy," *Harvard Business Review* (July–August 1987): 66–75; and "The Design School: Reconsidering the Basic Premises of Strategic Management," *Strategic Management Journal* (November–December 1990): 171–195; also Robert Simons, *Levers of Control: How Managers Use Innovative Control Systems to Drive Strategic Renewal* (Boston: Harvard Business School Press, 1995), 18–21.

4. David Garvin, "Building a Learning Organization," *Harvard Business Review* (July–August 1993): 78–91.

5. James L. Heskett, Thomas O. Jones, Gary W. Loveman, W. Earl Sasser, Jr., and Leonard A. Schlesinger, "Putting the Service-Profit Chain to Work," *Harvard Business Review* (March–April 1994): 164–174.

6. Peter F. Drucker, "The Theory of the Business," *Harvard Business Review* (September–October 1994): 95–104.
7. Jon R. Katzenbach and Douglas K. Smith, *The Wisdom of Teams: Creating the High-Performance Organization* (Boston: Harvard Business School Press, 1993).

Chapter Twelve

Implementing a Balanced Scorecard Management Program

*"I tried to tell my boss that a Balanced Scorecard
was about management not measurement."*

THIS MANAGER had been asked by his CEO to lead a middle-management task force to develop a Balanced Scorecard for the division. He sensed that this effort was doomed to failure, because the CEO viewed the scorecard as a narrow effort to improve the organization's performance measurement system, not as a new way to manage the business.

Our experience corroborates and reinforces this manager's concern. The goal of a scorecard project is not to develop a new set of measures. Measurement—how we describe results and targets—is indeed a powerful motivational and evaluation tool. But the measurement framework in the Balanced Scorecard should be deployed to develop a new management system. This distinction between a measurement and a management system is subtle but crucial. The measurement system should be only a means to achieve an even more important goal—a strategic management system that helps executives implement and gain feedback about their strategy. We have seen senior executives mobilize the power of the measurement framework in the Balanced Scorecard to create long-term organizational change.

Management processes and programs are built around frameworks. Traditional management systems have been built around a financial framework, usually the ROI model originated at the turn of this century by DuPont. The financial framework worked well as long as financial measures could capture the great majority of value-creating (or value-destroying) activities that occurred during quarterly and annual periods. This framework became less valuable as more and more of an organization's activities involved investments in relationships, technologies, and capabilities that could not be valued in the historical-cost financial model. Organizations adopt the Balanced Scorecard because it retains a focus on short-term financial results, but also recognizes the value of building intangible assets and competitive capabilities.

The scorecard provides a new tool for senior executives to focus their organizations on strategies for long-term success, an important task that until now has been difficult to accomplish. By identifying the most important objectives on which an organization should focus its attention and resources, the scorecard provides a framework for a strategic management system that organizes issues, information, and a variety of vital management processes (see Figure 12-1). As Part Two has illustrated, each component in this strategic management system can be linked to strategic goals. Objectives for customers, internal business processes, and employees and systems are linked to achieve long-run financial performance. Departmental, team, and personal goals are aligned with achieving strategic performance. Resource allocations, strategic initiatives, and annual budgets are driven by the strategy. And management reviews become opportunities for feedback and learning about strategy. The Balanced Scorecard does not eliminate a role for financial measurement in a management system. But it embeds financial measurement in a more balanced management system that links short-term operational performance with long-term strategic objectives.

LAUNCHING THE BALANCED SCORECARD PROGRAM

Organizations launch scorecard programs for a variety of reasons (see Figure 12-2). Some examples of the rationales used by particular companies we are familiar with appear in the Appendix. Note that none of the reasons in Figure 12-2 relates solely to improving the measurement system. Each reason is part of a broad, overarching goal—mobilizing the organization to new strategic directions.

In our experience, CEOs have adopted the Balanced Scorecard for a specific strategic purpose. And, in each case, the initial scorecard exercise

Figure 12-1 Using the Balanced Scorecard as a Strategic Framework for Action

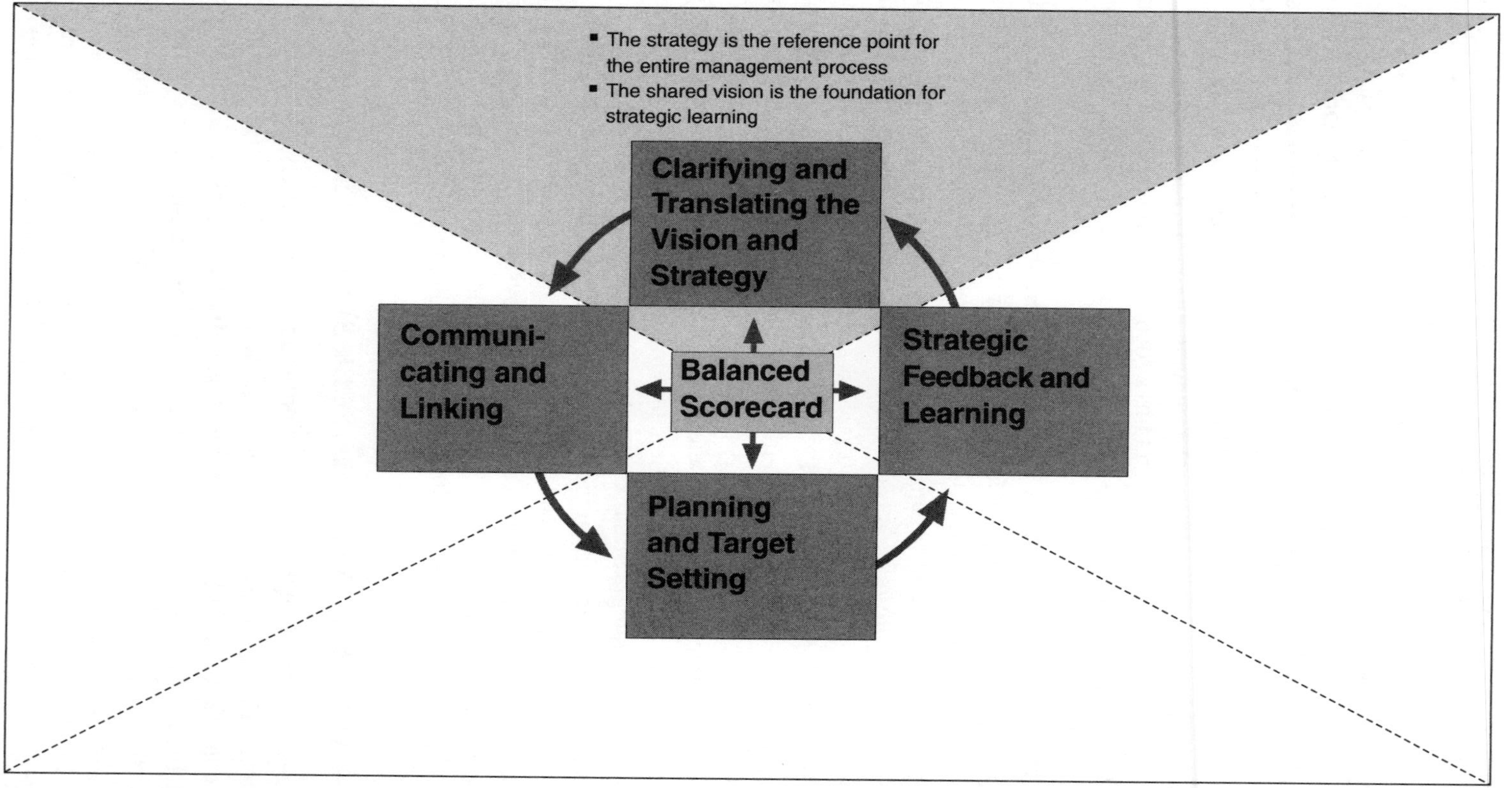

- The strategy is the reference point for the entire management process
- The shared vision is the foundation for strategic learning

Clarifying and Translating the Vision and Strategy

Communi-cating and Linking

Balanced Scorecard

Strategic Feedback and Learning

Planning and Target Setting

accomplished that purpose. But in none of the companies did the Balanced Scorecard continue to focus only on that initial purpose. Instead, the first application seemed to start a process of change that went well beyond the original aim of constructing a scorecard. Within a year after starting the scorecard effort, each organization was using the scorecard as the cornerstone of its management system.

Figure 12-2 Most Companies Introduce the Scorecard to Drive Single Pieces of the Management Process

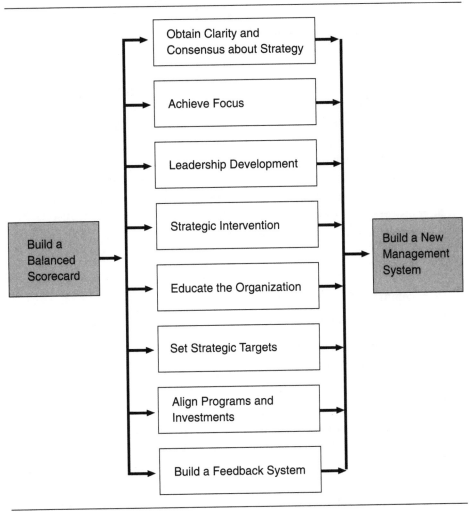

THE DYNAMICS: MOBILIZING THE ORGANIZATION

A management system does not appear instantaneously. Because of its scope, complexity, and impact, a new management system must be phased in over time. This approach is preferable since, as each element of the system is changed or embedded, the CEO has an opportunity to unfreeze the organization from its previous processes and send a message about the new process. If each change is linked to a consistent message—such as a new strategy for the organization—each transformation reinforces and builds upon the previous ones. When the Balanced Scorecard is used as the central organizing framework for the new management system, all the changes can be consistent and coherent. The result can be dramatic, as the National Insurance story illustrates.

We first discussed National Insurance in Chapter 7. Recall that the new management team, brought in by the corporate parent to turn around a dismal situation, concluded that National had to focus on niches, where existing staff already had special expertise and comparative advantages. Its initial attempts to communicate the change in strategy to the organization, however, had little impact. Most people could not understand the new vision—they thought they already were specialists. The management team, at this point, launched the development of National's Balanced Scorecard, which led logically and inexorably to a sequence of actions (see Figure 12-3) that ultimately succeeded in transforming National into a profitable insurer.

The first few steps in the implementation process

- clarified the company vision and strategy,
- communicated the corporate strategy,
- launched cross-business strategic initiatives, and
- led to each SBU developing its own strategy, consistent with that of the company.

These steps all occurred during the first year.

The corporate review process (see step 5 in Figure 12-3) created some unanticipated benefits. As the individual SBUs developed specific strategies, they identified several cross-business issues that were not included in the original corporate scorecard. For example, many of the SBUs realized that they must understand their customers better and needed to solicit feedback on customer satisfaction. Since many SBUs would be selling to the same customers, they identified the opportunity for developing a new business process, an integrated selling approach to targeted market segments. This experience was an excellent example of strategy emerging from within the organization, as discussed by Mintzberg and Simons (see Chapter 11). The bottom-up strategy formulation at the SBU level, within the context established at the company level, led to an entirely new approach for accomplishing the SBUs' strategy. Several such strategic initiatives emerged from the SBUs, and were then incorporated into an updated corporate scorecard.

Immediately upon approval of their scorecards, the SBUs began a monthly review process (step 8 in Figure 12-3). The monthly reviews were supplemented with quarterly reviews that focused more heavily on strategic issues. Initially, information was available on only two-thirds of the measures. Management reviews focused more on the measures where data were available. The lack of data for a scorecard measure, however, did not prevent an issue from being discussed. The group felt that discussion, even without data, kept members focused on strategic issues, and was certainly superior to the alternative of no discussion on a particular strategic process, objective, or measure. The measurement gap also motivated management to develop a plan to acquire the missing data. In general, the plan required that a more basic management system be developed, since the lack of data indicated the general lack of an adequate management process.[1] For example, the lack of a measure on underwriting quality revealed that there were no processes to specify, to measure, and to audit underwriting quality. Thus, the building of the complete Balanced Scorecard required National's managers to develop a more complete management system. Most of this development was completed over a six-month period.

After two years, the Balanced Scorecard had become integrated into the regular management cycle at National. The organization had achieved its short-term objective—survival. The new management measures and processes had facilitated a shift of the entire organizational culture, from an unfocused generalist strategy to a targeted specialist one.

At the start of the third year, National's CEO declared that the initial strategy had achieved its short-term goals. Organizational survival was no longer in doubt. The strategy now had to be refined and updated so that it could focus on achieving aggressive growth and profitability objectives. The executive committee drew up a list of 10 strategic issues. These were posed in the form of questions, such as "How do we achieve a preferred relationship with agents?"

Figure 12-3 Using the Management System to Orchestrate Change

2A *Communicate to Middle Managers:* The top three layers of management (100 people) are brought together to learn about and discuss the new strategy. The Balanced Scorecard is the communication vehicle. *(months 4–5)*

2B *Develop Business Unit Scorecards:* Using the corporate scorecard as a template, each business unit translates its strategy into its own scorecard. *(months 6–9)*

4 *Review Business Unit Scorecards:* The CEO and the executive team review the individual business units' scorecards. The review permits the CEO to participate knowledgeably in shaping business unit strategy. *(months 9–11)*

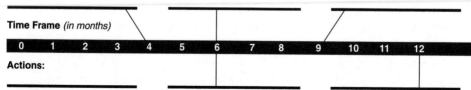

Time Frame *(in months)*

| 0 | 1 | 2 | 3 | 4 | 5 | 6 | 7 | 8 | 9 | 10 | 11 | 12 |

Actions:

1 *Clarify the Vision:* Ten members of a newly formed executive team work together for three months. A Balanced Scorecard is developed to translate a generic vision into a strategy that is understood and can be communicated. The process helps build consensus and commitment to the strategy.

3A *Eliminate Nonstrategic Investments:* The corporate scorecard, by clarifying strategic priorities, identifies many active programs that are not contributing to the strategy. *(month 6)*

3B *Launch Corporate Change Programs:* The corporate scorecard identifies the need for cross-business change programs. They are launched while the business units prepare their scorecards. *(month 6)*

5 *Refine the Vision:* The review of business unit scorecards identifies several cross-business issues not initially included in the corporate strategy. The corporate scorecard is updated. *(month 12)*

6A *Communicate the Balanced Scorecard to the Entire Company:* At the end of one year, when the management teams are comfortable with the strategic approach, the scorecard is disseminated to the entire organization. *(month 12–ongoing)*

6B *Establish Individual Performance Objectives:* The top three layers of management link their individual objectives and incentive compensation to their scorecards. *(months 13–14)*

9 *Conduct Annual Strategy Review:* At the start of the third year, the initial strategy has been achieved and the corporate strategy requires updating. The executive committee lists ten strategic issues. Each business unit is asked to develop a position on each issue as a prelude to updating its strategy and scorecard. *(months 25–26)*

7 *Update Long-Range Plan and Budget:* Five-year goals are established for each measure. The investments required to meet those goals are identified and funded. The first year of the five-year plan becomes the annual budget. *(months 15–17)*

8 *Conduct Monthly and Quarterly Reviews:* After corporate approval of the business unit scorecards, a monthly review process, supplemented by quarterly reviews that focus more heavily on strategic issues, begins. *(month 18–ongoing)*

10 *Link Everyone's Performance to the Balanced Scorecard:* All employees are asked to link their individual objectives to the Balanced Scorecard. The entire organization's incentive compensation is linked to the scorecard. *(months 25–26)*

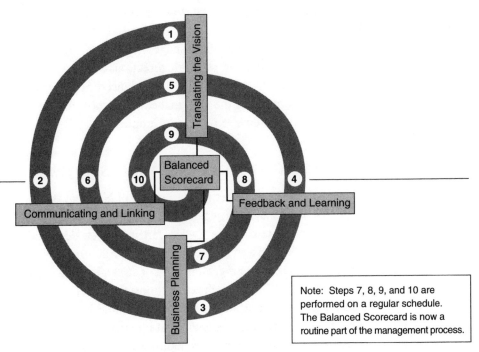

Note: Steps 7, 8, 9, and 10 are performed on a regular schedule. The Balanced Scorecard is now a routine part of the management process.

Source: Robert S. Kaplan and David P. Norton, "Using the Balanced Scorecard as a Strategic Management System," *Harvard Business Review* (January–February 1996): 78–79. Reprinted with permission.

Each SBU director had to develop answers to the questions raised by each issue. The SBU director met for a half-day with a member of National's executive committee. These discussions were meant to stretch the thinking of the SBU and company leadership. They culminated with an agreed-upon set of directions for the next three to five years. These directions were documented so that they served as guidelines for developing new long-range plans and updated scorecards (step 9 in Figure 12-3).

The linked sequence of 10 action steps at National Insurance occurred over a 24-month period. During this time, National's CEO and senior management team not only introduced a new strategy; they completely revised the management system by which the organization functioned. What started out as an attempt to clarify the vision resulted in a comprehensive new approach to management. Anticipating the radical changes that were to come, the CEO announced, in his letter introducing the program to the organization: "The Balanced Scorecard, and the philosophy that it represents, is the way we have elected to manage the business."

In the past, most organizations, when they attempted to change directions and introduce new strategies and processes, failed because their management systems and processes were not linked, via a central framework, to their strategy. Because it provides a coherent framework, executives can use the Balanced Scorecard as an ongoing management tool to mobilize and guide their organizations around new strategic directions and to accomplish their agendas for change. In our opinion, the Balanced Scorecard's most important role arises from filling the void that exists in most management systems—the lack of a systematic process to implement strategy.

BUILDING AN INTEGRATED MANAGEMENT SYSTEM

Many organizations have had experiences similar to that of National Insurance: the introduction of a Balanced Scorecard creates pressure to broaden its role in the management system. Once a scorecard has been designed and introduced, concerns soon arise if the scorecard is not tied into other management programs, such as budgeting, alignment of strategic initiatives, and setting of personal targets. Without such connections, the effort devoted to developing a Balanced Scorecard may not deliver tangible benefits.

Most companies have a management calendar that identifies the different management processes being used and the schedule for the operation of each process. Typically, the calendar is organized around the budgeting and operational review process. Strategy formulation and review is usually disconnected from the scheduled periodic management processes. The Balanced Scorecard provides a vehicle to introduce strategic thinking into ongoing management processes, but such a linkage must be made explicit.

Figure 12-4 is the management calendar at Kenyon Stores. The CEO established this calendar after he had redesigned the management process to incorporate the Balanced Scorecard and the strategic perspectives that it represented. The management calendar incorporates four essential features of a strategic management system:

1. Strategy formulation and strategic issue update
2. Link to personal objectives and rewards
3. Link to planning, resource allocation, and annual budgets
4. Feedback and strategic learning

Strategy Formulation and Strategic Issue Update

The strategy formulation and strategic issue update is a means for top-down guidance for the heads of the operating divisions. During this process, senior management can either initiate the development of a Balanced Scorecard linked to a new long-range plan, or it can update the strategy annually. At Kenyon Stores, the CEO had outlined 10 strategic issues at the end of the first quarter, raised in part by the strategic-scorecard reviews that had been performed at the end of the previous year and, in part, by the functional leaders of the organization. The issues were corporate in scope and reflected shared corporate priorities and themes. The CEO asked the SBU presidents to take the list and develop a plan on how the updated corporate themes and priorities should be implemented in their organizations. The presidents presented their ideas in a four-hour "Strategic Dialogue" meeting with the CEO. The meeting itself was intimate and informal; the goal of the meeting, however, was tangible and specific. The CEO and each SBU president were to reach agreement on the strategic approaches to each of the 10 issues; for example, How would the SBU maintain fashion leadership? How would the SBU develop its key people?

After the strategic dialogue meeting, the SBU presidents worked with their management teams to develop or update their long-range plans and their SBU Balanced Scorecards. Generally, this development process occurred over a three-month period, during the second quarter of the fiscal

Figure 12-4 The Management Calendar at Kenyon Stores

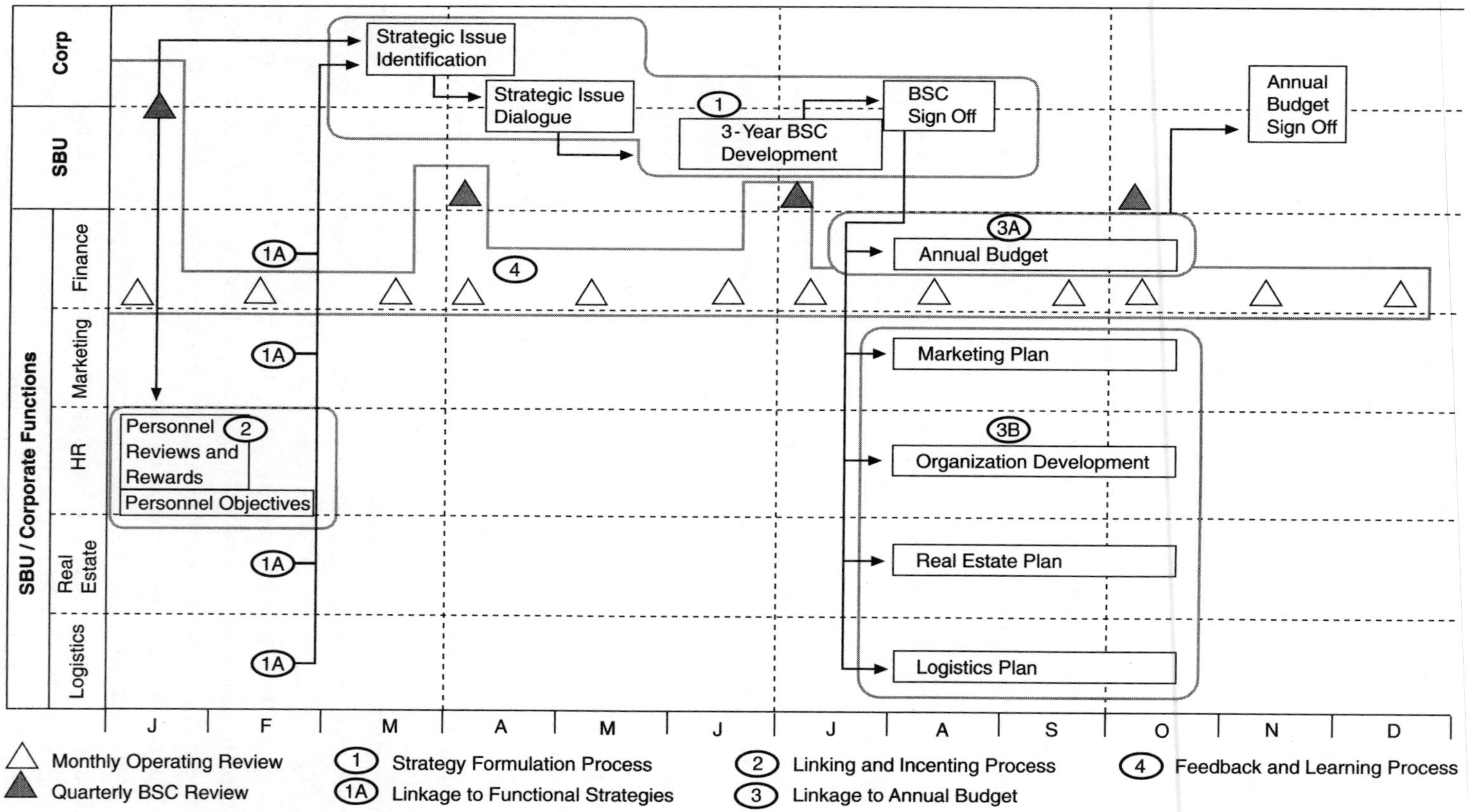

year. Linking corporate and SBU strategies to functional strategies is an important extension of the process. As discussed in both Chapters 8 and 10, corporations such as Kenyon Stores, often establish centralized, corporate-level functional departments to support their (otherwise) decentralized strategic business units. Corporate and SBU objectives are linked simultaneously to objectives for corporate-level functional departments during the long-range planning/SBU Balanced Scorecard development process.

Thus, by mid-year, both functional department and SBU heads have clearly specified mutually consistent, long-range objectives and targets. The process culminates with a final review and sign-off between the CEO and each SBU or functional department president at the end of the second quarter. The completion of the long-range plan/Balanced Scorecard in mid-year allowed the management process to shift gears into the operational planning process that would occur during the second half of the year.

Link to Personal Objectives and Rewards

As companies attempt to implement new strategies—building relationships, developing new fashions or technologies, and accessing new customers and consumers—managers must continually take risks and experiment so that they can learn and grow. Executives must encourage this innovative behavior by managing the second integration issue—linkage to personal objectives and rewards. As long as personal incentives and rewards are tied to short-term performance measures, especially financial ones, management thinking will remain risk-averse and short-term. Senior executives will find it difficult to keep focused and committed to building long-term capabilities and relationships.

Clearly, incentive compensation motivates performance. But, as discussed in Chapter 9, the organization may wish to get some experience in managing with the Balanced Scorecard before explicitly tying compensation to it. Unless, however, reward and punishment are eventually tied, implicitly or explicitly, to the balanced set of objectives, measures, and targets on corporate and business scorecards, the organization will not be able to use the Balanced Scorecard as the central organizing framework for its management systems. In its early implementation, Kenyon Stores used the Balanced Scorecard to stimulate SBU strategy formulation and review but did not shift its formal incentive compensation to scorecard measures. After a year of experience with the scorecard, Kenyon began to link executive incentive compensation to the Balanced Scorecard.

Link to Planning, Resource Allocation, and Annual Budgets

Kenyon's third integration step, linkage to annual budgets, occurs during the second half of the year. Operating units and functional departments link the second quarter's strategic planning to budgeted targets and spending authorizations for the next fiscal year. If the strategy formulation and strategic issues update has been done well, the budgeting process should simply involve translating the first year of a multiyear (3–5 year) plan into an operational budget.

Feedback and Strategic Learning

The final component of Kenyon's management system—feedback and strategic learning—uses the two-level review process described in Chapter 11. This process links monthly operational reviews—where managers compare short-term performance with targets established in the annual budget—and quarterly strategic reviews that examine longer-term trends in scorecard measures to assess whether and how well the strategy is working.

By integrating various management processes centered on the Balanced Scorecard into its management calendar, Kenyon Stores' corporate- and SBU-level managers shifted their focus from tactics to strategy, and were now able to effectively translate their strategies into actions.

SOME CAUTIONS: IT'S NOT AS SIMPLE AS IT SEEMS

Managers in a variety of manufacturing and service organizations have attempted to build scorecards for their business units. Not all the experiences have been successful. Several executives have commented, "It's not as simple as it seems." Our analysis of their experiences reveals several ways in which scorecard projects can indeed fail. These factors include defects in the structure and choices of measures for the scorecard, and organizational defects in the process of developing the scorecard and in how it is used.

Structural Defects

Many senior executives feel that they already have a Balanced Scorecard because they supplement financial measures with nonfinancial ones, like customer satisfaction and market share. But these nonfinancial measures exhibit many of the defects of traditional financial measures they are meant to complement. They are lagging measures, reporting how well an organization's strategy worked in the past period. Also, they are generic, in that all companies are trying to improve along these dimensions. The measures are good for keeping score, but not good for communicating to employees what they must excel at to win future competitive games. They do not provide specific enough guidance for the future, nor are they a sound basis for resource allocation, strategic initiatives, and linkage to annual budgets and discretionary spending.

Fortunately, these structural defects are relatively easy to remedy. Chapter 7 described how to build scorecards that reflect unique strategies, targeted customers, and critical internal processes. The scorecards derived from specific strategies will have a balanced set of measures, both outcomes and performance drivers, lagging and leading indicators, and with all the measures eventually linked to achieving excellent long-run financial performance.

Organizational Defects

Other problems arise not from defects within the scorecard itself, but from the process used to implement the concept. Our worst fears are realized when we receive a phone call that begins:

> *Hello, this is John Smith. I'm an assistant controller [or manager of quality] at Acme Industries and am serving as chairman of a task force to improve performance measurement at the company. We've done an extensive literature survey and are attracted to your Balanced Scorecard approach. We are doing a benchmarking study and would like to come to talk with you about what the best performance measures should be for our scorecard and the types of measures that have proven most successful in other companies.*

We usually respond to such calls by expressing appreciation for their interest in the Balanced Scorecard, but suggesting that the proposed meeting is unlikely to be successful for either party. When asked to explain our reticence, we point out several problems. First, the scorecard development process should not be delegated to a middle-management task force. For the Balanced Scorecard to be effective, it must reflect the strategic vision of the senior executive group. Merely slapping performance measures on existing processes may drive local improvement but is unlikely to lead to breakthrough performance for the entire organization. In addition, if senior executives are not leading the process, they will be unlikely to use the scorecard in the important management processes described in Part Two of this book. The senior executives will continue to conduct operational reviews that emphasize meeting short-term financial targets, thereby by-passing and undermining the fundamental rationale for developing a score-card in the first place.

Most important, a Balanced Scorecard should not be created by emulating the best measures used by the best companies. If, as we have argued, the best scorecards are derived from strategies designed for breakthrough performance, measures chosen by even excellent companies for their own strategies are unlikely to be appropriate for other organizations that face different competitive environments, with different customers and market segments, and in which different technologies and capabilities may be decisive. When people tell us, "It's not as simple as it seems," they are referring to the hard, intensive work required to formulate a scorecard appropriate for their organization and to make that scorecard an integral part of their management processes. There are few shortcuts in developing a viable scorecard.

The other extreme, however, can also be detrimental to effective deploy-ment of the scorecard. Some organizations work too intensively and too long in searching for the perfect scorecard. When information is not available for several critical measures, they attempt to install reliable information systems to produce the desired data. This decision leads to significant delays in the introduction of the scorecard, destroying whatever momentum and enthusiasm had been established for the concept. Balanced Scorecards are not immutable. They are dynamic and should be continually reviewed, assessed, and updated to reflect new competitive, market, and technological conditions. By delaying introduction of the scorecard, companies lose the opportunity to gain feedback on the measures for which information is available, and, even more important, to get practice and insight in using the scorecard as a core management system. Our advice, when we find organizations delaying because they are not sure whether they have selected the right measures, or because data are not available for some of the measures, is "Just do it." Start the learning process of how to manage with a balanced set of performance drivers and outcome indicators.

MANAGING THE BALANCED SCORECARD STRATEGIC MANAGEMENT SYSTEM

Introducing a new management system centered on the Balanced Scorecard must overcome the organizational inertia that tends to envelop and absorb virtually any change program. Two types of change agents are required for effective implementation of the new system. First, an organization needs transitional leaders, the managers who facilitate the building of the scorecard and who help embed it as a new management system. Second, the organization needs to designate a manager to operate the strategic management system on an ongoing recurring basis. An additional difficulty of embedding the Balanced Scorecard as a strategic management system (yet another entry on the "It's not as simple as it seems" list) is that the responsibilities of both the transitional leaders and the manager of the ongoing system do not fall within traditional organizational boxes.

Transitional Management Role

We have identified three critical roles that must be played in building and embedding the Balanced Scorecard as a strategic management system:

1. Architect
2. Change agent
3. Communicator

The architect is responsible for the process that builds the initial Balanced Scorecard, and that introduces the scorecard into the management system. Since the scorecard represents a radical change in the philosophy of management, the architect must completely understand and be internally motivated by the new focus on long-term strategic objectives. This person must be capable of educating the executive team and guiding the translation of strategy into specific objectives and measures in ways that are nonthreatening and do not trigger defensive reactions.[2]

A successful scorecard program demands a high level of commitment and time from the executive team, which implies that the architect will likely have only one shot to launch the program. If the first attempt is not successful, the architect will generally find it difficult to obtain additional time at executive team meetings. In our experience, external consultants or knowledgeable internal practitioners can play a critical role in launching a successful scorecard program. Typically, the relationship involves experienced external and internal consultants working closely on a pilot program at the SBU level, where the CEO of the SBU has already bought into the concept. The pilot program serves two purposes. First, it demonstrates the value of the Balanced Scorecard, and, second, it builds the competency of an internal consulting group that can then manage the rollout of the program to the rest of the organization.

The internal consultants also support the change agent who will embed the scorecard into ongoing management processes. The change agent should have a direct reporting relationship to the CEO since he or she serves as the chief of staff to guide the development of the new management system over the two- to three-year period during which the new management processes triggered by the Balanced Scorecard unfold. The change agent's role is critical since he or she serves as the surrogate for the CEO, shaping the day-to-day use of the new management system. The change agent helps managers redefine their roles, as required by the new system.

The communicator is responsible for gaining the understanding, buy-in, and support of all organizational members, from the most senior levels down to teams and employees on the front lines and in the back offices. The new strategies articulated on the Balanced Scorecard generally require new values and ways of doing work that are built around customer focus and satisfaction, quality and responsiveness, innovation and service, and enhanced roles for employees and systems. The manager of the scorecard communication process should perform this task as an internal marketing campaign. The communication program should also motivate employees and teams to provide feedback about whether the proposed strategy is feasible and desirable. While the communication department traditionally would be responsible for such an educational program, the scorecard communication function is so important for effective implementation of the concept, we urge that a specific individual, perhaps actively supported by the communication department, be designated to manage the strategic communication campaign until the awareness and motivation objectives have been achieved.

Managing the Ongoing Strategic Management Process

Once the 24–36 month process of embedding the Balanced Scorecard into an organization's ongoing management processes is over, how can an organization maintain its strategic management system in the steady state? Figure 12-5 illustrates how various parts of the strategic management system influence the traditional responsibilities of several members of the executive team. The vice presidents of strategic planning, human resources, finance,

Figure 12-5 Who Should Manage the Strategic Management System?

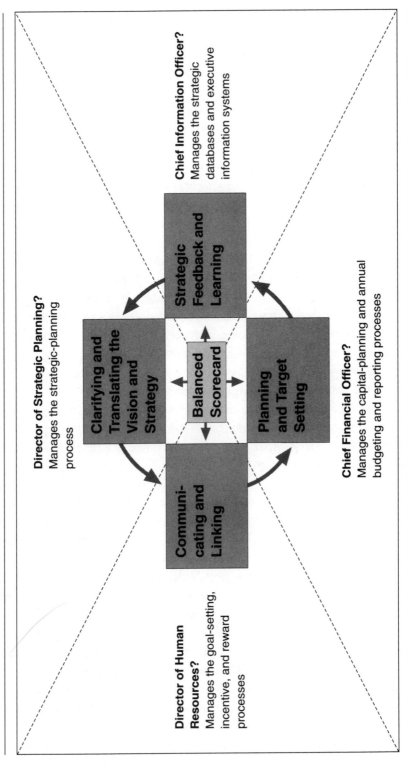

Director of Strategic Planning?
Manages the strategic-planning process

Chief Information Officer?
Manages the strategic databases and executive information systems

Clarifying and Translating the Vision and Strategy

Strategic Feedback and Learning

Balanced Scorecard

Communi-cating and Linking

Planning and Target Setting

Director of Human Resources?
Manages the goal-setting, incentive, and reward processes

Chief Financial Officer?
Manages the capital-planning and annual budgeting and reporting processes

and information systems are the traditional "owners" of pieces of the strategic management process. Yet today no one has responsibility for operation of the total system.

Clearly, the chief executive officer of the business unit is the ultimate "process owner." As the system that specifies the goals and objectives of the entire unit, sets performance targets and allocates resources and initiatives to achieve these targets, monitors results, and rewards or punishes realized performance, the strategic management system must be the personal responsibility of the CEO and the senior executive team. But the ongoing operation of the system must be assigned to a particular person; otherwise, gaps will develop in measurement, reporting, and monitoring.

As illustrated in Figure 12-5, the operation of the strategic management system draws upon the skills, experience, and responsibilities of several traditional management functions. It would be easy for the ongoing operation of the scorecard strategic management system to be decomposed into these traditional functional roles, with each department doing its individual job well. We feel, however, that effective maintenance of the system is so important to its success that, as with the case of the communicator, it should be in the hands of a single, qualified individual.

Most organizations today have a leadership void for this system. No executive in a traditional organization has the responsibility or perspective to manage a strategic management process, and it is unclear who should assume this responsibility.

The chief financial officer (CFO) is one logical custodian of the new process. Many CFOs, however—particularly those who come from an accounting, internal control, and audit background—have reached their current positions because of their ability to manage a rigorous, disciplined, and focused financial system. These are not necessarily the traits required for managing a holistic, innovative, judgment-based, people-intense management process built around achieving stretch targets for customers, internal processes, employees, and systems.

An alternative candidate would be the director of strategic planning. But the traits of the current occupant of this position represent the flip side of the characteristics of the CFO. Traditionally, strategic planning has been an annual event, and the function emphasizes strategy formulation, not strategy implementation. The director of strategic planning, if he or she is to assume the role for managing the strategic management system, must lead a continual, not an event-driven process, with the same discipline and adherence to an ongoing reporting and review schedule that is currently used for the financial reporting and management system. The chief information officer has, obviously, the systems background for being the custodian of the strategic management system but generally lacks the linkage to strategy and, perhaps, active membership in the business unit's senior executive team.

At this time, therefore, the specific identity of the manager of the strategic management system is unclear, but unless organizations place someone in this role, they may fail to capture all the benefits from operating an integrated system. Such a manager serves an important and visible role for the organization, and the function provides new experiential and growth opportunities for the individual. Someone will eventually assume this position. In the interim, the transitional change agent, who helped to embed the scorecard into the strategic management system, will likely take initial responsibility for managing the ongoing process.

SUMMARY: TRANSLATING STRATEGY INTO ACTION

Companies initially adopt the Balanced Scorecard for a variety of reasons, including clarifying and gaining consensus on strategy, focusing organizational change initiatives, developing leadership capabilities at strategic business units, and gaining coordination and economies across multiple business units. In general, organizations can achieve these targeted objectives with the development of an initial Balanced Scorecard. But the development of the scorecard and, especially, the process among senior managers to define the objectives, measures, and targets for the scorecard, ultimately reveals an opportunity to use the BSC in a far more pervasive and comprehensive manner than originally intended.

The Balanced Scorecard can be the cornerstone of an organization's management system since it aligns and supports key processes, including:

- Clarify and update strategy
- Communicate strategy throughout the organization
- Align departmental and personal goals to the strategy
- Identify and align strategic initiatives
- Link strategic objectives to long-term targets and annual budgets

- Align strategic and operational reviews
- Obtain feedback to learn about and improve strategy

Further, by integrating the Balanced Scorecard into the management calendar, all management processes can be aligned with and stay focused on implementing the organization's long-term strategy.

Over the past few years, as our experience with scorecard programs has accumulated, we have been (pleasantly) surprised at the impact and generality of the concept. What started out as a quest to improve performance measurement systems has evolved into an approach that helps executives solve perhaps their most central issue: how to implement strategy, particularly one that requires radical change. In retrospect, we now understand why this behavior is so consistent and pervasive. The process of developing a good Balanced Scorecard gives an organization, usually for the first time, a clear picture of the future and a path for getting there. In addition to producing and developing an organization's pathway to its vision, the development process has engaged the energy and commitment of the entire senior management team. Given this clarification and management consensus about what the future organization should look like, enthusiasm and momentum have been created. Expectations have been raised. The inevitable question is, How can we make sure that we achieve our vision?

When organizations make the critical transition, from vision to action, they experience the real excitement and gain the real value from developing a Balanced Scorecard. The initial development of a scorecard should always lead to an ongoing series of management processes that ultimately mobilizes and redirects the organization. Each management process involves linking the Balanced Scorecard to drive some aspect of longer-term, strategic, balanced behavior.

Robert Simons, in his seminal work on the design of management systems, notes: "Everyone familiar with organizations knows implicitly that myriad control systems influence day-to-day organizations. But there is little systematic understanding of why or how managers use these systems to accomplish their agendas."[3] While we have a long way to go before developing a complete "systematic understanding," we have observed the phenomenon mentioned by Simons. Executives use the many elements of their management system to orchestrate their agendas. By building the management system around the scorecard framework, they can achieve the ultimate payoff—translating strategy into action.

NOTES

1. This is an example of the "missing measurement" program, described in Chapter 10.
2. For discussion of defensive reasoning—how to recognize it and overcome it—see C. Argyris and D. Schön, "Defensive Reasoning and the Theoretical Framework That Explains It," Part II, *Organizational Learning II: Theory, Method, and Practice* (Reading, Mass.: Addison-Wesley, 1996), 75–107.
3. Robert Simons, *Levers of Control: How Managers Use Innovative Control Systems to Drive Strategic Renewal* (Boston: Harvard Business School Press, 1995), 11.

Building a Balanced Scorecard

CONSTRUCTING AN ORGANIZATION'S first Balanced Scorecard can be accomplished by a systematic process that builds consensus and clarity about how to translate a unit's mission and strategy into operational objectives and measures. The project requires an architect who can frame and facilitate the process, and collect relevant background information for constructing the scorecard. But the scorecard should represent the collective wisdom and energies of the senior executive team of the business unit. Unless this team is fully engaged in the process, a successful outcome is unlikely. Without the active sponsorship and participation of the senior executives, a scorecard project should not be initiated. It will surely fail without leadership and commitment at the top.

We are aware of two instances where an excellent scorecard was built by a very senior staff executive without actively engaging the senior management team in the process. In one company, the scorecard was developed by the chief financial officer, and in the other by the senior vice president of business development. In both companies, the executive was a member of the most senior executive team, an active, contributing participant in all senior executive strategy-setting and management meetings. Because of their high-level involvement with corporate strategy, both individuals produced scorecards that accurately captured the strategy, customer focus, and critical internal processes of their companies. Their scorecards were accepted as accurate representations of the organizations' critical objectives and measures. But in both instances, the scorecard ultimately did not drive change or become an integral part of the companies' management processes. We believe this disappointing outcome occurred because of the lack of senior executive involvement in the process and a lack of consensus about the role for the Balanced Scorecard. The scorecard project was likely viewed, in both organizations, as a staff-led initiative to improve a measurement system, not to make fundamental changes in the way the organization viewed or managed itself.

ESTABLISH OBJECTIVES FOR THE BALANCED SCORECARD PROGRAM

The first step for building a successful Balanced Scorecard is to gain consensus and support among senior management on why the scorecard is being developed. Many managers find the conceptual appeal of a Balanced Scorecard to be obvious. They see the shortcomings of limited financial measurement and need little prompting to develop a more balanced approach. The conceptual appeal of the scorecard, however, is not a sufficient reason to embark on such a program. When the process is launched, the senior executive team should identify and agree on the principal purposes for the project. The program objectives will help to:

- guide the construction of objectives and measures for the scorecard,
- gain commitment among the project participants, and
- clarify the framework for implementation and management processes that must follow the construction of the initial scorecard.

We illustrate here, with actual examples, some of the many initial reasons for developing a Balanced Scorecard.

Obtain Clarity and Consensus About Strategy

Chem-Pro, a manufacturer of polymer-based industrial products, had recently reorganized to become more customer-focused. Its traditional functional organization had been replaced by one designed around lines-of-business (LOB) and business processes. In addition, senior management had also identified four critical business processes that it must improve and excel at: order generation, product management, order fulfillment, and production. Each of the five lines-of-business had different requirements for the four processes. For example, the consumer group distributed large numbers of standardized products through retail channels, while the precision group worked with the engineers of a small number of very large customers to define the product specifications for new chemicals. Obviously, each of the four critical business processes had to be customized to the different needs of each LOB.

The Balanced Scorecard for Chem-Pro began by defining a standard corporate template that clarified the strategic priorities for all the LOBs in the new organization. Each line-of-business then developed its particular strategy, consistent with corporate priorities. At that stage, the LOB scorecards were communicated to the new managers of the four business processes so that they could develop programs that would meet the specific objectives of the individual LOBs. The sequential process of:

- defining objectives and measures at the corporate level,
- linking corporate objectives to individual LOB objectives and measures, and
- linking LOB objectives and measures to critical business processes

enabled Chem-Pro to introduce a complex organizational change—from functional specialization to customer-based line-of-businesses and customer-focused business processes—in a manner that gained acceptance, buy-in, and involvement by everyone.

Achieve Focus

Metro Bank initiated its Balanced Scorecard to achieve focus. Metro was the surviving entity of a merger of two highly competitive banks in the same region. The agendas of the two parents had never been fully rationalized into a common vision. At the same time, without having achieved a synthesis or consensus on an operating style and strategy for the new Metro Bank, managers had launched a major transformation program in order to be more innovative and to create a bank tailored for the twenty-first century. Unfortunately, the transformation program had gone wild, leaving the bank with more than 70 different action programs, each competing for management time and resources.

The CEO of the bank saw the Balanced Scorecard as a way to bring the organization together. By clarifying the strategic objectives and identifying the critical few drivers, Metro was able to create consensus and teamwork among all the senior executives, regardless of which bank they came from or which functional organization they represented. Further, the scorecard created a vehicle to set priorities, to consolidate and to integrate the many change programs currently under way. The result was a much more manageable set of strategic initiatives, all focused on achieving specific objectives of acknowledged strategic importance.

Decentralization and Leadership Development

The CEO of Pioneer Petroleum wanted to decentralize and disperse the power currently invested in a highly centralized functional organization. He created 14 new strategic business units whose mission was to be intensely customer-focused, and to reduce and eventually eliminate all unnecessary (non-value-added) costs. The leaders of the new SBUs, however, had all grown up in the old, centralized Pioneer culture, where they had learned to carry out orders. They had no experience in formulating their own strategies and managing the process by which these strategies would be implemented. Pioneer's CEO was concerned that the new SBU heads did not have enough executive experience to implement the new decentralization strategy.

The CEO engaged the senior management team in a scorecard process to facilitate the development of executive leadership among the 14 SBU heads. The team developed a corporate template that defined the strategic priorities. This template became the corporate Balanced Scorecard. Each SBU head then used the corporate scorecard as the starting point to formulate the unique SBU-level strategy. The SBU executive teams began with an off-site session to clarify the mission, vision, and values of their new organizations. The session continued by developing an SBU Balanced Scorecard that could be reviewed at the corporate level. The development of the scorecards brought the executives of the 14 new businesses together to begin working as a team. The articulation of the shared vision for the SBU proved to be the perfect vehicle for the team-building and strategy development processes. The corporate template was helpful in guiding their thinking and in reducing the risk associated with independently developing an SBU strategy for the first time. The creativity and energies of the SBU executive team could be focused along the dimensions defined in the corporate strategy.

The corporate review was also valuable in ensuring, before implementation, that the SBU strategies were acceptable to corporate. The entire process gave the CEO an opportunity to develop new skills among the SBU executives about how to formulate and manage business unit strategies. Although leadership development is an ongoing process, Pioneer's CEO used the preparation of corporate and SBU Balanced Scorecards as an effective first step.

Strategic Intervention

Kenyon Stores, unlike Pioneer Petroleum, was already decentralized. Its market-based SBUs specialized in fashion apparel for different customer segments. Each pursued its own strategy for fashion, targeting markets, and sourcing goods. Kenyon's CEO was convinced, however, that the highly decentralized approach led to lost opportunities for higher growth and increased profitability. The decentralized approach was ideal when the organization was smaller and its mission was to be close to trends and fashion requirements for targeted customer segments. But each SBU was approaching the size that the corporation itself had been only five years earlier. This scale dramatically changed the strategic agenda, requiring an SBU president to become more of a strategist and less of a merchant. The CEO saw the Balanced Scorecard as a way to get personally involved with the SBU presidents, helping them develop as business heads and assisting them in developing strategies for future growth.

Kenyon's CEO used the Balanced Scorecard to create a corporate strategic agenda. Along with the SBU presidents, he defined 10 issues (see Chapters 8 and 12) for which each SBU had to establish its own specific objectives and mechanisms for achievement in their individual Balanced Scorecards.

The corporate and SBU executive teams launched the annual long-range planning process around discussion of how each SBU would deliver on these 10 issues. This dialogue enabled the SBU presidents to build their long-range plans around the scorecard framework. The 10 issues provided a mechanism for integrating the SBU strategies into the corporate agenda. The process engaged the CEO in shaping the strategy of the organization instead of just reviewing results after the fact. More important, the process gave the CEO a vehicle to work with the previously autonomous SBU presidents. He used the process to help educate, stretch, and stimulate them.

In summary, the initial impetus for constructing a Balanced Scorecard can arise from the need to:

- clarify and gain consensus about vision and strategy,
- build a management team,
- communicate the strategy,
- link reward to achieving strategic objectives,
- set strategic targets,
- align resources and strategic initiatives,
- sustain investment in intellectual and intangible assets, or
- provide a foundation for strategic learning.

The selection of the objectives for the scorecard project at the outset is not to constrain the subsequent uses of the scorecard. In general, as described in Chapter 12, we have seen the role of the scorecard grow and expand through the implementation process. But the initial set of objectives will serve to motivate and communicate why the organization is going through the exercise, and will help sustain the program if interest and commitment should decline.

THE PLAYERS

Once agreement on the objectives and future role for the Balanced Scorecard has been reached, the organization should select the person who will serve as the architect, or project leader, for the scorecard. The architect will own and maintain the framework, philosophy, and methodology for designing and developing the scorecard. Of course, any good architect requires a client, which in this case is the senior management team. As in any building project, the client must be totally engaged in the development process, since the client will assume ultimate ownership of the scorecard and will lead the management processes associated with using it.

The architect guides the process, oversees the scheduling of meetings and interviews, ensures that adequate documentation, background readings, and market and competitive information are available to the project team, and, in general, serves to keep the process on track and on schedule. The architect, over the course of facilitating the construction of the initial scorecard, must manage both a cognitive, analytic process—translating soft, general statements about strategy and intent into explicit, measurable objectives—and an interpersonal, even emotional, process of team building and conflict resolution.

The architect, in our experience, has been a senior staff manager in the organization. We have seen people from a broad range of backgrounds managing and facilitating the development process of a Balanced Scorecard in their firms:

- Vice president of strategic planning or business development
- Vice president of quality management[1]
- Vice president of finance, or divisional controller[2]

Some organizations have used outside consultants to assist the internal architect for the scorecard development process.

BUILDING A BALANCED SCORECARD: THE PROCESS

Each organization is unique and may wish to follow its own path for building a Balanced Scorecard. We can describe, however, a typical and systematic development plan that we have used to create scorecards in dozens of organizations. If executed properly, the four-step process will encourage commitment to the scorecard among senior and mid-level managers and produce a "good" Balanced Scorecard that will help these managers achieve their program objectives.

Define the Measurement Architecture

TASK 1. SELECT THE APPROPRIATE ORGANIZATIONAL UNIT

The architect must, in consultation with the senior executive team, define the business unit for which a top-level scorecard is appropriate. Most corporations are sufficiently diverse that constructing a corporate-level scorecard may be a difficult first task. The initial scorecard process works best in a strategic business unit, ideally one that conducts activities across an entire value chain: innovation, operations, marketing, selling, and service. Such an SBU would have its own products and customers, marketing and distribution channels, and production facilities. It should be one where it is relatively easy to construct summary financial performance measures, without the complications (and arguments) related to cost allocations and transfer prices of products and services from or to other organizational units.

Figure A-1 shows a typical structure for a hierarchically organized multinational company. The natural setting for a Balanced Scorecard is at level III of such an organization.

If the organizational unit is defined too narrowly (say, within an SBU at level III of Figure A-1), it may be difficult to define a coherent, self-contained strategy. For example, a scorecard for a single functional department or for a single initiative may have too narrow a scope. A set of key performance indicators would likely be sufficient for such a narrow purpose. But Balanced Scorecards have been developed for complex support functions, joint ventures, and not-for-profits. The relevant question is whether the proposed organizational unit has (or should have) a strategy to accomplish its mission. If yes, the unit is a valid candidate for a Balanced Scorecard.

In one application, we worked with a large gas and chemical company. The operating units of the company included:

- a regulated, monopoly-provider of natural gas to local customers

Figure A-1 Define and Clarify the Business Unit

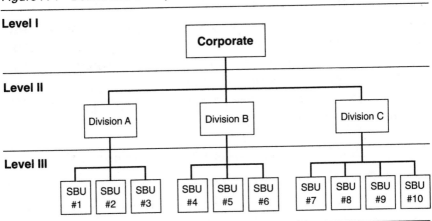

- an unregulated, competitive supplier of natural gas to national customers
- a basic chemicals company
- a gas services consulting company

Originally asked to facilitate the development of the company scorecard, we soon determined that even though many corporate resources and services served all operating units, the operations of each unit company were so diverse that separate scorecards for the different units made more sense than attempting to start by building a corporate scorecard.

TASK 2. IDENTIFY SBU/CORPORATE LINKAGES

Once the SBU has been defined and selected, the architect should learn about the relationship of the SBU to other SBUs and to the divisional and corporate organization. The architect conducts interviews with key senior divisional and corporate executives to learn about:

- Financial objectives for the SBU (growth, profitability, cash flow, harvest)[3]
- Overriding corporate themes (environment, safety, employee policies, community relations, quality, price competitiveness, innovation)
- Linkages to other SBUs (common customers, core competencies, opportunities for integrated approaches to customers, internal supplier/customer relationships)

This knowledge is vital to guide the development process so that the SBU does not develop objectives and measures that optimize the SBU at the expense of other SBUs or the entire corporation. The identification of SBU/corporate linkages makes visible both constraints and opportunities that might not be apparent if the SBU were considered as a completely independent organizational unit.

Build Consensus around Strategic Objectives

TASK 3. CONDUCT FIRST ROUND OF INTERVIEWS

The architect prepares background material on the Balanced Scorecard as well as internal documents on the company's and SBU's vision, mission, and strategy. This material is supplied to each senior manager in the business unit—typically between 6 and 12 executives. The architect should also acquire information on the industry and competitive environment of the SBU, including significant trends in market size and growth, competitors and competitor offerings, customer preferences, and technological developments.

After the senior executives have had an opportunity to review the material, the architect conducts interviews of approximately 90 minutes each with the senior managers. During these interviews, the architect obtains their input on the company's strategic objectives and tentative proposals for Balanced Scorecard measures across the four perspectives. While we, for simplicity, will refer to the architect as a single person, in fact, the interview process and subsequent synthesis of information is best done by a group of two or three individuals. The architect, as the leader of the team, will typically conduct the actual interview, asking questions and probing after responses. One person may concentrate on the actual objectives and measures specified by the executive; another attempts to capture quotes that serve to flesh out and give more meaning and context to the objectives and measures. The interviews can be free flowing and unstructured, but the interview process, as well as the aggregation of information supplied by the executives, will be facilitated if the architect uses a common set of questions and offers a common set of potential responses.

The interviews accomplish several important objectives, some obvious, others less so. The explicit objectives are to introduce the concept of the Balanced Scorecard to senior managers, to respond to questions they have about the concept, and to get their initial input about the organization's strategy, and how this translates into objectives and measures for the scorecard. The implicit objectives include beginning the process of having top management think about translating strategy and objectives into tangible, operational measures, learning about the concerns that key individuals may have about developing and implementing the scorecard, and identifying potential conflicts among the key participants either in their views of the strategy and objectives or at a personal or interfunctional level.

TASK 4. SYNTHESIS SESSION

After all the interviews have been conducted, the architect and other members of the design team meet to discuss the responses in the interviews, highlight issues, and develop a tentative list of objectives and measures that will provide the basis for the first meeting of the top management team. The team members can also discuss their impressions about the personal and organizational resistance to the Balanced Scorecard and to the change in management processes that will follow the introduction of the scorecard.

The output of the synthesis session should be a listing and ranking of objectives in the four perspectives. Each perspective and objective within the perspective will be accompanied by anonymous quotes from the executives that explain and support the objectives, and that identify issues for the executive team to resolve. The team should attempt to determine whether the tentative list of prioritized objectives represents the business unit's strategy, and whether the objectives across the four perspectives appear to be linked in cause-and-effect relationships. These observations can serve as discussion questions during the executive workshop to follow.

TASK 5. EXECUTIVE WORKSHOP: FIRST ROUND

The architect schedules and conducts a meeting with the top management team to begin the process of gaining consensus on the scorecard. During the workshop, the architect facilitates a group debate on the mission and strategy statements until a consensus is reached. The group then moves from the mission and strategy statement to answer the question, "If I succeed with my vision and strategy, how will my performance differ for shareholders, for customers, for internal business processes, and for my ability to grow and improve?" Each perspective is addressed sequentially.

The architect shows the proposed objectives, their rankings, and associated quotes from the interviews. The architect can show videotapes of interviews with shareholder and customer representatives to add an external perspective to the deliberations. Usually, the group will be deliberating on far more than four or five measures for each perspective. Each objective should be discussed in its own right, not compared to other candidates, so that its specific relevance, strengths, and weaknesses can be fully explored. At this time, narrowing the choices is not critical, though straw votes can be taken to see whether some of the proposed measures are viewed as low priority by the group.

After all the candidate objectives for a perspective have been introduced and discussed, the group votes on the top three to four candidates. This can be done in a variety of ways: written ballots, show of hands, or giving each person three green dots and asking him or her to place a dot next to each objective considered the most important. For the highest-ranked objectives, the architect and the team will draft a one-sentence or one-paragraph description. If time permits, the architect can ask the group to brainstorm on measures for the objectives.

The executive team should be divided into four subgroups, each responsible for one of the perspectives. One executive from each subgroup is chosen to lead the subgroup for the next stage of the process. In addition to the senior executives, representatives from the next levels of management and key functional managers should be included in the four- to six-person subgroups to broaden the base of deliberations and consensus.

By the end of the workshop, the executive team will have identified three to four strategic objectives for each perspective, a detailed descriptive statement for each objective, and a list of potential measures for each objective. After the meeting, the architect prepares and distributes a post-workshop document that summarizes the accomplishments, and lists the composition and leader of the four subgroups.

Select and Design Measures

TASK 6. SUBGROUP MEETINGS

The architect works with the individual subgroups for several meetings. During these meetings, the subgroup attempts to accomplish four principal objectives:

1. Refine the wording of the strategic objectives in line with the intentions expressed in the first executive workshop.

2. For each objective, identify the measure or measures that best capture and communicate the intention of the objective.

3. For each proposed measure, identify the sources of the necessary information and the actions that may be required to make this information accessible.

4. For each perspective, identify the key linkages among the measures within the perspective, as well as between this perspective and the other scorecard perspectives. Attempt to identify how each measure influences the other.

In facilitating these meetings, a skilled architect draws upon the underlying frameworks for the four perspectives discussed in Part One, as well as the linkages between measures, both within and across perspectives, that describe the cause-and-effect relationships underlying the strategy.

THE ART OF SELECTING AND DESIGNING MEASURES

The essential objective in selecting specific measures for a scorecard is to identify the measure that best communicates the meaning of a strategy. Since every strategy is unique, every scorecard should be unique and contain several unique measures. As we discussed in Chapter 7, however, certain core outcome measures appear repeatedly on scorecards. We have identified these as:

Core Financial Measures

- Return-on-investment/economic value-added
- Profitability
- Revenue growth/mix
- Cost reduction productivity

Core Customer Measures

- Market share
- Customer acquisition
- Customer retention
- Customer profitability
- Customer satisfaction

Core Learning and Growth Measures

- Employee satisfaction
- Employee retention
- Employee productivity

While most scorecards will draw heavily from the core outcome measures, the art of defining measures for a scorecard rests with the performance drivers. These are the measures that make things happen, that enable the core outcome measures to be achieved. The discussion of objectives and measures in Chapters 3 through 7 (including the appendices to Chapters 4 and 5) should help the architect and the subgroup team devise performance driver measures in the four perspectives that will communicate, implement, and monitor the business unit's unique strategy.

The final output from the subgroups should be, for each perspective:

- A list of the objectives for the perspective, accompanied by a detailed description of each objective;

- A description of the measures for each objective;

- An illustration of how each measure can be quantified and displayed; and

- A graphic model of how the measures are linked within the perspective and to measures or objectives in other perspectives.

When these outputs have been accomplished, the architect can schedule the second executive workshop.

TASK 7. EXECUTIVE WORKSHOP: SECOND ROUND

A second workshop, involving the senior management team, their direct subordinates, and a larger number of middle managers, debates the organization's vision, strategy statements, and the tentative objectives and measures for the scorecard. The output from the subgroups should be presented by executives in the subgroups, not by the architect or external or internal consultants to the subgroup. The presentations help build ownership for the objectives and measures, as well as for the entire scorecard-development process. The participants, either in a plenary session or in working groups, comment on the proposed measures, and start developing an implementation plan. A good focus for this second workshop is to be able, at the end, to sketch out a brochure to communicate the scorecard intentions and contents to all employees of the business unit. A secondary objective would be to encourage participants to formulate stretch objectives for each of the proposed measures, including targeted rates of improvement. Depending on the type of measure under consideration and the organization's philosophy about target setting, a variety of approaches can be employed—from benchmarking to rates of change—for specifying targets to be achieved by the next three to five years.

Build the Implementation Plan

TASK 8. DEVELOP THE IMPLEMENTATION PLAN

A newly formed team, often made up of the leaders of each subgroup, formalizes the stretch targets and develops an implementation plan for the scorecard. This plan should include how the measures are to be linked to data base and information systems, communicating the Balanced Scorecard throughout the organization, and encouraging and facilitating the development of second-level metrics for decentralized units. As a result of this process, an entirely new executive information system that links top-level business unit metrics down through shop floor and site-specific operational measures could be developed.

TASK 9. EXECUTIVE WORKSHOP: THIRD ROUND

The senior executive team meets for a third time to reach a final consensus on the vision, objectives, and measurements developed in the first two workshops, and to validate the stretch targets proposed by the implementation team. The executive workshop also identifies preliminary action programs to achieve the targets. This process usually ends up by aligning the unit's various change initiatives to the scorecard objectives, measures, and targets. The executive team, by the end of the workshop, should agree on an implementation program to communicate the scorecard to employees, integrate the scorecard into a management philosophy, and develop an information system to support the scorecard.

TASK 10. FINALIZE THE IMPLEMENTATION PLAN

For a Balanced Scorecard to create value, it must be integrated into the organization's management system. Our recommendation is that management begin using the Balanced Scorecard within 60 days. Obviously a phase-in plan must be developed, but the "best available" information should be used to focus the management agenda, consistent with the priorities of the scorecard. Ultimately, the management information systems will catch up to the process.

TIME FRAME FOR IMPLEMENTATION

A typical scorecard rollout project can last for 16 weeks (see timeline in Figure A-2). Obviously, not all of this time is taken up with scorecard activities. The schedule is largely determined by senior executives' availability for interviews, workshops, and subgroup meetings. If people are available, on demand to the project—an admittedly unlikely situation—the time schedule can be compressed. An advantage of doing the project over a 16-week period is that the senior executive team has time between scheduled events—interviews, executive workshops, and subgroup meetings—to contemplate and reflect on the evolving structure of the Balanced Scorecard and the strategy, the information system, and, most important, the management processes that it will signify.

The architect's (and consultants') involvement is heavy at the front end of this timetable, up to about the end of week 6 when the first executive workshop is held. In the second half of the timetable, the client, the senior executive team, should be taking more responsibility for development of the scorecard. The architect then shifts to a staff and facilitating role, helping schedule the subgroup meetings and assisting in the conduct of these meetings. The more that the senior executive teams are responsible for the subgroup meetings and the subsequent executive workshops, the more likely that the Balanced Scorecard project will culminate in a new approach for managing the business.

Figure A-2 A Typical Balanced Scorecard Timeline

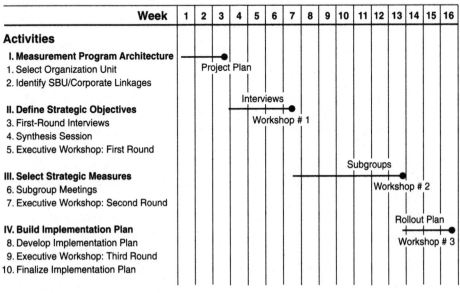

Week	1	2	3	4	5	6	7	8	9	10	11	12	13	14	15	16
Activities																
I. Measurement Program Architecture																
1. Select Organization Unit																
2. Identify SBU/Corporate Linkages																
II. Define Strategic Objectives																
3. First-Round Interviews																
4. Synthesis Session																
5. Executive Workshop: First Round																
III. Select Strategic Measures																
6. Subgroup Meetings																
7. Executive Workshop: Second Round																
IV. Build Implementation Plan																
8. Develop Implementation Plan																
9. Executive Workshop: Third Round																
10. Finalize Implementation Plan																

This schedule assumes that the business unit has already formulated its strategy and has market and customer research available that can inform decisions on market segmentation and the value propositions to be delivered to customers in targeted market segments. If the business unit must do a strategic analysis of its industry so that it can make fundamental choices about market, product, and technology strategies, or if it must conduct more detailed market research, the schedule will be extended by the amount of time required for these tasks.

At the completion of the project schedule, the senior and top middle managers of the business unit should have obtained clarity and consensus on the translation of the strategy into specific objectives and measures for the four perspectives, agreed on a rollout plan to implement the scorecard, including, perhaps, new systems and responsibilities for capturing and reporting data for the scorecard, and have a broad understanding of the management processes that will be changed as a result of having scorecard measures at the heart of the organization's management systems.

SUMMARY

Our experience has shown that an organization's first Balanced Scorecard can be created over a 16-week period. At that point, an organization is moving toward implementation where it can make the Balanced Scorecard the cornerstone of its management systems, as described in Part Two of the book.

NOTES

1. The title of such a person varies. We have seen such titles as VP quality improvement and productivity, VP continuous improvement, VP business process redesign (or reengineering), and VP process improvement.
2. Simplifying, but only slightly, we have seen two types of financial officers in organizations. The first type views his or her role as a change agent in the organization. This person understands the limitations of using only financial measures of past results for guiding the organization in its new competitive environment, and wants the finance group to use its capabilities in data gathering, information systems, measurement, and auditing to develop and operate new systems of measurement, communication, and control. Such a finance executive could indeed be an architect and, subsequently, the process owner of the unit's Balanced Scorecard. The second type of financial officer, however, jealously guards the objectivity, auditability, and integrity of the financial numbers cur-

rently being produced. This officer feels that adding softer, more subjective, and less auditable numbers to the responsibility of the finance organization will dilute its fundamental mission and compromise its ability to measure and control the financial numbers to the high-quality standards established over decades of practice. This second type of financial officer, typically from an accounting and auditing background, is not a good candidate to be the architect for the Balanced Scorecard project, nor, subsequently, to maintain it as a central management system.

3. The chief financial officer and either the chief executive officer or the chief operating officer should be interviewed to learn about the financial objectives for the SBU.

Index

About the Authors

Robert S. Kaplan is the Arthur Lowes Dickinson Professor of Accounting at the Harvard Business School. Formerly he was on the faculty of the Graduate School of Industrial Administration at Carnegie-Mellon University and served as dean of that school from 1977 to 1983. He consults on the design of performance and cost management systems with many leading companies in North America and Europe; regularly offers seminars in North America, Europe, and Israel; and has lectured throughout the world. Currently he serves on the boards of the J. I. Kislak Organization (in Miami) and Renaissance Solutions and on the Academic Committee of the Board of Trustees of the Technion (Israel Institute of Technology). His research focuses on new cost measurement and performance management systems for the rapidly changing environment of manufacturing and service organizations. The author or co-author of eight books and more than 100 articles, Kaplan is the recipient of numerous awards for both his teaching and his publications.

David P. Norton is president of Renaissance Solutions, Inc., an international consulting firm specializing in performance measurement and organization renewal. Previously he cofounded Nolan, Norton & Company, where he spent 17 years as president, prior to the firm's acquisition by Peat Marwick. He is a trustee of Worcester Polytechnic Institute and a former director of ACME (The Association of Consulting Management Engineers). He has served on numerous client steering committees and received an Award for Excellence for his support to the Department of Defense on its approaches to corporate information management.